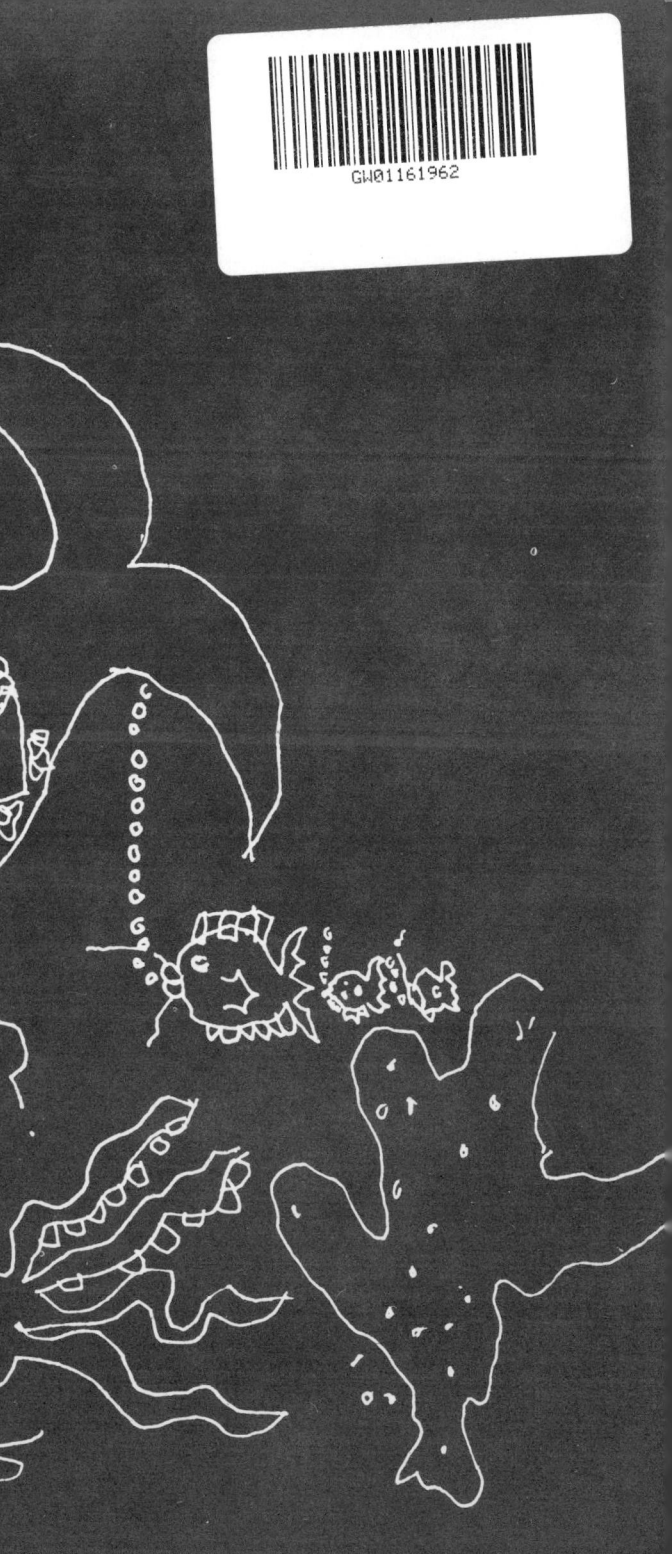

INSIDE THE WHALE
Ten Personal Accounts of
Social Research

INSIDE THE WHALE

Ten Personal Accounts of
Social Research

Edited by
Colin Bell and S. Encel

PERGAMON PRESS

Pergamon Press (Australia) Pty Limited,
19a Boundary Street, Rushcutters Bay, NSW 2011
Pergamon Press Ltd,
Headington Hill Hall, Oxford OX3 0BW
Pergamon Press Inc,
Maxwell House, Fairview Park, Elmsford, New York 10523
Pergamon of Canada Ltd,
75 The East Mall, Toronto, Ontario M8Z 2L9, Canada
Pergamon Press GmbH,
6242 Kronberg/Taunus, Pferdstrasse 1, Frankfurt-am-Main, West Germany
Pergamon Press SARL,
24 rue des Ecoles, 75240 Paris, Cedex 05, France

© 1978 Colin Bell and S. Encel

Cover design by Allan Hondow
Typeset in Australia by Savage and Co.
(Printed in Hong Kong by Toppan Printing Company (H.K.) Pty Ltd.)

Inside the whale.

ISBN 0 08 022244 7
ISBN 0 08 022243 9 Paperback

1. Social science research. I. Bell, C.R., ed.
II. Encel, Solomon, joint ed. III. Title.

300.72

All rights reserved. No part of this publication may be reproduced, stored in a retrieval system or transmitted in any form or by any means: electronic, electrostatic, magnetic tape, mechanical, photo-copying, recording or otherwise, without permission in writing from Pergamon Press (Australia) Pty Limited.

PREFACE

Australian publishing owes many debts to Andrew Fabinyi, and we have dedicated *Inside The Whale* to him as a token of recognition. This book, in particular, owes a great deal to him.

Our task was made all the more pleasant by Jerry Mayer and Christine Boden of Pergamon Press. Our secretaries, Nadia Massoud and Suzi Houseman, handled the many chores associated with the production of the book with their usual efficiency and good nature.

Authors do not generally have the pleasure of collaborating with their own children. All the more reason, therefore, to acknowledge their participation. We thank Rachel Bell and Sarah Encel for their assistance with the cover design and Fiona Thompson for her striking endpaper design which captures the whole enterprise so well. To all those mentioned, and to the authors of the various chapters, our grateful acknowledgments.

C.B.
S.E.
Sydney, August 1977

For Andrew Fabinyi

CONTENTS

INTRODUCTION
   Colin Bell & S. Encel   1

STUDYING THE LOCALLY POWERFUL:
Personal Reflections on a Research Career
   Colin Bell   14

IN SEARCH OF POWER
   S. Encel   41

CAPITAL MISTAKES
   Hugh Stretton   67

REFLECTIONS ON *AN AUSTRALIAN NEWTOWN*
   Lois Bryson & Faith Thompson   93

TAKING THE QUEEN'S SHILLING:
Accepting Social Research Consultancies in the 1970s
   Eva Cox, Fran Hausfield & Sue Wills   121

WORKING IT OUT TOGETHER:
Researching Academic Women
   Bettina Cass, Madge Dawson, Heather Radi,
   Diana Temple, Sue Wills & Anne Winkler   142

NATIONALISM, RACE-CLASS CONSCIOUSNESS
AND SOCIAL RESEARCH ON BOUGAINVILLE
ISLAND, PAPUA NEW GUINEA
   Alexander F. Mamak   164

THE BACKGROUND TO *BRADSTOW*:
Reflections and Reactions
   Ron Wild   182

WORDS, DEEDS AND POSTGRADUATE
RESEARCH
   Bill Bottomley   216

A MARXIST AT WATTIE CREEK:
Fieldwork Among Australian Aborigines
   Hannah Middleton   238

INTRODUCTION

Colin Bell & S. Encel

The title of this book needs explanation. *Inside the Whale* (Secker & Warburg, 1940) is one of George Orwell's longer essays, written in the first instance as a critical review of the work of Henry Miller. Orwell used this ostensible topic, however, to ventilate two of his favourite themes, the sterility of party politics and the baneful influence of political commitment on literature. The metaphor of the whale comes from Miller, who used it to describe his own detachment from politics and his refusal to deal with political topics in his writing. Orwell agreed that this was now the formula which any sensitive writer would have to adopt in order to write literature, particularly novels, that was not emotionally spurious. 'Get inside the whale', counsels Orwell. 'Give yourself over to the world-process, stop fighting against it or pretending that you control it; simply accept it, endure it, record it.'

Whereas Miller coined the metaphor of the whale to denote withdrawal from society, Orwell's use of it implies that the whale *is* society, and that we should spy out the interior. Despite his pessimism about writing in the 1930s, which he declared to be the barrenest period for imaginative literature in 150 years, Orwell observed that this same period had been productive of good sociological studies. In a later essay, 'Writers and Leviathan' (*Politics and Letters,* Summer 1948), which uses similar imagery, he stressed that writers *should* involve themselves in political and social issues, provided that they retained their intellectual independence. For the contributors to this book, the whale is also society, and each of them has tried, in his or her own way, to spy out the interior; in doing so, they have all experienced the problems of commitment, independence and interpretation which social scientists share with imaginative writers.

Writing a personal account of research is more difficult and more delicate than simply expounding the findings of a work of scholarship. The conventions of scientific exposition dictate that the results of research be presented in an impersonal style; a hypothesis is stated and the steps involved in testing it are laid out in logical order. As Sir Peter Medawar observed, in a famous article 'Is the Scientific Paper a Fraud?' (*The Listener*, 12 September 1963) the picture of scientific enquiry so presented is mythical; see also his article 'Hypothesis and Imagination' (*The Art of the Soluble*, Methuen, 1967). Nonetheless, like other myths, this one demands passionate adherence and deviation from it attracts anger and derision — witness the reception of James D. Watson's *The Double Helix* (Weidenfeld & Nicolson, 1968). The myth persists, among other reasons because it protects the research worker from queries about his/her motives, methods and assumptions. Impersonality confirms professional detachment and scholarly rigour. A personal account involves self-revelation and implies that the writer feels his or her work to be important. Art historians have noted the influence of romanticism on the painting of self-portraits, which painters came to use as a way of asserting that they were different from other people. Courbet made himself look like a Bohemian, Van Gogh like a proletarian, and the surrealist painters tried to portray not only their outward appearance but their unconscious minds and dream selves. The contemporary social role of the scientist, like that of the artist, dates from the Romantic period, but in the twentieth century the professionalisation of science has steered the individual research worker firmly away from romantic conceptions of social reality or personal role. Self-portraiture is an indulgence, permitted to distinguished elderly figures whose personal reflections no longer impinge on their scientific reputation.

INTRODUCTION 3

The reaction against positivism and objectivism in the social sciences which became strongly marked in the 1960s has led to an insistence on the exposure of personal assumptions and on the 'reflexive' nature of social enquiry. For a long time there was very little to set against the Lynds' self-critique in *Middletown in Transition* (Harcourt Brace, 1937). The 1960s saw a wave of reflexive self-examination, including Hammond's *Sociologists at Work* (Basic Books, 1964), Vidich, Bensman and Stein's *Reflections on Community Studies* (Wiley, 1964), Sjoberg's *Ethics, Politics and Social Research* (Routledge, 1965), Lazarsfeld, Sewell and Wilensky's *The Uses of Sociology* (Weidenfeld & Nicolson, 1968) and Horowitz's *The Rise and Fall of Project Camelot* (MIT Press, 1967). Other books have followed this first upsurge, which was exclusively American and touched off by political developments, especially the so-called 'war on poverty' and the real war in Vietnam. So far as we know, the present volume is the first of its kind to reflect upon the preoccupations of social research in Australia. What does it tell us?

The Lynds were prompted to do their heart-searching because they returned to Middletown after ten years and had to face people whose life they had exposed in their original study (published in 1928). It is this kind of participant observation, living in a community without being part of it, which clearly imposes a stress on the self-image of the researcher and summons up the familiar worries about subjectivity, morality, abuse of confidence and preservation of anonymity. It is hardly surprising that five of our ten accounts deal with just this situation, and that two of the five involved a wide cultural gap between the researcher and his/her subjects. Alex Mamak's references to reciprocity between the researcher and his informants, to honesty and freedom, difficulty and tension, the political convictions of the researcher and the problems of sponsorship, illustrate common concerns which affect every outsider whose involvement with the object of the research is essentially finite and external. In their own several ways, all five students of community social structure found their own answers to these problems and also to the subsequent problem of 'feedback' from the people they were involved with. The crucial conclusion, as Hannah Middleton writes, is the use to which all the material gathered in the field is put: 'if you are not part of the solution, you are part of the problem'. Lois Bryson and Faith Thompson ask a similar question when they note that the disparity between the values of professionals and the majority of their clients has become part of the conventional wisdom, and that social scientists must ask themselves whether they are not helping to widen the schism between theory and practice.

It is not our intention, even if it were possible, in this introduction to rehearse all points made in the chapters that follow. Rather we wish to draw out some of the purposes they collectively serve. These contributions are a complaint against the ways in which social research normally is written up, published and taught. Fieldwork manuals don't worry how fieldworkers are to keep sober enough to remember and record their observations and yet not spoil the sociable reciprocity required to actually observe an ongoing system of interaction. So, for instance, the comments about beer in Bill Bottomley's and Ron Wild's accounts are a welcome reminder that there's more to fieldwork than to 'behave like a gentleman, keep off the women, take quinine daily and play it by ear' in Evans-Pritchard's classic prescription.

That prescription is not just a joke. Research methodologies abound in prescriptive, normative statements about how research should or should not be done. Indeed, the function of most social science methods texts is to provide recipes for doing social research — and such texts are known in the trade as cookbooks. Yet all practising social researchers know that social research is not like it is presented and prescribed in those texts. It is infinitely more complex, messy, various and much more interesting. These accounts do, of course, also expose the soft underbelly of social science — unprotected by the hard shell of quantitative science as normally presented to the world through those texts, books and monographs. That social science also takes place in a political context you would never guess from the methodology texts.

Put at its simplest, all these contributions show that social research is a social and political activity; not a set of techniques to be applied to the world 'out there'. So all the chapters reflect social and political concerns *first* and techniques only later, if at all. Eva Cox's piece nicely illustrates the dilemmas that those who 'sell' their expertise to enquiries, commissions and so on often find themselves in. It is not just whether those that pay for research get what they pay for, but as her chapter shows, it is not always clear they know what they want. Social scientists all too frequently find themselves in the situation of having to define the objectives of those who hire them and then find themselves blamed for distorting the original objectives of the organisation. 'Taking the Queen's shilling' will remain problematic for *both* social researchers *and* their hirers, whilst the nature of social research is so poorly appreciated by those who see it as a solution to all their problems. There is, as Cox says, in a masterly understatement, a 'lack of clarity in role definition'. This book ought to go some way to demystify what social research is really like — but it might make social research less easily saleable, which would be no bad thing. With less money about, both social researchers and those who hire them will no doubt be defining their objectives much more closely.

We set out quite deliberately to cover as wide a range of styles of research as we could — wider than other recent collections of personal accounts of social research such as *The Organisation and Impact of Social Research*, Shipman (Longmans, 1976) (which is only about the sociology of education). We regret that we do not have a piece in this book on 'in-house' research — though, of course, Stretton's chapter comes close. That is why we have been reflecting on the relationship involved in 'Taking the Queen's shilling'. We did try to publish a piece on doing research on the inside — on being a full-time member of a governmental research unit. This proved to be impossible. The person approached agreed and indeed drafted his tale, so we are in the tantalising position of knowing what he was going to say but not being able to say it ourselves. He believed, in the last analysis, that it would harm future research prospects if he were to reveal the internal workings and the political context in which that particular research unit operated. We regret his decision to withdraw his piece very much indeed.

The reason for mentioning it here is that despite our intentions to include chapters that covered as wide a range of research situations as possible, they were thwarted. No matter how much we may now protest that existing accounts do not reveal enough to understand the social and political context of social research and our intention to do something about it, there are fairly clear limits to what we can achieve. There is, as we have suggested, a great personal (and very understandable) reluctance to give accounts that might prejudice future research prospects. Yet that reluctance means that potentially misleading accounts of social research are given — not only by commission (and as editors we have tried to prevent that), but also by omission. Accounts of the behaviour of sponsors, both public and private, are necessarily circumspect or even absent totally.

We need many more frank accounts, as varied as those of Stretton and Mamak, of going for the well-known ride on a tiger without enjoying the fate of the unfortunate young lady from Riga. Anybody who reads and ponders the accounts of Stretton and Mamak — and Cox, for that matter — will be much better prepared for establishing a satisfactory working relationship with their sponsors, be they in government or private industry. To achieve an authentic relationship with the sponsor/hirer *and* those one is studying must be the honest open ambition of all social researchers. How this can be done is extraordinarily difficult to prescribe, yet Stretton's and Mamak's accounts do describe how in their different ways they came near to having this satisfactory relationship.

What this shows is that social science has become part

of the structure of power — with all the dangers of incorporation, co-option and just plain exploitation. Mamak could have been used by the copper companies (but wasn't); Stretton's uneasy relationship with Canberra shows just how problematic this can be; and it is a central theme of Cox's chapter. No one would imagine that trying to change a nation's housing policy was an unpolitical act. Stretton's chapter is discouraging, partly for its account of the practical difficulties involved in dealing with bureaucrats, and partly for its explanation of these difficulties, that is, the dominance of neo-classical economic concepts among the officials and experts. Stretton thus raises a point of great theoretical importance, which touches also on the issue of disparity between those who make the decisions and those who are affected by them. Neo-classical economics, and the sociology that is closely linked with it, operates with an abstract model of individual and collective motivation, which generates its own resistance to the kind of information about social dynamics collected in the field by trained observers who are acutely aware of the limitations of abstract models. In Stretton's view, the government economists who refused to listen to his arguments were themselves victims of dogma about scientific certitude, who had not been taught to recognise their theories and methods as optional, controversial, value-structured instruments. But Stretton's is not merely a theoretical critique. We would have been less interested in it as a contribution had it remained at that level. It goes on to link theory with action, and in doing so provides an exceptionally revealing account of the possibilities and frustrations of working for government, comparable with the Crossman diaries quoted in Encel's chapter.

Most of the chapters recount stories of far lesser ambition than Stretton's. Social scientists should not delude themselves by thinking that they can easily effect a 'social change'. And some have had no such ambition anyway. As Bryson and Thompson say of those they studied, 'the local residents, whom we naively wished to assist, seem to have been supremely unaffected by the work'.

Four chapters are about that most familiar research situation — that of the postgraduate student (those of Bottomley, Bryson and Thompson, Wild, and Middleton). And when we say familiar, perhaps we should say statistically frequent, for to many social researchers it is quite unknown other than from their own personal experience and the anecdotes of others. These four accounts will strike familiar chords in anyone who has done postgraduate work. Most have faced the painful dilemmas described in detail by Bottomley and yet few tell their tales. Rarely do any researchers, even in the usually ovorverbal social sciences, reflect publicly (as opposed to informally within and through the gossip networks) on what their research careers mean to them in terms of personal and political development. That this development reflects the familiar intersection of autobiography and social structure should also become clear in the body of the book. The institutional setting — mainly university social science departments — is also familiar, but this does not mean that reflections on what happens in them are often made very public. Yet this is where so much research does actually get done — and most methodology texts, of course, totally ignore this setting.

What Bottomley's account particularly draws to our attention is that research is not just a social process but also a learning experience for those who do it. A doctorate is, we learn from Bottomley, also an education — even if you are not awarded the degree. The researches of Wild, and of Bryson and Thompson, also began as doctorates. The constraints under which distinguished pieces of work were produced are brought out by these writers. *Bradstow* (Angus & Robertson, 1974) and *An Australian Newtown* (Kibble Books, 1972) are significant contributions to what we know about Australia. Now we know considerably more about how those researches were done. Both, too, had to face acutely the problem that their research, once published, would generate a life of its own — though *Bradstow* gave Wild a far worse time than *An Australian Newtown* gave Bryson and Thompson. There are salutary lessons that their accounts teach us. Social research will be reacted to by those who are studied, especially if they are powerful. This is a theme that runs implicitly through Bryson and Thompson's chapter, and is elaborated at length in the two chapters written by the editors.

Lone, virtually unaided research students, have the doubtful advantage that at least they don't have to worry unduly like others about their relationship with sponsors and grant givers in quite the same way. That's why Middleton's problems were different to Mamak's, Wild's to Cox's and Stretton's. Yet doctoral students have supervisors, universities and, most significantly, examiners to worry about. This is a theme that could be developed further. Given that so much social research is actually an examination (for a doctorate), the role of the examiners surely requires more attention than it has been given up to now. University regulations frequently force researchers to work by themselves. Yet Bryson and Thompson explain just how much they gained from working together and so, of course, did Cass *et al.*

Social research can be lonely. Middleton, though integrated into the kinship system of the Gurindji and despite the constant social interaction in which she was involved, was essentially and existentially by herself. That fieldwork can be extraordinarily stressful (and joyful we hasten to add) is not something that the textbooks lay all that much emphasis on. 'A Marxist at Wattie Creek' should comfort those who have chosen to go through similar experiences. We still have far too few accounts of what fieldwork is really like and that is why we are especially pleased to publish the pieces by, for instance, Wild and Middleton.

Middleton, unlike those cookbooks, but like most of the rest of the contributors here, is not concerned to hide her commitment. That is how it should be. Just as we believe that the development of social research has been seriously distorted by underemphasising or ignoring its social and political context, so also has the pretence that social researchers are disinterested value-neutral automatons. The contributors to this book are just like its readers. We have political allegiances, prejudices, histories and experiences that shape our lives. And most of us do not sharply distinguish between our activities as social researchers and the rest of our lives. For Middleton and Wild most sharply, and others only to a lesser extent, the research had to dominate their lives. Or rather their lives became the research. That is not an uncommon experience, yet the effects of this on researchers are not often revealed. It also emphasises that research does not all take place on the same day — that seemingly simple point is ignored in the usual textbooks. Commitment, rather than a pretence of disinterested pursuit of knowledge, is the real motivation to social research. Otherwise why put up with the nastiness, the 'detailed drudgery' in Bryson and Thompson's phrase, and the enormous expenditure of effort required?

That's what took Middleton to Wattie Creek and Wild to Bowral. Few make much money out of research consultancies. As Cox says of her frustrating experiences, 'without commitment to the necessity for the kinds of research undertaken . . . the researchers would not have persevered'. Commitment is also what led Bettina Cass and her co-workers to fight against the odds and overcome the lack of resources to do their study of academic women. The research literally could not have been done without it. With value-neutrality (a concept we no longer understand) that research would never have started and if started would not have been continued, let alone finished. Though at some personal cost, that account does show what can be done without much aid — with only the labour power of the researchers. That needs underlining as it is too frequently assumed that all research must cost a lot of money. The implications of 'big research' are drawn out in Bell's chapter — team research like that described by Cass, though it desperately needed some funding, can avoid some of the grosser difficulties that immediately present themselves when sponsors are involved.

So all these contributions do emphasise the personal in the research process. We would all readily agree that we became different people through the experiences revealed here. Bell emphasises in his chapter that the social research experiences described have reoriented his view of sociology and of society. The same is true for Bottomley. In Encel's case, the orientation gained as a student was reflected in his choice of research interests and theoretical assumptions. It was, however, the experience of detailed research on the structure of power and inequality which finally shaped those assumptions into a firmly held set of views about society, politics and people, and the further experience of being attacked and criticised which made him reflect even more deeply on those views and decide to stick to them. Others' experiences are not necessarily so dramatic or far-reaching, yet without accounts such as those published here it is difficult for people to realise that we also learn about ourselves through social research and not only about others.

The chapters collectively allow a window into a normally closed world. They describe the ethos and the milieux of social research. They will provide rich data for those interested in the taken-for-granted worlds inhabited by the social researchers themselves — rather than the more usual insights into the taken-for-granted worlds of those studied. *Sociologists at Work* is the title of a distinguished predecessor to *Inside the Whale*. It is a measure of the change in social science since 1964, when *Sociologists at Work* was published, that the personal accounts published here are so political and publicly aware. Many of the accounts in *Sociologists at Work*, important as they are, are almost as if given by chemists describing their work in a laboratory, ignoring the world outside. Such accounts, whilst still possible, would now seem very unsatisfactory if not actively misleading. It was precisely because those accounts accurately reflected the state of American sociology in the early 1960s that it was possible later in that decade to talk about the 'crisis' in sociology — they represent the failure of the sociological imagination.

The chapters of this book are all marked by a concern to link social research with the public issues of the wider society. Although they are personal accounts, they demonstrate that the personal is frequently very political. Personal concerns become political because of this linkage between research and public issues, be it housing policy, land rights, the consequences of mining operations, or the situation of women. This is most obvious in the cases of Stretton and Cox because of their direct involvement in social policy. But even with the research carried out for doctorates, as in the cases of Bottomley, Bryson and Thompson, Middleton and Wild, it would be futile to give a purely 'internalist' account.

Related to this is the fact that these chapters frequently reflect a debate with Marx — indeed, the whole of sociology is sometimes seen as a debate with that hirsute ghost. What these chapters show is just how fruitful that debate has been — Encel clearly owes great debts to an early engagement and so do most of the others, for example Mamak and Middleton. Again, it is a simple point but bears repeating here — a debate with Marx is a *theoretical* debate and though these are accounts of social *research*, they all belie the conventional distinction between theory and research. This comes over, time and again, and yet as we all know the teaching of theory and method are frequently separated. This is another element of the *unreality* of much of conventional social science. These are accounts of social research and yet they all talk about theory. One of the reasons perhaps that we have stayed 'inside the whale' is that we have emasculated both our theories and methods through their separation.

Although Marx can be perceived in the background, perhaps the most important influence in the foreground is that of C. Wright Mills. This fact, evident to us on reading all the contributors, is not the result of design. We did not mention Mills, or indeed any other scholar, in the notes we sent our contributors to outline the purpose of *Inside the Whale,* yet most of the essays in this volume have a distinctly Millsian flavour. This is partly because of Mills' concept of the sociological imagination as a bridge between public issues and the private concerns of social science; partly because of Mills' central concern with the structures of power and inequality and his insistence that social scientists have a duty to expose these structures and use their knowledge for public purposes. If we had all remained truer to Mills, we would have less to answer for. As Stretton puts it, we would have taught our students not to treat their theories and methods as the accumulating dogma of the one true science. In this spirit, we hope that *Inside the Whale* will contribute to a livelier, significant and more politically relevant social science.

STUDYING THE LOCALLY POWERFUL

Personal Reflections on a Research Career*

Colin Bell

Introduction

Let us start by taking the metaphor seriously — we *are* inside the whale. If we think of Jonah helplessly carried across oceans with perhaps the feelings of *individual* lack of control, even of understanding, that many people seem to experience, then the point is made. It is twenty years since C. Wright Mills wrote in *The Sociological Imagination*, 'Nowadays men [today perhaps he would have written people] often feel that their private lives are a series of traps'.[1] Social science has not been very much help in springing those traps, nor in increasing our understanding of the navigation of the whale that we are all inside. It is a radical commonplace that most social science swims with the tide — more like a jellyfish than a whale. Its assumptions are those of society — social science shares the prejudices, biases, delusions, hopes, aspirations, faiths and ideologies of society as a whole. As a *whole*? No, not as a whole — only of some.

It does make sense to write of society as a whole — paradoxically though, only for some is it possible to speak of society as a whole. Society — as an all-inclusive notion, as something (like a whale) that we are all in needs some careful thought. It is in fact, far too liberal democratic in what it evokes.

---

*Dedicated gratefully to Bob Woodward and Carl Bernstein.

Not everybody, not every group counts for equal. Some, in another classic Orwellian phrase, are more equal than others. In such situations (and when have there been any others?), some control others. Indeed, the controllers define who the others are. And what is more, they control the ideas about the parts *they play*, that the others play, as well as notions about 'society' as a whole — the interlocking and interrelationships of both or the many, or all sides. 'Society' then suggests that 'we are all in the same boat' — if not inside the same whale. And yet, of course, it is in the interests of the controllers, the powerful, to encourage such notions, for if we don't all pull together, won't we all drown? In liberal capitalist societies it is most frequently at this level that such control is exercised — at the level of ideas, normative control in Etzioni's terms. It would be a mistake, though, to overemphasise this as coercive control, violence — the army, military and the police (and husbands in families) — is ever present in even the most liberal of liberal democracies. And utilitarian control — put crudely, money — is still one of the key bonds in these societies. However, as has been remarked, the cash nexus is remarkably fragile and hardly holds society together alone in the face of the basic and fundamental contradictions. Even when backed, albeit at some distance, by coercive control and reinforced by all the means of normative control that the State's ideological apparatus can mobilise — through the Church, schools and the media — the cash nexus is not always enough to hold 'society' together.

This should not be an unfamiliar view of 'society'. I was provoked, for instance, to write the following a few years ago:

> Conflict is an ineluctable and inevitable component of all societies and this is reflected in, and frequently worked out in, the various social institutions in those societies. Conflict is a reflection, not of the 'inefficiency' of the social system but of the inescapable existence of differential opportunities to achieve valued objectives. Societies and their social insti-

tutions (including universities) are not, then, inert masses, disturbed only occasionally by unrest, but are volatile wholes, seething with discordant ideas, opposing interests and competing social groups.

This view of society and its institutions, is in opposition to that of society united by a dominant pattern of values. This is not to deny that some values in society and especially within social institutions (including universities) are held in common. It is, however, necessary to point out that these values are constantly being exploited for their power to legitimate a variety of patterns of behaviour. Those values are so general that they appear to support great diversity of action — witness the free speech debate. Instead of the apparently dominant view of society based on consensus, the view supported here stresses the *normalcy* and pervasiveness of conflict between different interest groups. This conflict is expressed in a variety of ways.[2]

However, if ideological control (that prevents the emergence of divergent and contradictory elements) takes place at what, for want of a better phrase, can be called the 'macro-level', then it may be necessary I believe, to go on to analyse how this occurs at the 'micro-level'. Actually what is meant here is how do the locally powerful maintain their positions at the level of individual relationships? The assumption here is that there are, within systems of interpersonal relationships, mechanisms by which the controllers, the powerful, translate their might into right. And that they do not have to do it coercively, though it helps if you are big and strong. And that they do not just buy utilitarian acceptance through money, though it helps if you are rich. And that both of these material interests are obscured by the locally powerful's control and maintenance of the normative or ideological system. The very stability of so many local inequalities is an eloquent testimony to the success of the locally powerful in converting might into right within local systems. The point of this chapter is to suggest that we do not know all that much about how that is done because the locally powerful are extraordinarily difficult to study.

This chapter is, as those who have seen earlier versions were quick to point out, a slightly uneasy mixture of autobiography and political manifesto. As my research career led me to the political, ideological and scientific positions that I am displaying here, I don't find that surprising. I do insist, though, that this chapter cannot be divided into two parts. There is a relationship between my biography and my current political and scientific positions. I have been strengthened in my resolve to try to put them together by the other chapters in this book, which also illustrate this relationship in a variety of ways.

It is not my intention to claim all that much for the reorienting or, to use a key term in the account that follows, *redirecting* potential of the experience of working in universities in advanced capitalist societies. And yet the fact remains that the experience of working in one, the University of Essex in England, did clarify for me all sorts of things about the nature of society and of social organisations that I had only read about in books. My practical experience of being Chairman of a Sociology Department in a university wracked with prolonged conflict between the 'students' and the 'university' taught me more, much more quickly than my extensive and protracted reading. The statements about the inevitability of conflict that I made in the introduction of this chapter were originally written in a submission to Lord Annan who was enquiring into the 'troubles' at Essex. I find my remarks there now rather crude, but they do have for me, sufficient immediacy and relevance to the redirection of sociological enquiry so as to make me still feel that they are worth quoting. The point I am making is that they emerged through confronting the actions of the locally powerful power holders — those who were running the University of Essex. I was forced, in an expression that I will elaborate, to 'study up', to examine the actions, motives and ideologies of the locally powerful; for *they* were determining events, rather than the locally powerless — the students. In true hegemonic style, my locally powerful were busy blaming the victims, in this case the students, rather than themselves. I introduce these remarks here just to show how intimately involved intellectual and political development can be, even in such usually sterile environments as universities.

Autobiography

I *became* a sociologist through being a postgraduate student; I had read History and Geography as an undergraduate. For two years I 'did research' in Swansea in South Wales — and wrote *Middle Class Families*.[3] The book, which was also an M. Sc. Econ. thesis, was meant to be a contribution to a number of discrete, but interrelated topics that reveal some aspects of the nature of advanced capitalist society: what the relationship is between social and geographical mobility, what functions extended family aid plays (indeed, does the extended family even exist?) for different families with differing mobility experiences, what the local social structure of the housing estates/developments was where I was carrying out the field research. The book has been modestly successful — it illuminates some of the processes that maintain stratification in our kind of society. It has added significantly to ethnography of the middle class — any addition would be significant, as the middle class was then and is still largely unstudied. *Middle Class Families* is, also as John Westergaard recognised in a paper given to the British Sociological Association in 1975 at Canterbury, England, one of the very few British empirical studies that takes property transmission seriously and confronts the interrelationships between property and occupational position. Shortly after *Middle Class Families* was published, in 1968, I was asked by a distinguished British sociologist to write a much more general book on the British middle class — I found the prospect very unattractive and unjustifiable — feeling a sort of personal, moral and political distaste for the exercise. I said to him (and he quotes me, unattributed, in one of his publications) 'how could I justify that to my students?' — for by then I was at the University of Essex.

I hurried to complete the middle-class family research because I had had the opportunity to run a major research project. This was a restudy of the town of Banbury in England. Banbury was the locale of one of the very best British community studies, *Tradition and Change,* which was written by Margaret Stacey.[4] We wanted to study that community again and say something about the social changes that had occurred between 1950, when the first research was done, and 1966-68, when we returned to the town. Our study, called *Power, Persistence and Change,* is now, belatedly, published.[5] The reasons for the delay, and the difficult nature of the organisation of that research, I have written about extensively in a chapter in a book I edited with Howard Newby called *Doing Sociological Research.*[6] The Banbury restudy describes the changing nature of the local social system. It concentrates on such matters as the local political system, religion and voluntary association membership, as well as the informal organisation of neighbourhoods. It says a great deal, rather mechanically I now think, about stratification. Our conclusions were that Banbury 'can be seen to be composed of two or three social levels, has no neat class system, but is dynamic, stratified, cross-cut by ties within and without. It is an ordered society, without a formal social order'.[7] I would suggest now that that conclusion was of necessity a theoretical imposition on the data. It was also a political judgement.

In 1968 I went to the University of Essex and remained there for seven years until I came to Australia in 1975. Besides writing up some of the Banbury research, I was involved in a number of other projects. The first was an extraordinary piece of contracted research for the Roskill Commission on the siting of a Third London Airport.[8] Extraordinary first and foremost for the speed at which it was done: from conception, in April, to publication, in December 1969.[9] It involved comparing the local social structures of the four sites of rural England that were on the final short list. The background to the Commission and its whole methodology are well described and criticised by Self,[10] Hall,[11] and Perman.[12] We accepted largely unquestioned the really basic assumptions of the Commission — whilst at the same time seeing ourselves as largely detached and setting our own terms of reference (which we did actually write ourselves). My personal position then about consultancies and doing this kind of work was approximately that elaborated with style by Edward Shils in 'The Calling of Sociology'.[13] I engage in a critique of that position later in this chapter.

Soon after the 'airport research' (and whilst still writing up the Banbury project) I wrote, with Howard Newby, a textbook called *Community Studies*.[14] That book is far from uncritical of the dominant traditions that we discerned in the literature on communities or local social systems. (Ron Wild's chapter in this book is a reflection on a particularly good community study.) While *Community Studies* does provide a critique of sociology, it does not provide a critique of society nor is informed by a particular theoretical view of society. Later I quote one of the more startling naive remarks that we then made about the nature of local political systems. *Community Studies* never really gets to grips with ideologies. The text is still widely used and has been, in publishing terms, very successful.

During this period I was also supervising Howard Newby's doctoral research on agricultural workers in East Anglia — now published as *The Deferential Worker*.[15] It was through that experience, as well as what was happening in the University of Essex at the same time, that I began to arrive at my current position on social research. Together we wrote a paper[16] for a British Social Science Research Council conference on 'The Occupational Community of the Traditional Worker', the proceedings of which are now published as *Working Class Images of Society*, edited by Martin Bulmer. At that conference it became increasingly clear that enormous research efforts were being expended on analysing (usually in a fairly theoretically and methodologically sophisticated manner) the life styles, attitudes and ideologies of the British working class. The direction of sociological attention was *down*, towards the relatively powerless. There was no corresponding interest and attention in the powerful, in the definers and controllers of the social situation. There was an interest in the social system as a whole — say, in the conflicts and contradictions between capital and labour — and yet the focus of attention was on labour, not on the bourgeoisie. We all recognised this *lacuna* and would agree with Ronnie Frankenberg's remark that the working class were those that the sociologists wrote about most and mixed with least, whilst the middle class were those we mixed with most and wrote about hardly at all. That conference strengthened Howard Newby and myself to *redirect* our personal research attention towards the powerful, towards the objects of deference (if that is indeed what they were), towards the controllers and definers of the local social situation. We felt that it was neither realistic, nor scientifically possible, to go on making remarks about the system as a whole, whilst focussing our research attentions more or less exclusively on only one side. We successfully applied for funds to study not farm workers in the class structure, but capitalist farmers in the class structures. We decided, at last, to study directly and overtly the locally powerful. This is published now as *Property, Paternalism and Power*.[17]

This significant reorientation was occurring at the same time as I was heavily involved in the conflicts within the University at Essex. Whilst doing the general background reading to our future work on farmers, we began to look for other comparative social structures — not just agrarian, though the peasant literature made us sharply aware that we ought to consider patron-client relationships. The literature on American negro slavery, particularly the work of Eugene Genovese[18] — with the title 'The World The Slaveholders *Made*' [my emphasis] — led us to think much more widely about what social structures would lead the powerless to endorse the conditions of their own inferiority. At the same time as we were feeling our way in this direction, we used to talk a great deal with Leonore Davidoff (also at Essex) who was doing brilliant social historical work on nineteenth-century domestic servants — yet another group who at least seemed to endorse a moral order within which they were forever condemned to a subservient position.

I can also illustrate usefully and further elaborate my reorientation by the parallel changes that occurred over the same period in my thinking on the sociology of the family and on the sociology of marriage. I had a long interest in the sociology of the family – indeed, I had been teaching courses on it all the time I was at Essex, and I had founded and then convened the British Sociological Association Family and Kinship study group.

For many sociologists the sociology of the family was for years an intellectually moribund area; but by 1972 or 1973 the critiques that were emerging out of the women's movement from one side, and from the followers of R.D. Laing and David Cooper on the other, were making it much more lively. Like many British sociologists of the family, I had tended very much to treat the 'family' as a sort of black box into which I rarely peered. I taught what the family's functions were, how they had changed over time, as well as lots of stuff about kinship and the extended family and so on. I talked a lot about the 'emerging conjugal form'. Like most other sociologists, I said very little about sex or the erotic dimension of relationships and also precious little about child rearing and socialisation (that could safely be left to social psychologists elsewhere). In 1970 I had written, with Patrick Healey, a paper on 'The Family and Leisure' in which we pointed out that women had been relegated to a subsidiary and residual category.[19] Quite rightly (and very early in the history of what is an ongoing debate), we began to face the 'problem of definition surrounding women's domestic activities'.[20] There were at that time almost no data on what actually occurred within marriages – Elizabeth Bott's *Family and Social Network* being a rare exception, yet hardly being able to bear the weight of interpretation that was frequently put on its relatively thin data base.[21] So being pushed, just a little by the first critiques from the women's movement, my course on the sociology of the family began to change. I wrote another chapter, simply called 'Marital Status' (written after 'The Family and Leisure' chapter, but confusingly published before it, should anyone ever be interested in reconstructing my intellectual biography!).[22] I went on record as saying that marriage did different things for men as opposed to women; for instance, I wrote that 'most women are still denied alternative arenas for social validation'.[23] However, I go on to quote, approvingly, Berger and Kellner's famous remark that the small family is an 'innocuous "play area" in which the individual can safely exercise *his* world-building proclivities, without upsetting any of the important social, economic and political applecarts. Barred from expanding *himself* into the area occupied by these major institutions, *he* is given plenty of leeway to discover *himself* in *his* marriage and *his* family'.[24] (I have drawn attention to the unconscious sexism in that quotation by adding my own italics.) Again though, there were precious little data on which to base those remarks. I then began to put together my thoughts on the family and my other work on farmers, peasants and slaves. Were not wives, within families, also endorsing the conditions of their own inferiority? Perhaps families as play areas were not quite so innocuous — what was happening was that the locally powerful within families (i.e. the husbands) were 'doing social work' in the ethnomethodical sense to maintain their positions. At the 1974 British Sociological Association Conference in Aberdeen, Scotland, Howard Newby and I presented a paper, 'Husbands and Wives: the dynamics of the deferential dialectic', that represents the redirectional focus of our sociological thinking on the sociology of marriage.[25] What were the local and interpersonal mechanisms by, and through which, the locally powerful operated — and again whilst we still believe that paper to be adequate, theoretically we don't have much data on which to base and illustrate our argument. As we remarked there:

> Demeanour is of critical importance in conveying the correct balance between identification and differentiation in relationships characterised by traditional authority. All superordinate

individuals in a deferential relationship are faced by a dilemma that reflects the contradictions inherent in the deferential dialectic: in the coming together involved in face-to-face interaction certain mechanisms must be employed that maintain social distance. What are these mechanisms? Some are ritualized and easily observable — bowing, curtsying, saluting and so on — whilst other mechanisms can be observed without too much difficulty — etiquette, forms of address, degree of physical contact for example. The problem is that in the most particularistic of relationships, such as that between husband and wife, the norms of demeanour are extremely difficult to investigate. Even the more generalized attributes of demeanour referred to above are likely to be inappropriate. We need to know a great deal more about the obeisances, condescensions and ceremonial taboos which prevail between husbands and wives. We know that the behaviour of men and women is often different when members of the opposite sex are absent, whilst certain forms of behaviour, verbal and non-verbal, are traditionally taboo 'in front of the wife' or the husband. But our knowledge is little beyond the level of social anecdote. The insights of Goffman need to be extended beyond the mental hospital and the outermost Shetland Islands and brought into an examination of sexual stratification in the family.[26]

We went on to emphasise that deference stabilises the hierarchical nature of the husband and wife relationship, and that this relationship was embedded in a system of power — power both of the hand and of the purse.

It is clear, then, that it is vitally important to study the activities of these locally powerful people. We need to understand how their 'world-building proclivities' operate *on* others, how the local hegemonic structures are imposed on and then accepted by the relatively powerless. Of course, for all sorts of reasons this is no easy task — the very basic notion of family privacy is a strong ideological defence against such research and can easily be used to deny *access*. This, as I shall argue below, is a vital weapon in the hands of the locally powerful — be they farmers, university authorities or husbands — and it has shaped the formation of sociological knowledge. That we know so little about the locally powerful is no accident, but both a direct and indirect consequence of their very power. The functions of ignorance are no joke. If we are 'inside the whale' — and the metaphor really does seem very apt for the role of families in the lives of many women — then we should exercise ourselves in understanding those who control it.

Redirecting Sociology
Sociology typically looks down the social structure from the top — there are far more studies of workers than there are of owners in capitalist society. It also tends to look outwards from metropolitan areas towards the peripheries. This is not the place to elaborate that sociology rarely reaches the *real* peripheries of society (see Galtung,[27] Appendices B and D). The potential for social control that it is suggested this gives the powerful has frequently been commented on: sociology is done *on* the relatively powerless *for* the relatively powerful. Sociology can be easily seen as thoroughly implicated in the power structure of society. This does not mean that individual sociologists have anything but the best of intentions — they may even believe themselves to be true radicals.

The *directional* character of sociology is another consequence of the 'scientific' nature of the activity. It is a complex subject, only understood and capable of being practised after years of training (or professionalisation, with all the implications of trained incapacity that that should suggest). It is expensive: needing large samples, expensive equipment and libraries. It typically takes place in universities and similar institutions. When this is stressed, it is hardly surprising that knowledge of welfare bureaucracies is not widely distributed amongst welfare recipients, and that appreciations of patterns of ownerships of transnational industrial and commercial conglomerates do not pervade the working class. The powerless do not have, at the most basic levels, the resources of time, energy or money to 'do sociology'. Indeed, it is no accident that this is so and it could be suggested that it is naive utopianism to believe that it could be otherwise. Sociology, like science as a whole, has not been for the people. It has been primarily, largely and almost exclusively for the powerful and for those who control our societies — and that is true of both liberal capitalist as well as State socialist societies. This has been both an intended *and* an unintended consequence. It has been only secondarily for the sociologists; though it often seems as if much more research has been done to meet the career needs of sociologists than for any other reason. The nature of modern sociology has been determined more by these sorts of considerations than by any others — such as the disinterested pursuit of knowledge that the 'scientific' model of sociology suggests.

Yet, it is possible to *turn the direction of sociological attention round.* This is not to underestimate the continuing and important demystifying nature of conventional (or even 'bourgeois') sociology: the working class have not become embourgeoisified, more working-class children have not made it to universities, work is meaningless and dissatisfying, schools are mechanisms for the reproduction of labour power, women are discriminated against formally and informally in the labour market, urbanisation has created new tyrannies of distance for the working class, many poor people in our social formations are actually *in* work (not dole bludgers[28] or unemployed), and so on and so on. These findings emerge from a sociology that is frequently informed by a kind of marxified Fabianism: a belief in the reformist political possibilities that will follow from demonstrations that the facts are facts. (Just how many people are in poverty?, Just how class-biased is police activity?, Just how many accidents happen at work?) The *direction* of this sociology's attention rarely wavers: it is down and out. George Orwell was *Down and Out in London and Paris* and, to labour the point, sociology because it looks down and out has become down and out too. This is one principal reason for much of the current dissatisfactions with sociology — the purposes that it can serve are all too clear.

Studying Up
Of course, this is not a new critique — but it has emerged for me through a conscious reflection on a personal research career that started in 1964. I would now argue that a number of research projects that I have been involved in were vitally moulded by the activities of the locally powerful. Until recently, I rarely saw this moulding, perhaps I should write *determination*, of the research by the locally powerful as good data in their own right. The locally hegemonic consequences of the husbands within the families that I wrote about in *Middle Class Families* were (when I did that research from 1964-66) so totally taken for granted by me and so unquestioned (as far as I can now see by their wives as well as by me) that they were invisible. Within a local interaction system — families on a middle-class housing development — the husbands were so powerful that they did not have to be studied.

Sociologists should begin, in Laura Nader's phrase addressed to anthropologists, 'studying up'.[29] By 'studying up' — that is to say, turning the direction of social science enquiry and imagination round — she feels, and I agree, that we are much more likely to make our students feel energetic about what we and they are doing. Her second reason for advocating studying up is that such a social science would become much more scientifically adequate. As she hopes (about anthropologists) that they

> might indeed ask themselves whether the entirety of fieldwork does not depend upon a certain power relationship in favour of the anthropologist, and whether indeed such dominant subordinate relationships may not be affecting the kinds of theories we are wearing. What if, in reinventing anthropology, anthropologists were to study the colonizers rather than the colonized, the culture of power rather than the culture of the powerless, the culture of affluence rather than the culture of poverty?[30]

Such a social science Nader believes would have much more democratic relevance, for ' "studying up" seems to be one track for integrating paramount social concerns with the goals and aims of the science of man'.[31] Yet such a social science would be unable to meet some of the normative criteria of a science.

It could be argued that the ideologies of normative sociology are the crucial mechanisms of social control that prevent the redirection of sociological attention — it just would not be science or sociology. If that can be satisfactorily rebutted, then the possibilities of 'doing sociology' by the people might well be increased and the old and current image of sociology would be changed. As was pointed out, this image is one of sociologists fondly believing they were doing sociology for themselves (or for other sociologists). Yet when their work was pertinent enough, which perhaps it frequently is not, it is used openly or secretly by the powerful. Maybe its most significant use is to channel off, and therefore contain, a large amount of moral indignation and even radical intention into the relatively harmless activity that sociology is today. If it 'studied up' it would be a lot less harmless — but its scientific legitimacy would be threatened, such is the power of the ideology of science.

There are many, many differences between the social sciences and the natural sciences and this is not the place to rehearse them all again. Yet two points do need to be made more explicit and systematic than I have yet made them in this chapter. Firstly, the social scientist, as opposed to the natural scientist, is part of the system being studied. True, we often try to study society from outside the whale as if *we* are not in it, but unlike the natural scientists we cannot manipulate or 'control' it from outside. Society can only be manipulated and controlled from within. Secondly, and to use the functionalist terminology, when compared with the fields of the natural sciences, society exhibits low integration. Elements of society (be they individual, groups or classes) exhibit a remarkable independence — when compared to molecules or whales. They can think and feel for themselves and as I made clear earlier, I view society as made up of elements that have different needs and *incompatible interests*. Political choices about whose side we are on are therefore essential and necessary. Where is sociology to be located? The choice of such a point of departure is a political choice, because it decides for what interests the sociologist's knowledge can be used. This is not just about the institutional setting of sociological research projects, because a sociologist who appears to be independent of all policy makers has to choose a perspective which, to put it at its mildest, is of different relevance to different social groups. Sociology that looks down (with its large samples, easy access and adequate funding) appears 'scientific' and is legitimated as such. Sociologists, including myself, who have done such research tend naturally to stress our political commitment — marxified Fabianism again. Are we not trying to promote the common good rather than just being a tool of management, the power elite or the State? However, sociology that 'studies up' often won't be seen as scientific — funds will be difficult to obtain, sampling frames non existent, access (unlike to the working class) well-nigh impossible and so on. Indeed, the whole activity may not even be deemed worthy of the name of science. Legitimating seals of approval may well be withdrawn from a sociology that looks up and not down.

Sociology that only studies down and out has, as far as suggested above, generated a family of theories that are consistent with its directional nature: problems of integration, pattern maintenance, tension management, goal attainment and adaption. What these theories and concepts have in common, as has often been pointed out before but bears repeating, is that they all see the system from the point of view of the powerful, of the manipulators of the system (that is why the farmers I studied in East Anglia — in what was, for me, an important personal redirection of sociological research — bemoaned the local loss of community). But a sociology that studies up turns out to be relatively theoretically impoverished — in itself no accident, as so little studying up has been done. The Marxist theory of class struggle, of course, looms large — and at the interpersonal level much of Simmel's work shows remarkable insights (again largely ignored and forgotten by sociologists). What has happened, though amongst those social scientists who study up is that, in Herman Schmid's (of the University of Lund in Sweden) felicitous phrase, 'Science in the ordinary sense of the word is often replaced with what could be called political thinking by scientifically trained persons'.[32] What I would add is that the definition of what is to pass as science in a society (or within the sociological profession) also reflects the interests of the power holders in society (and in the sociological establishment). I stress this because judgements about what is and what is not good sociology, on apparently ideologically neutral (i.e. 'scientific') definitions, are usually also political judgements. Such is the detachment and isolation of so much sociology from society that these judgements, say over ethnomethodology, may often only have relevance within sociology.

The best example I can think of for sociologists being 'scientifically' rubbished are the followers of C. Wright Mills, like Domhoff; while it seems quite clear that the dismissals by the academic establishment are mystifying political judgements. As Domhoff himself has recently expressed it,

> The pluralist's single-minded way of studying power has a long and honourable history in American political science. Its roots are deeply imbedded in certain streams of philosophical thinking *which try to tell us how science must be done.* Empirical studies such as this book represents here little or no bearing on the arguments of this tradition.[33] (The italics are mine.)

All I am doing is applying a Mertonian commonplace of the sociology of science to the sociology of sociology: there is a normative system within sociology (as there is within science) that functions to control the activities of individual sociologists. The consequence for sociology has been that sociology rarely studies up and so is scientifically inadequate, theoretically impoverished, and politically and socially emasculated. Sociology that studies up in society as a whole will frequently be dismissed as political pamphleteering under the label of science.

These concerns and causes for concern have long been recognised by the sociological establishment — though not always with the consequences they would like. Edward Shils — in his magisterial essay 'The Calling of Sociology' that concludes *the* paradigmatical collection of establishment sociology, *Theories of Society* — is a fine example (see ref. 13). He distinguishes between manipulative sociology, alienated sociology and consensual sociology. His third category is a kind of synthesis of the other two, and for him (and for me in the past) is a way out of the dilemma that he perceived facing sociology. He wrote that 'Neither manipulative nor alienated sociology can meet the requirements of a policy that respects human dignity and is therefore adequate to aspirations of universal validity. Consensual sociology is alone capable of satisfying the requirements of an adequate theory and of proper relationship with policy.'[34] Since if it is true, as Shils claims, that the research procedures of sociology 'are equally open to the observers and the observed' and since manipulation 'is indispensable to the effective conduct of the affairs of any organisation . . .', there is no reason why sociology should not place itself at the disposal of a manipulation that is in principle accepted as legitimate.

It is particularly relevant to my personal reflections that I first read that Shils essay when I was acting as consultant to the Roskill Commission on the siting of the Third London Airport. They were trying to decide which of four sites in rural England should be concreted over — would more or less 'social damage' be done here or there? 'Cost Community' I was exhorted. Britain, it then seemed, needed a third London airport, it had to go somewhere after all. But this is not all there is to it. If it were, Shils would not perceive a dilemma. The real calling of sociology is to 'participate in those forms of co-ordinated activity that involve insight, reasonable persuasion, loyalty and mutual detachment'. Was I not doing just that when I worked for the Roskill Commission? This may sound somewhat vague, but Shils proceeds to a clearer formulation: 'The function of sociological research and of sociological theory in the working of society is to enrich the *empathic* element in opinion, to provide insight into the self as well as others, and to *unite* the self and others through a better appreciation *of the ties that bind them together'* (the italics are mine).

In other words, the functions of sociology are to create an attitudinal and behavioural integration; or, to use the words of what Shils would call an alienated sociologist, to indoctrinate public opinion. Shils, like most sociologists, bases his reasoning on an assumption of common interests among the members of society, as well as on the assumption that there are no important conflicts built into the structure of society. So Shils does not solve his dilemma. He deceives himself and others, and presents a formulation of manipulative sociology under a new label. Of course he does: after all manipulation 'is indispensable to the effective conduct of the affairs of any organisation'. I don't wish unfairly to pillory Shils. I refer to him merely because his way of thinking has long been so representative and so dominant in contemporary social science. If you believe what Shils believes, why study up? True, Shils clearly senses the political nature of his dilemma but then 'solves' it by assuming a harmony of interests. The 'proof' of this harmony is attitudinal integration (consensus) and behavioural integration (conformity) and social sciences' purpose — its true function in advanced industrial societies, whilst inside the whale, is to do what it can to produce these proofs. The structurally determined incompatibilities and contradictions between groups and individuals in society are forever minimised by this tradition. Indeed, they are systematically obscured by much of current sociology. It might be possible to argue even further — but this would take me too far from the concerns of this chapter — that the heavy emphasis on manipulative social science is a consequence as well as a cause of a consensual society.

For, as we all know, what people define as real is real in its consequences. And the people who do the defining in our society are the powerful — with a little help from their friends, the social scientists.

Reconsiderations
This is not just a further example of the ruling ideas about society being those of the ruling class — about what is science, what is sociology and what is the fundamental nature of society.[35] But also, as was earlier referred to in passing, the locally powerful also control access to the fields of investigation. This control of access is an extraordinarily powerful weapon in determining the overall nature of research findings. To misuse the metaphor even further, to get into the whale in the first place may need their permission and sponsorship, and so open the way to control. Any advocacy of 'studying up' has to face this problem. The locally powerful, if they come to our attention as a legitimate focus for sociological investigation in the first place, can vitally control what is known about them. The evidence of corporate criminal activity is all around us and that many politicians are crooks is now widely believed, yet the systematic investigation of such centrally significant activity is hardly ever the subject of sociological study. We know more about shoplifting, teenage vandalism and pot-smoking than we do about 'the theft of the nation' — CIA involvement in Chile, Italy, Greece as well as Australia, and about the heroin trade. That, too, is no accident.

If, when we did the Banbury restudy, we had really been studying up, we would have had to know a lot more about the interconnection of the local political elite and property speculations. We would have (as was much more true in our study of large-scale agriculture in East Anglia) concentrated our attention on the *systematic* manipulation of the local housing and labour markets in the interests of the local economic elite. We would not, surely, have made remarkably silly (and empirically quite unjustified in the light of later evidence about what was going on in British local government) statements as we did in *Community Studies;* such as 'In Britain, politics is a formal game played it would seem, almost entirely by the rules. It is remarkably uncorrupt'.[36] One of the central rules was 'don't get caught' — another was that 'you can't ask about that'. What we were doing implicitly during the Banbury community study was to play the research game by *their* rules — the rules of both the locally powerful and normative rules of the sociological profession. To have gone after data about graft in local politics would have prejudiced our already precarious position with the local political establishment. They just captured and then controlled us and our findings — of course, this was not done explicitly. How could we (I'm asking this ironically, it is necessary to stress, for fear of being misunderstood) have asked about personal gain from prior knowledge of town planning decisions, and still collected data about the sociographic background of political leaders which at the time almost seemed our sole purpose? And in accepting and then working within the behavioural bias of so much sociology that purports to study community power, we missed almost entirely the structural determinants of who gains and who loses from local decisions. Indeed, to focus on local decisions at all may well have been mistaken. The locally powerful were certainly powerful enough not to have their position seriously challenged by the ordinary workings of the local political system. We could have produced, indeed I think we did, an accurate description of how that system worked. Yet we so rarely, if ever, challenged the interests of the locally dominant groups that our account reveals virtually nothing about power in Banbury. 'Politics', which was what we studied, was such an innocuous play area that we were allowed to study it.

I have tried elsewhere[37] to systemise what may be called 'the problem of access' and this needs to be discussed again here in this chapter, for there is no possibility of 'studying up' until these problems are understood. Any social system can be conceived as varying in its degree of 'closure' — by which is meant here ease of access to the researcher. For

STUDYING THE LOCALLY POWERFUL

instance, communities, as normally understood, are much more open than, say, factories or prisons. The housing developments I studied in South Wales were open in that I was free to wander on and off them. Getting anyone to talk to me was a much different matter. The wives — who typically were around during the day — often made it very difficult for me to see their husbands in the evenings, as they saw one aspect of their role as being the protection of their husbands from people like me. I noted then, but never really used nor reflected upon how different the wives were when their husbands were present. The competent, quite literally 'mistress in their own homes appearance' during the day changed to an appearance often of being quite timid and deferential during the evening. For instance, I found it totally impossible frequently to complete an interview with a wife when her husband was present because whether or not he gave the answers, she expected him to.

All social structures vary in the degree of encompassing (the word is Goffman's and he uses it to describe total institutions[38]). The more encompassing — and this characteristic is not only to be found in informal organisations — a social structure, frequently the more difficult it is to study. Or more precisely, the more the sociologist who wishes to study such a structure is likely to be dependent upon the locally powerful, who have accomplished and work this symbolic and sometimes physical encompassment. Husbands accomplish this encompassment in families. Farmers in East Anglia also traditionally 'worked' this encompassment to their own advantage, using it to control totally the social environment of their workers. In the face of the industrialisation and urbanisation of the English countryside, farmers have reconstituted these total institutions *on the farm*. A higher and higher proportion of farm workers now lives in tied cottages on the farm. Access is now even more controlled by the locally powerful.

'Studying up', then, is going to face problems of access — to the powerful themselves and to data about their activities. As Nader put it, 'the powerful are out of reach on a number of different planes: they don't want to be studied; it is dangerous to study the powerful; they are busy people; they are not all in one place, and so on'.[39] She goes on to make rather light of these difficulties — my personal experience both during the Banbury research and that during the capitalist farmers project would suggest that access problems can be potentially crippling to any piece of research that is designed to be based on fieldwork or interview data. Just how could families and/or marriages be observed[40], without field work or interviews? (Maybe the answer is to compare the number of battered wives with battered husbands.) Much of sociology's research edifice is based upon questions directed at real people and if they won't talk — as many locally powerful political leaders would not, both in Banbury and in East Anglia — then the sociologist can be in trouble. Of course, I am suggesting strongly that it is usually not in the interest of the locally powerful to talk to social scientists and to be studied anyway. Their notorious reticence and sheer difficulty and hostility towards researchers is also no accident.

Not all research on the locally powerful necessarily has to come face to face with them. The schematic statements that I have made about conflict and the necessity of taking sides means that there can be other possibilities. For instance, in our study of the locally powerful in East Anglia, we maintain that we can see the system working in the interests of the powerful and against the interests of the less powerful through an analysis of local government expenditure.[41] It is possible in this way to get away from intimately linking power and behaviour. For too long, as Lukes has eloquently argued in his *Power: A Radical View,* behavioural approaches to the operation of power have dominated the field.[42] In addition, studies of 'power' in advanced industrial societies are often based on little more than 'positional' data (e.g. endless lists of directors and club memberships); that is, *secondary* sources. Elites find it easy to deny access to themselves; that is, they can control access by social scientists to *primary* sources. So despite the behavioural bias of studies of power that Lukes discerns, there has rarely been any analysis of real observed behaviour.

Many of the social structures in which I have been interested, have investigated and have written about have been face to face, local and small. What I have often sought to do is to build up a sociology that was based on 'observed interpersonal events' — the phrase is William Whyte's in his reflection on *Street Corner Society*.[43] There are, I now see, even greater limitations to such a sociology than I had earlier appreciated. For whilst I would still maintain that observed interpersonal events — say in marriage, in villages, on farms and so on — are vitally important for the maintenance of local power in particularistic social structures, there are limits to how far this can go. It is difficult, for instance, to appreciate the cumulative nature of such events, both over time and across a class of locally powerful — to all husbands and to all farmers. What such an approach lacks most of all is a political economy.

My position now, where I have reached inside the whale, is to believe that whilst it is possible to start from some political economy to move down to a sociology of observed interpersonal events, it is not possible to reverse this process. If the locally powerful are only studied 'in action' as it were, much will be missed — and not just backstage behaviour, which almost by definition the sociologist will not be allowed to see. However, I now believe that much behaviourism — in the sense of sociology that focusses exclusively on the actual behaviour of real people in natural social settings — can be extraordinarily trivial. Sociology's attention should, for a while at least, be focussed on the powerful and the consequences of their power on us all. For if it is not, then sociology will continue to be shaped by the powerful and will continue to obscure and mystify their power. Such a sociology will continue to make remarks about companionate marriages, communities, expedient decisions over airport sites, lack of corruption in local politics and so on and so on. I am drawing these examples, of course, from my own work.

Reflections such as these are necessary, though rare. Sociology's perpetual state of crisis for the last decade — exemplified by its 'methods without substance',[44] and its political naivity and complicity — won't be cured by such reflections. Indeed, perhaps only disciplines as uncertain of themselves as sociology currently is could produce them. I think, though, they are necessary both for its practitioners and its students so that with the collapse of the hegemonic positivistic empire in sociology, some of the alternatives can begin to be sketched. It is important to know how we became what we are.

NOTES AND REFERENCES

1. Mills, C.W. *The Sociological Imagination,* Oxford University Press, 1959.
2. Unpublished submission to Lord Annan's enquiry into the troubles at the University of Essex, England. For background, read successive issues of the *Times Higher Education Supplement* through Spring/Summer, 1974.
3. Bell, C. *Middle Class Families,* Routledge, 1968.
4. Stacey, M. *Tradition and Change,* Oxford University Press, 1960.
5. Stacey, M., Batstone, E., Bell, C. & Murcott, A. *Power, Persistence and Change: A Second Study of Banbury,* Routledge, 1975.
6. Bell, C. 'Reflections on the Banbury Re-Study', in C. Bell & H. Newby (eds), *Doing Sociological Research,* Allen & Unwin, 1977.
7. Stacey *et al.,* p.135.
8. Commission of Enquiry into the Siting of a Third London Airport, 1969–1971.
9. Abell, P., Bell, C. & Doriean, P. *The Disruption of Community Life,* HMSO, 1970.
10. Self, P. 'Cost-benefit analysis and the Roskill Commission', *Political Quarterly* 41, 3 (1970).
11. Hall, P. 'Roskill and Airports', *New Society,* 28 January 1971.

12. Perman, D. *Cublington: A Blue Print for Resistance*, Bodley Head, 1973. See particularly pp.60-65, which are based on an interview with me.
13. Shils, E. 'The Calling of Sociology', in T. Parsons, E. Shils, K. Naegele & J. Pitts (eds), *Theories of Society*, Free Press, 1965.
14. Bell, C. & Newby, H. *Community Studies*, Allen & Unwin, 1973.
15. Newby, H. *The Deferential Worker*, Allen Lane, 1977.
16. Bell, C. & Newby, H. 'The Sources of Social Imagery of Agricultural Workers', in M. Bulmer (ed.) *Working Class Images of Society*, Routledge, 1975.
17. Newby, H., Bell, C., Rose, D. & Saunders, P. *Property, Paternalism and Power*, Hutchinson, 1977.
18. Genovese, E. *The World The Slave-holders Made*, Allen Lane, 1970.
19. Bell, C. & Healey, P. 'The Family and Leisure' in M. Smith, S. Parker & C. Smith (eds), *Leisure and Society in Britain*, Allen Lane, 1973.
20. Bell & Healey, p.159.
21. Bott, E. *Family and Social Network*, Tavistock, 1957.
22. Bell, C. 'Marital Status', in P. Barker (ed.), *A Sociological Portrait*, Penguin, 1972.
23. Bell, 'Marital Status', p.69.
24. Berger, P. & Kellner, H. 'Marriage and the Construction of Reality', *Diogenes* 46 (1964).
25. Bell, C. & Newby, H. 'Husband and Wives: The Dynamics of the Deferential Dialectic', in D.L. Barker & S. Allen (eds), *Dependence and Exploitation in Work and Marriage*, Longmans, 1976.
26. Bell & Newby, 'Husbands and Wives', p.163-64.
27. Galtung, J. *Theories and Methods of Social Research*, Allen & Unwin, 1967.
28. Welfare cheats or welfare scroungers.
29. Nader, L. 'Up the Anthropologist — Perspectives gained from studying up', in D. Hymes (ed.), *Rethinking Anthropology*, Random House, 1974..
30. Nader, p.289.

31. Nader, p.293.
32. Schmid, H. 'Sociology and Political Action', Mimeo, n.d.
33. Domhoff, G.W. *The Bohemian Grove and Other Retreats: A Study in Ruling Class Cohesiveness,* Harper, 1974, p.110.
34. It should be clear that I now view 'consensual sociology' as a logical absurdity.
35. 'The ideas of the ruling class are in every epoch the ruling ideas: the class, which is the ruling material force of society, is at the same time its ruling *intellectual* force. The class which has the means of material production at its disposal, has control over the means of mental production'. Marx, K. & Engels, F. *The German Ideology,* International Publishers, 1970, p.39.
36. Bell & Newby, *Community Studies,* p.220.
37. Bell, C. 'A Note on Participant Observation', *Sociology,* 3 March 1969.
38. Goffman, E. *Asylums,* Pelican, 1968.
39. Nader, p.302.
40. Ethically, I would add, this raises more problems than I have space to discuss adequately here.
41. Bell, C. & Newby, H. 'Community Power in Rural Areas', Mimeo: paper presented to 47th ANZAAS Conference, Hobart, 1976.
42. Lukes, S. *Power: A Radical View,* Macmillan, 1974.
43. Whyte, W. *Street Corner Society,* Chicago University Press, 1943.
44. Lewis Coser's title for his presidential address to the American Sociological Association in 1975.

IN SEARCH OF POWER

S. Encel

Bertrand Russell once argued that man's chief desire is for power and glory. The business of the social sciences should be to seek the laws of transformation of one form of power into another, just as physics deals with the transformation of one form of energy into another.[1]

As Partridge has noted, we do not need to accept Russell's naturalistic definition of power in order to recognise that it is central to an understanding of social processes.[2] The social sciences, products of bourgeois society and with their intellectual horizons defined by bourgeois liberalism, have to a large extent been able to ignore this central role, and with it the awkward fact that the exercise of power is frequently marked by force and violence. Relatively few social scientists seem to have heeded Martin Luther's injunction that the world cannot be ruled without violence: 'the civil sword shall and must be red and bloody'. Some years ago, the political scientist Harry Eckstein organised a conference to distil the collective wisdom of American social science on the question of violence, and confessed himself sadly disappointed with the results.[3]

In an address to the American Psychological Association in October 1976, Ralph Nader acknowledged pragmatic reasons for avoiding the topic. People refrain from 'studying up', he remarked, because it might lead to retribution, demotion or subtle ostracism. But he also criticised social scientists for constructing 'ideological cages' for themselves, and avoiding real problems by retreating into specialisation. Alfred McClung Lee, giving the presidential address to the

American Sociological Association at the same time, accused his colleagues of serving the interests of profit and power by giving their discipline a sham legitimacy provided by scientism.[4] These statements echo the words of earlier critics like Loren Baritz, which have lost none of their force since they were originally uttered.

This avoidance of the issues raised by power, force and violence is common to all the social sciences, but takes varying forms in different disciplines. In economics, generally regarded as the oldest-established and most influential, Gunnar Myrdal pointed out more than forty years ago that the problems of power and inequality had been side-stepped by the pretence that economic choices could be separated from social and political preferences.[5] Following Myrdal, Kapp has demonstrated that the political framework on which capitalism depends is obfuscated by neo-classical orthodoxy, through the assumption that social returns from production can be separated from private returns, which alone are the business of economic theory. He called instead for a 'new science of political economy' to expose the real forces which control the economic system. The soundness of Kapp's view may be seen from his argument (published in 1950) that capitalism was an economy of unpaid social costs which would ultimately overtake private returns based on profit.[6]

Political science, despite its apparent concern with the nature, distribution and use of political power and influence, has been less helpful in illuminating these matters than might be expected. Machiavelli, generally treated as the founder of political science, was certainly interested — or, rather, fascinated — by power, but few political scientists have been Machiavellians. Because the academic role of political science is largely to serve as an adjunct to the teaching of law and administration, its choice of themes reflects this relationship. The governments of bourgeois societies are constitutional governments; hence, what is meant by 'political institutions' is the formal structure of constitutional government. The fashionable obsession with election results and opinion surveys is an extension of these assumptions, as it implies that elections are politically decisive.

Psychology is particularly well placed to avoid these awkward questions, since it can take the social framework for granted and concern itself with individual behaviour, role theory, socialisation and 'adjustment', a key word with profound ideological implications. At the most conservative end of the theoretical spectrum, psychology retreats even from the study of human beings into the observation of animal behaviour, neurophysiology and neurochemistry. Anthropology, possibly the least reflexive of all the social sciences, has consistently ignored its historical derivation from European colonialism and imperialism, although the shock of seeing it pressed into service as an agent of counter-insurgency operations in South-East Asia prompted a wave of rethinking.

The case of sociology is more complicated and more perplexing; understandably so in view of the diffuse nature of the subject. In principle, sociology ought to be concerned with power, since its origins lie at least partly in criticism of the social order. Most of this criticism, however, is directed at improvements within an existing structure rather than radical change or replacement of that structure. Especially in the circumstances of continuing economic growth and comparative social stability, at least in the affluent industrial countries, in the twenty-five years following 1945, it was easy for sociologists to drift into an acceptance of 'piecemeal social engineering' and the theoretical assumptions underlying it. In these circumstances, the powerful conservative impulse which is also part of the sociological tradition could assert itself even more effectively than in earlier periods. This tradition, emphasising social solidarity, positive knowledge and ethical neutrality, lends support to a view of society as a system in equilibrium, whose imbalances can be corrected by social technology.

Autobiography
What led me to embark on the study of power was not a

well-formed theory. My conception of the social world was formed as a schoolboy in Melbourne in the closing years of the 1930s. Looking back, it seems that a series of traumatic incidents occurred within a few months: the German march into the Rhineland, the Italian invasion of Ethiopia (subject for a class geography project), the Spanish civil war, the Stalinist purges, the Anschluss with Austria, the Munich crisis, the Japanese invasion of China (topic for a history project), the IRA bomb outrages in England, the Nazi occupation of Czechoslovakia, the Hitler-Stalin pact, the Danzig crisis. The school debating society organised a special discussion about the defence of Australia in the event of a world war. I took part in an inter-school debate about the inevitability of war in capitalist society. A German official in Paris was shot by a young Jewish student, and an orgy of reprisals was unleashed by Nazi stormtroopers. German-Jewish refugees began to arrive in Australia. It was in the home of one of them that I heard a broadcast of Neville Chamberlain's speech announcing war with Germany.

The world I learnt about from the daily press and from my parents' friends was one of conflict, unemployment, violence, dictatorship, repression, racial prejudice, war and the threat of war. It was unnecessary to read books to find out that these things were going on. In the atmosphere of the 1930s, however, books were of the greatest importance. Penguin Specials were available for ninepence, Left Book Club volumes for one shilling. By the time I left school, I had read a number of Marx's pamphlets and had started on *Capital*. Yet I never became a Marxist; there were too many things unaccounted for in the theory, and too many things about its living embodiment, the Soviet Union, which disturbed me. John Strachey's book *The Nature of Capitalist Crisis*[7] provided a convincing application of Marxian economics to explain the great depression, but his predictions of revolution in *The Coming Struggle for Power*[8] were wildly astray. The doctrinal and tactical disputes between the Russians and the Chinese communists, described in Edgar Snow's *Red Star Over China*,[9] made it clear that Marxist principles did not necessarily lead to the same conclusions. Nor could I accept the orthodox Marxist description of Nazism as no more than a cloak for monopoly capitalism.

After interrupting my studies for a spell in the armed services, I returned to the University of Melbourne after the war and found myself in classes with Marxist students, arguing about historical materialism, Soviet industrialisation, socialist realism, the Trotsky-Stalin conflict, Orwell's *Animal Farm*, Koestler's *Darkness at Noon*, the Cominform and Yugoslavia. When these discussions resolved themselves into disputes about specific cases which defied orthodoxy, the standard Marxist ploy was to fall back on the plea of 'ultimate' determination by the material framework. The standard comeback, how ultimate is ultimate? — to which there was no satisfactory response — became too tedious and I soon found myself avoiding sterile arguments. It was at this point that I discovered Weber. I had become aware of him years earlier, when I acquired the Pelican edition of Tawney's *Religion and the Rise of Capitalism*,[10] but knew little of his wider interests. With admirable timing, Routledge and Kegan Paul published the Gerth and Mills translation of his essays while I was in my second year as an undergraduate at the University of Melbourne.[11]

Weber's insights into the complexity of the relations between class, status and power provided the necessary corrective to the Marxist oversimplifications which had troubled me from the beginning. Weber's account of bureaucracy corresponded to my own observation and linked up with the Trotskyist critique of Stalinism. His emphasis on the role of ideas was a welcome antidote to determinism and relativism. Although I found his discussion of status inadequate and rather dated, it pointed the way to an effective analysis of contradictions in the class structure, much more than the mechanical Marxism by which the Russian peasantry were transformed into a 'stratum' rather than a 'class', or the unconvincing sleight-of-hand which could distinguish 'non-antagonistic' from antagonistic contradictions. I was also unconvinced by his account of ethical neutrality, but again it was a corrective to the fashionable Sartrean ideas about commitment which were, at that time, the trendiest posture among the student Left. Perhaps, also, I responded to the ambiguities and uncertainties that could be sensed in Weber's work, much more appealing to my taste than the dogmatic certainties of the Marxists and the vile language in which they were expressed.

I left university with no thought of an academic career. A long time passed before I was able to draw on this stock of ideas; fortunately, they had matured like government bonds in the days before double-digit inflation. More than two years later, I found myself working as a junior clerk in the Commonwealth Public Service in Canberra. For nine months, I was on the staff of the Public Service Board, which gave me valuable insights into the growth of the bureaucratic elite that was beginning to develop as a result of the spectacular expansion of the Commonwealth bureaucracy – a process I later described as the 'bureaucratic revolution'. For a further nine months, I worked in the Prime Minister's Department, drafting replies to letters from all corners of the country addressed to the Prime Minister (Menzies) and preparing contributions to Cabinet submissions on a variety of matters, from a new Australian flag to the arguments in favour of appointing serving public servants to the boards of statutory corporations. As my official duties left considerable time on my hands during working hours, I was able to use it in collecting data on the growth of the bureaucracy since 1939. My official position also gave me privileged access to the Parliamentary Library, so my needs for reference books were excellently provided. I discovered, incidentally, that the library was well stocked with fiction, which was the principal reading matter for a large number of parliamentarians.

Under these conditions, I was able to finish my M.A. thesis in less than a year, using a basically Weberian framework to examine the growth of a complex hierarchy in what had been, originally, a fairly small and fairly simple organisation, in which a former chairman of the Public Service

Board was able to devote time to the important matter of checking on the punctuality of his subordinates in returning from lunch. Not long after completing my master's thesis, I took up my first academic appointment (at Melbourne University) and started on a doctoral dissertation. For the next twelve to fourteen years, I worked within a fairly well-established set of research interests — the role of bureaucracy in modern society, the relations between elites and class structure, the formation and execution of policy within government, and a number of specific issues related to these main concerns.

Hazards of Research
The explorer of power structures confronts many difficulties. Voltaire described the hero of one of his stories as a person whose principal talent lay in discovering the truth, which all men seek to obscure. People in power have more reason for obscuring the truth than others, although not always for the same reasons. Politicians and businessmen are alike concerned, at times, to exaggerate their own influence and achievements; at other times, they obstruct efforts to penetrate the details. The structure of wealth is notoriously difficult to examine. Official records can be misleading. Journalistic accounts range from the totally dishonest to the merely ignorant.

My first experience of probing these obscurities came with the study of Cabinet government which I originally wrote for my doctorate and was later published.[12] On leaving the Prime Minister's Department for an academic appointment, I was presented with a copy of the new edition of Sir Ivor Jennings' *Cabinet Government,* the gift being intended to encourage me to do a similar task.[13] Jennings' work was heavily based on biographies and autobiographies of ex-ministers, monarchs and civil servants. I tried to follow this example, only to find that relatively few Australian politicians had similar memorials. For a long time, I felt disadvantaged by this lack. Great was my relief, therefore, to read the diaries of Richard Crossman and to find that I could stop fretting about the comparison.[14] I had, of course, discovered early that politicians' accounts of themselves were unreliable. Disraeli once remarked that the practice of politics could be summed up in one word — dissimulation. Disraeli avoided the problem of dissimulating *after* the event by writing novels, whereas many other politicians mislead posterity in their books after having misled their contemporaries by their actions. Crossman's work is unusual because he attempted, and succeeded, in exposing the real workings of government to public view, and thus earned himself an enduring niche in the literature of politics which he could not have gained either as a minister or as a don. It is easy to recognise the flavour of authenticity in his work, especially when it is checked against contemporary newspaper stories.

Crossman's diaries, because of their exceptional character, underline the dangers of relying on politicians' memoirs, which are exposed as trivial and self-indulgent when they are not positively dishonest. He gives little comfort, also, to those people who think that more access to official records, especially Cabinet minutes, will remedy the problems of official secrecy and political dissimulation. He confesses that he was surprised by the discovery that Cabinet minutes were a 'travesty' and that this applied also to the minutes of Cabinet committees.

In my own case, I read all the biographies and autobiographies available, and was little the wiser. Even a relatively good biography, like L.F. Crisp's book on J.B. Chifley (Labor Prime Minister, 1945–49), left out far too much.[15] The two volumes of Sir Robert Menzies' autobiography were almost totally uninformative.[16] When he does admit to a little local difficulty, like his deposition as Prime Minister in 1941, his account is not only misleading but factually inaccurate, as one can see by comparing it with that given by Sir Paul Hasluck in the official war history.[17] A surprisingly good autobiography was that of Sir Earle Page, a politician whose principal achievement was to have stayed in office for a total of more than twenty years.[18] On the other hand, his version of the events following the death of J.A. Lyons[19] is mendacious in the extreme, omitting all reference to his biting attack on Menzies, whom he accused of moral responsibility for Lyons' death. At the time, Page denied that he had consulted the Chief Justice of the High Court, Sir John Latham, in an apparent attempt to retain the Prime Ministership and thus keep Menzies out of it; in his autobiography, Page simply ignored the incident, which was described by Latham in an article several years after Page's death.[20]

Having gained little illumination from written accounts, I tried personal interviews with surviving ex-ministers, and located approximately ten of them. This was an educational experience, but mainly in a negative sense, as I learnt almost nothing of any real value. Generally speaking, my respondents had only the vaguest recollections of the policies for which they were theoretically responsible; they claimed credit for actions with which they had only tenuous connections; their memories for dates and other details were frequently wrong; and whatever juicy scandals they might have known about were not disclosed to an outsider. I did, however, meet one sprightly old gentleman who had been a minister before the 1914-18 war, and was delighted to give me verbal portraits of all the prime ministers of that period.

I turned to the official archives. At this time, in the mid-1950s, there were no proper archives; and although an archival policy existed on paper, there was no effective administration. Personal contacts, as an ex-official of the Prime Minister's Department, were of considerable assistance. At the time, the British fifty-year rule was supposedly in force; in practice, a file might have papers on it dating all the way from the early years of the Federal Government up to the day before yesterday. Having obtained a catalogue of files stored in the archives, I selected a list of promising titles which I sent to the Prime Minister's Department, one of whose officials was designated to read through the files I had nominated and to pass them on to me if they contained nothing explosive. During university vacations, I was allowed to visit Canberra and sit in an office adjoining this gentleman. As I read them, he would reclaim them from me, visibly twitching with relief every time a precious bundle was restored to him.

From all this, I gained a certain amount, though much less than I had initially hoped. Many files contained nothing more than the original versions of reports which were available as parliamentary papers. Others were full of press cuttings, many of which repeated verbatim the text of official handouts, thoughtfully filed in the same folder. There were no secrets and few surprises.

If official archives were so unrevealing, what about private letters? A few collections, lodged in the National Library, Canberra, or in the Mitchell Library (part of the State Library of NSW), Sydney, were useful and interesting. There were, however, difficulties in gaining access to other collections which had not been deposited in libraries. One of these was the Deakin[21] collection, deposited at the University of Melbourne after the death of his last surviving daughter, who wished the material to be used as the basis for a detailed biography. I asked for access, but was denied. After further efforts, both by my supervisor and myself, I was permitted to read the diary of Cabinet proceedings which Deakin had kept, there being no other form of record. To maintain the security of these privileged documents, I was required to sit in the office of the custodian and make notes from the diary under his watchful eye. This was my first experience of the jealousy with which scholars have been known to guard the sources to which they have privileged access, but it was not the last.

A few years later, I tried to gain access to the papers of W. M. Hughes, Prime Minister from 1915 to 1923, which had been deposited in the National Library, Canberra, after his death in 1952. It was generally believed, wrongly, that Hughes had willed his papers to the library on condition that they be used for an official biography to be written by L. F. Fitzhardinge, then Reader in Australian History at the

Australian National University, Canberra.[22] Hughes had, indeed, arranged that Fitzhardinge should write his biography, but his will does not mention the fact, and the papers were presented to the National Library by his widow, Dame Mary Hughes, who wrote to the executors at the time declaring her wish that the documents should be retained by the library after the biography was completed. (Even after twenty-five years, this has still not been finalised, as the second volume, though completed in 1974, remains unpublished at the date of writing.) One of the curious consequences of these actions by Hughes' widow is that access is still not untrammelled. According to the executors, legal advice is that quotation from the papers cannot be permitted unless they have first considered the matter, and that costs would be involved in such a consideration.[23]

I made several requests to examine the Hughes papers, and was refused on each occasion. I discovered, however, that graduate students at the Australian National University had been allowed to use them as source material. At this time, I was on the staff of an institution called the Canberra University College, established at Canberra in 1930 as a branch of the University of Melbourne, with which it enjoyed a somewhat uneasy, semicolonial relationship. I did not join the staff of the Australian National University until 1960, when the College was merged into it (an event referred to at the time as a union of 'gentlemen' and 'players'). By that time, I had been awarded my doctorate, the thesis had been accepted for publication, and my own passions over the incident had evaporated. They were aggravated by the fact that one of the graduate students concerned had agreed to let me see his notes, but later contracted cold feet and withdrew his offer.

I was also unsuccessful on a third occasion, when I approached a retired public servant who had been private secretary to several Prime Ministers and then permanent head of the Prime Minister's Department. He had an extensive collection of letters and documents, but after a long interview in which he gave me some valuable insights into the personality of Hughes, it became obvious that his condition for letting me use the papers was that I should write a biography of himself. As I had no wish to add this to my existing commitments, I was obliged to decline the implied invitation.

So far, I have referred almost entirely to the obstacles to research. How, then, does one obtain information? Fortunately, most matters of importance do get written down and become available sooner or later. Many years ago, the editor of the London *Times*, John Delane, described how he refused to pay for a confidential memorandum which had been offered to him under certain conditions, pointing out that it was not the business of the press to consider the needs of 'statecraft', and that the information was sure to reach him in due course from one source or another. The development of photocopying and tape-recording has made the last remark even truer than in Delane's lifetime. Despite the capriciousness and unreliability of the mass media, their importance as a means of disclosure must never be underrated. But even without them, recorded information is never short in western societies in which the 'information industry' encompasses something like one-third of the total workforce. The student of power who feels that access to private sources will open up special insights is likely to find that the harvest is relatively meagre.

Backlash
One of the consequences of studying power is that, from time to time, one is impelled to describe and comment on the behaviour of powerful people. If they dislike what is said about them, they can strike back.

In 1965, I was one of a regular panel of commentators who broadcast notes on the news during the midday radio programmes of the Australian Broadcasting Commission (ABC). In August of that year, I discussed the manoeuvres of Sir John McEwen, then Minister for Trade and Deputy Prime Minister in the Menzies Government, who was reportedly endeavouring to upgrade the importance of his department. In 1964, McEwen had extended the functions of the department to cover manufacturing industry, and it was consequently renamed Trade and Industry. To consolidate this expansion, McEwen proposed that it should have two joint permanent heads, one responsible for trade policy and the other for secondary industry. The move was opposed by the Public Service Board and also by the Treasury, which was recurrently at loggerheads with McEwen's department because of its aggressively protectionist stance. Like most bureaucratic intrigues, this story leaked out to the press and, as a result, questions were asked in Parliament. The Prime Minister, Sir Robert Menzies, replied that he knew nothing about the matter. This was an evasion, but it also indicated that Menzies was not prepared to support McEwen. Apart from this parliamentary question and answer, I had other sources of information which confirmed the details. McEwen's Press Secretary heard the broadcast and demanded a copy of the script from the ABC. Not long afterwards, I received a letter from the ABC, informing me that they were reviewing their panel of commentators, that it was their policy to rotate the membership, and that I would consequently not be required for the present. I knew this to be a specious excuse, since most of the ABC's news commentators remain on the panel for many years. Moreover, the ABC has a long history of yielding to pressure of this kind, especially from politicians. In 1952, my former colleague, Professor Macmahon Ball, was summarily dropped from his regular weekly news commentary after a broadcast in which he suggested that Chinese allegations about the use of germ warfare by the Americans in Korea should be investigated by the International Red Cross. The then Minister for External Affairs, Mr R. G. Casey [later Lord Casey] heard the broadcast and promptly rang the ABC demanding an explanation. Whether he received one I do not know, but Professor Ball was suddenly removed.[24]

Not every student of politics has the experience of being abused under cover of parliamentary privilege. This happened in 1972, when the former leader of the Australian

Labor Party, the late Mr Arthur Calwell, made a farewell speech in the House of Representatives, in which he objected to my use of the word 'larrikin' to describe both himself and the former Liberal Prime Minister, John Gorton.[25] In an article published in the fortnightly review *Nation* in 1968, I pointed out the frequency with which two polar types of political leaders, whom I described as 'larrikins' and 'prima donnas', crop up in national political life.[26] I noted that these categories transcended party affiliation. In a later article published in 1969, I observed that while Sir Robert Menzies was Prime Minister and Mr Calwell leader of the Labor opposition, we had both types in action at the same time.[27] Since then, Mr E. G. Whitlam had replaced Mr Calwell, and I remarked:

> Since Mr Holt's [the Liberal Prime Minister after Menzies] death and Mr Calwell's retirement there has been a striking reversal of roles. It is the prima donna who is leading the Labor Party and the larrikin who is leading the Liberal Party, whereas under Sir Robert Menzies the reverse was true.[28]

My classification of types was taken up by other political commentators, like Mr Edward St John, who was a Liberal MP under Prime Minister Gorton and attacked him violently as a larrikin in a book published before the 1969 general election.[29] The term 'prima donna' was widely applied to Mr Whitlam, especially after he became Prime Minister. A cartoonist in the *Sydney Morning Herald* used the caption for a drawing of Mr Whitlam, pictured appropriately in front of the Opera House. Whether Mr Whitlam resented the appellation, I have no certain knowledge, but Mr Calwell's language in his speech on the adjournment left no doubt about his reaction. He described my articles as 'vindictive, bitter and full of lying rubbish', and continued:

> Encel, who is a professor in the University of New South Wales, is a dishonoured and unrespected academic ... It is

he, not I, who is ... not only a larrikin, but a liar and a lout ... Because I am a socialist who believes that the strength upon which the Labor Party is built lies with the trade union movement and not with middle class voters, Encel had the temerity to call me an incompetent larrikin ... he has been hanging round the Labor Party for many years, smelling like a piece of rotten meat, in the hope that with a change of government he might be made head of a government department or given an ambassadorial post. Furthermore, I resent any character like Encel calling the Prime Minister of Australia, whoever he is, a larrikin.[30]

For good measure, Mr Calwell went on to abuse two members of the Parliamentary Press Gallery who had attacked Mr Gorton in similar terms — Alan Ramsey of the *Australian* and Laurie Oakes of the *Sun-Pictorial*. Mr Oakes, using the categories I had suggested, noted the same reversal of roles in the leadership of the two parties. Mr Calwell attributed to Mr Oakes the same motive as myself — that is, an important job under a Labor government — and described him as 'nothing better than a mental prostitute'.

Rather less dramatic was the communication I had from Mr Gorton's successor as Liberal Prime Minister, Mr William McMahon. The second edition of *Cabinet Government in Australia* contains a number of references to Mr McMahon's actions and statements as Prime Minister, most of them critical.[31] One Friday afternoon in February 1977, while working quietly at home, I received a telephone call from Mr McMahon, who had apparently just read the book in connection with a parliamentary debate on ministerial responsibility, and was most anxious to disabuse me of grave errors I had made concerning his actions in a case involving the sale of aircraft to the government of Cambodia. He was also concerned that I should not misunderstand his relationship with Sir John McEwen, with whom he claimed to have been 'good friends'. As the McEwen-McMahon 'feud' was a staple topic of political discussion throughout the 1960s, and the evidence for it is overwhelming, I was not particularly impressed by this avowal. Mr McMahon followed up this call with a letter which repeated a number of points he had made on the phone. This, at least, is one way of obtaining a collection of private papers.

Theory

The problem of theory was not of great significance in the writing of *Cabinet Government in Australia*, as the objective existence of the phenomenon was beyond doubt. The main theoretical aim was to show that the formal exercise of power through the Cabinet system must be related to a broader political culture, especially the party system and the mechanisms of selecting the political class. The writing of *Equality and Authority*,[32] however, involved much wider and more ambitious theoretical perspectives, which had concerned me since I was a student, when I had chosen to adopt a position derived from Weber rather than from Marx.

Emphasis on the central importance of power, force and violence has been due principally to the influence of Marxism. Marxian concepts of the State, ideology, c 'ture, mode of production, dialectical transformation and class struggle provide an alternative conception of reality hose major characteristics are conflict, inequality and exploitation. Because Marxism does confront the problem of power, it fills a theoretical vacuum and generates repeated challenges to liberal orthodoxy. The limitations of Marxism are, however, as notable as those of the 'bourgeois' social science to which it addresses its challenge. These limitations arise from two principal sources. A theory of society and of history, predicated upon the inevitable collapse of capitalism, is *ipso facto* insulated against evidence and arguments that do not treat this collapse as a certainty, and look for sources of power and authority which are not axiomatically dependent upon the private ownership of the means of production. A second weakness, the fatal flaw at the heart of Marxist-inspired intellectual movements, is their incorporation into authoritarian political structures with prescriptive powers over intellectual criticism. In all communist countries, power is an approved theme for social enquiry in some spheres but not in others. Imperialism, neo-colonialism and the threat of capitalist aggression are approved, but studies of power and inequality in the communist countries themselves are, to put it mildly, unwelcome. During the great Soviet purges of the 1930s, a number of professors of political science were arrested and condemned for poisoning the minds of students who had been accused of conspiracy to murder Stalin. In the 1960s and 1970s, economists and sociologists in Czechoslovakia, Hungary and Poland were arrested, exiled or deprived of their official posts for questioning the orthodox version of relationships between the government and the governed. In the capitalist countries, the official communist movement has been intellectually stultified for years, while the 'unofficial' Marxist groups are afflicted with varying forms of sectarianism which, like orthodoxy, does not encourage intellectual independence. The most recent and most fashionable variety of neo-Marxist criticism of bourgeois social science, deriving from the work of Louis Althusser, has had an immediately powerful impact, which is likely to become progressively attenuated because of the besetting tendency of Althusser and his followers to elevate theory above facts. Since social science depends upon both, its receptivity to the Althusserian 'problematic' will decline.

The shortcomings of Marxism and neo-Marxism are largely responsible for the enduring influence of ideas deriving from Weber, whose analyses of power structures manifest a clear recognition of the multiple sources of power and inequality. The most important single influence on studies of power in recent social science has been the work of C. Wright Mills, who chose to work in a Weberian rather than a Marxian framework. Mills began by rejecting the conventional imagery of American political science and of Parsonian sociology, which sees politics as a shifting equilibrium of pressure groups, calling it, dismissively, 'romantic pluralism'.[33] Instead, he placed the structure of power at the centre of his social analysis, recognising that the sources of social and political inequality on which power structures rest are multiple in character, and can be accounted for only in terms of a matrix of relationships. Although he became more sympathetic towards Marxism at the end of his life, his essential position was that which he stressed in replying to his 'radical' critics; that is, that men are not dominated solely by their relationships to the means of production.[34] Although Mills never solved his theoretical problems, his perspectives have remained influential. A recent American student of power structures argues, very much in the same vein as Mills, that 'culture' is an essential part of the analysis of power. 'Culture is a symbolic framework which must be shared by all those who operate within it. Cultural meaning systems cannot, therefore, be easily or unilaterally changed by a minority'. Culture mediates between interest and action, and can shape class actions as much as those actions in turn shape mass attitudes.[35] To take a relevant instance, the seizure of power by the Bolsheviks in 1917 did not transform, and shows no sign of transforming, Russian society into an egalitarian, democratic, socialist society as envisaged by Lenin in *The State and Revolution.* It would be more accurate to describe post-revolutionary Russia in terms of the replacement of the Czarist autocracy by the Communist autocracy.

Weber was mistaken in thinking that the revolutionary regime would collapse, as he wrote in 1918, because no government could manage without a bureaucratic apparatus. The regime became bureaucratised, as Trotsky recognised many years after the revolution, but did not collapse. This recognition has been a major stimulus to the study of elite groups in contemporary society. As Mills saw, the importance of elites arises from the great centralisation of political and economic power in large formal institutions, and is not inconsistent with the structural analyses of Marx. Other students have also recognised the complementary nature of the concepts of class and elite. Bottomore, for instance, notes that class and elite can refer either to different types of political systems or to different aspects of the same system. Hence, he proposed a threefold typology of class/elite structures, ranging from a tightly articulated ruling class to a multiplicity of elites, without a cohesive group of powerful individuals or families.[36] Giddens extends this to a fourfold classification, linking the type of elite with a power structure, from a cohesive oligarchy to a loosely articulated set of leadership groups, operating in an hegemonic/democratic power structure, with an 'abstract' elite rather than a visible aggregation of persons.[37]

Giddens also points out that even if political power depends upon economic power, the Marxist equation of the two distorts the fact that power must be mediated through institutional structures, and that the behaviour of elites is fundamental to the mediation process. A similar view is taken by Miliband, especially in his criticism of Althusserian 'structural super-determinism'. Miliband contends, as Mills did before him, that politics is an autonomous sphere of action which is influenced by, but never wholly reducible to, economic interest.[38] My experience of studying the actual operations of politics and bureaucracy had given me the same conviction. At the same time, I rejected the assumption that all inequalities between 'men' would be removed as the result of a proletarian revolution. I was already aware of the ambiguities inherent in the use of the word 'man' to refer to two sexes with widely differing social roles, whose equalisation demanded a much more fundamental change in social relationships than the abolition of the private ownership of the means of production. For different reasons, I did not accept the related assumption that racial prejudice was a social artifact of capitalism. Even as an adolescent, it was obvious to me that Marxism was quite unable to cope with the maniacal and sadistic racism of Nazi Germany, for which quite other forms of explanation were needed — if, indeed, that phenomenon can ever be explained. Despite the theoretical difficulties involved in the concept of 'status', it provided a necessary alternative category to subsume inequalities which were neither political in nature nor the result of ownership and control of the means of production. My concept of status was not the same as that of Weber, who in my view had never solved the logical problems of distinguishing between class and status.

The adoption of this theoretical perspective made the task of writing *Equality and Authority* more difficult, partly because it generated a host of theoretical problems, partly because it demanded a much wider search for material than might otherwise have been the case. The book attracted a correspondingly wide range of criticism, which reminded me of the three types of critics identified by Mills — the liberals, the radicals and the highbrows. The liberals, in this case, were mainly newspaper reviewers who disliked my emphasis on class differences and on the influence of institutions such as the private schools in accentuating and deepening these differences. The highbrow criticisms took a number of forms. One involved the objection that the book was concerned too much with elites and not enough with classes; in other cases it was reversed, so that I was criticised for being too concerned with the minutiae of class and status and not sufficiently with elucidating the structure of power. Another highbrow criticism was that my work was concerned with describing structures and not with the attitudes or motivations of individuals. The radical critiques, basically Marxist in character, objected to my refusal to identify a clear-cut ruling class and my preference for Weber rather than Marx, and accused me of being a Parsonian functionalist in disguise.

Two particular critiques are worth mentioning here because of their depth and rigour. Both of them are also characterised by a combination of the radical and highbrow perspectives. R. W. Connell has used his critique to strengthen the rationale of his own work on class structure in Australia.[39] He objects to my model of class and status as being essentially 'stratificationist' and based on occupational differences. The model, he asserts, is derived from Weber and from W. G. Runciman, to whom he attributes a 'pure stratificationist perspective'. This perspective involves a concept of society as made up of *ranks,* whose components include wealth, occupation, education and family membership. Connell's attack on the 'stratificationist' perspective is penetrating and effective, but he is wrong to attribute such a perspective to Weber or Runciman, or for that matter to myself. The model of class and status which I constructed in *Equality and Authority* depends partly on occupation, partly on ownership of the means of production, and partly on control of economic resources and political mechanisms. In other words, the structure of class and status at any given time is the outcome of conflict as well as the existence of established hierarchies. Connell notes that my work contains a 'mixture of perspectives', which I could hardly take as a criticism since I explicitly stressed the need for a variety of perspectives on such a complex problem. As a critic of other people, Connell operates from a Marxist standpoint. When he comes himself to deal with the many-sided nature of social reality, he veers towards a Weberian posture; for example, when he notes that the division of labour is embedded in an 'elaborate structure of status distinctions, income differences, customary privileges and differential recruitment'.

Connell also disputes my emphasis on bureaucracy as part of the power structure, and in particular my examination of the role of individual officials. 'The attitudes of senior officials', he asserts, 'are not normally a principal determinant of the way the bureaucracy functions'. This is simply not true, as even a brief consideration of administrative history would demonstrate, and it underrates the importance of bureaucracy in society. Moreover, Connell's position on this matter is inconsistent, because he goes on to say that the 'individual' power of bureaucrats is more important than their collective power as a unit within the social order. It is precisely because the collective weight of bureaucracy *is* important that individual officials have a lasting influence on policy and politics. The role of the bureaucrat is particularly significant during periods of rapid social change, when the interests of powerful groups become split up and confused. The impact of rapid technological change is an outstanding example. The growth of the so-called 'post-industrial society' (which is post-industrial in the sense that it entails new kinds of struggles over resources) provides another important perspective on increasing bureaucratisation. What Connell said about my work in a comparatively polite way was repeated at much greater length by Osmond.[40] Osmond's critique reflects the collective view of a group of neo-Marxists responsible for publishing the magazine *Arena*. Apparently, he and his colleagues felt so strongly about my work that they found it necessary to publish their critique in a polemical pamphlet of 52 pages. When I first read this pamphlet I felt personally attacked, not by the polemic, but by the vituperative intensity of Osmond's writing, which accused me not only of a wide variety of theoretical sins but also of intellectual shallowness and inability to comprehend the significance of some important writers and a number of key concepts. The tone of the pamphlet, however, is paradoxical, because Osmond appears determined to prove that my work is worthless, in which case it hardly seems to merit such a prolonged and rigorous attack. Perhaps the resolution of the paradox lies in a sentence on the last page, which asserts that my work is 'fatally undermined by the general weaknesses of Cold War social science'. In other words, the pamphlet is a political statement whose intent is to identify my work with the 'liberal establishment' of American social science and its involvement with American foreign policy under Kennedy and Johnson. This 'establishment' is associated with the well-known views of Daniel Bell about the 'end of ideology', which Osmond also ascribes to me. As I devoted a number of pages in *Equality and Authority* to attacking the Australian version of the 'end of ideology' school, which sees politics in terms of pluralistic competition between interest groups, I was unable to take this identification seriously.

It is interesting to observe that another of the contributors to this book, Alex Mamak, has also been involved in a controversy with contributors to *Arena* because of his participation in a project sponsored by a mining company, and his chapter deals in part with the issues ventilated in that controversy. These are essentially the issues put so eloquently in the two famous lectures by Weber, *Science as a Vocation* and *Politics as a Vocation*. Although, as I said earlier in this chapter, I am not convinced by Weber's discussion of ethical neutrality, my position is closer to his than it is to the Marxist theorem which treats all social science as ideological (except, of course, for Marxist social science). Behind that lies the more fundamental proposition that *all* science is ideological unless it is in harmony with dialectical materialism, a doctrine which would be no more than an occasion for good clean fun if it were not the basis for repression of unpopular opinions by Communist governments.

One curious feature of Osmond's pamphlet is its failure to examine the implications of an analysis of class, status and power in Australia derived from a basically Weberian perspective. Throughout his account, he describes me as a kind of crypto-functionalist or unconscious Parsonian.[41] Even as an undergraduate, I was unable to take Parsons seriously, for reasons similar to those advanced briefly by Hugh Stretton in his contribution to this volume and elaborated in his book *The Political Sciences*.[42] Like Connell, Osmond derides my emphasis on bureaucracy as a 'master-theme', without any real judgement about the validity of such an emphasis. He seems unable to accept the notion that there are positions which are neither Marxist nor Parsonian.

Conclusion
When the work is done and the book is published, it no longer belongs to the writer. Other people's reactions are now part of the relationship between the writer and his work.
> Between the conception
> And the creation
> Between the emotion
> And the response
> Falls the shadow.

The two books described above were written in an attempt to explore the nature of power, inequality and privilege.

Their existence continues to influence me in a double form — partly through my response to other people's reactions, as though I were seeing the world through a pair of spectacles with one lens of plain glass and one of refracting glass. I would not — could not — write either of these books again, but the experience of writing them confirms my profound belief that the justification for my work as a social scientist lies in these areas.

NOTES AND REFERENCES

1. Russell, B. *Power,* Norton, 1938, pp.11-15.
2. Partridge, P.H. 'Some Notes on the Concept of Power', *Political Studies* 11 (1963), pp.107-25.
3. Eckstein, H. (ed.). *Internal War,* Princeton University Press, 1968, Introduction.
4. *Science and Government Report,* 1 November 1976.
5. Myrdal, G. *The Political Element in the Development of Economic Thought,* transl. Paul Streeten, Routledge & Kegan Paul, 1953.
6. Kapp, K.W. *The Costs of Private Enterprise,* Harvard University Press, 1950.
7. Strachey, J. *The Nature of Capitalist Crisis,* Gollancz, 1932.
8. Strachey, J. *The Coming Struggle for Power,* Gollancz, 1935.
9. Snow, E. *Red Star Over China,* Gollancz, 1943.
10. Tawney, R.H. *Religion and the Rise of Capitalism,* Pelican, 1938.
11. Gerth, H.H. & Mills, C.W. (eds). *From Max Weber: Essays in Sociology,* Routledge & Kegan Paul, 1947.
12. Encel, S. *Cabinet Government in Australia,* Melbourne University Press, 1962; rev. edn, 1974.
13. Jennings, I. *Cabinet Government,* Cambridge University Press, 2nd edn, 1951.
14. Crossman, R. *Diaries of a Cabinet Minister,* vol. 1, Hamish Hamilton & Jonathan Cape, 1975.
15. Crisp, L.F. *Ben Chifley,* Longmans, 1961.
16. Menzies, R.G. *Afternoon Light,* Cassell, 1967; *The Measure of the Years,* Cassell, 1970.

17. Hasluck, P.M.C. *The Government and the People 1939-41*, Official War History, series 4, vol. 1, 1952.
18. Page, E. *Truant Surgeon*, Angus & Robertson, 1963. Sir Earle Page was leader of the Country Party in the Federal Parliament, 1923-39; Treasurer, 1923-29; Prime Minister, April 1939; Minister for Health, 1949-58.
19. J.A. Lyons was a minister in the Scullin (Labor) government 1929-31, and became Prime Minister in a conservative government, 1932-39. He died suddenly in March 1939.
20. Latham, J.G. Review of 'Truant Surgeon', *Quadrant* 7 (1963).
21. Alfred Deakin was Attorney-General in the first Federal Government, 1901-03; Prime Minister, 1903-04, 1905-08 and 1909-10.
22. Fitzhardinge, L.F. *W.M. Hughes, A Political Biography*, vol. 1, Angus & Robertson, 1964.
23. Letter from Perpetual Trustee Company Ltd, Sydney, 14 December 1976.
24. A number of recent cases of this kind are reviewed in the ABC Staff Association journal, *Channel* 1, 4 & 5 (1974).
25. Larrikin, a term which originated in the cities of Sydney and Melbourne about a century ago, means a flash, tough, aggressive and irreverent character.
26. Encel, S. 'The Larrikin Leaders', *Nation*, 25 May 1968.
27. Encel, S. 'The Leader of the Push', *Nation*, 13 December 1969.
28. Encel, 'The Leader of the Push'.
29. St John, E.H. *A Time to Speak*, Sun Books, 1969.
30. Commonwealth Parliamentary Debates, 11 October 1972, pp.2479-80.
31. Encel, *Cabinet Government in Australia*.
32. Encel, S. *Equality and Authority: A Study of Class, Status and Power in Australia*, Cheshire, Melbourne, 1970; Tavistock, London, 1970.
33. Mills, C.W. *The Power Elite*, Oxford University Press, 1956; Parsons, T. 'The Distribution of Power in American Society', in *Essays in Sociological Theory*, Free Press, 2nd edn, 1964.
34. Domhoff, G.W. & Ballard, H.B. (eds). *C. Wright Mills and the Power Elite*, Beacon Press, 1968.

35. Mollenkopf, J. 'Theories of the State and Power Structure Research', *Insurgent Sociologist* 5, 3 (1975), p.255.
36. Bottomore, T.B. *Elites and Society*, Watts, 1966, p.44.
37. Giddens, A. 'Elites in the British Class Structure', in P. Stanworth & A. Giddens (eds), *Elites and Power in British Society*, Cambridge University Press, 1974, p.7.
38. Miliband, R. 'Poulantzas and the Capitalist State,' *New Left Review* 82 (1973).
39. Connell, R.W. *Ruling Class, Ruling Culture*, Cambridge University Press, 1976.
40. Osmond, W. 'The Dilemma of an Australian Sociology', *Arena*, monograph, 1972.
41. Osmond, pp.10-11, 13, 26-28, 30, 32, 35.
42. Stretton, H. *The Political Sciences*, Routledge & Kegan Paul, 1969.

CAPITAL MISTAKES

Hugh Stretton

This chapter describes an attempt to reform some Australian housing and banking processes. In the 1970s, the new inflation hit those lines of business in a particular way that threatened severe suffering and trouble. During 1974 I arrived at an analysis of the trouble, partly familiar and partly new, which seemed to indicate a workable cure for it. The idea was offered to the Australian Government, then to the South Australian State Government. So it is possible to compare how two bureaucracies responded to identical advice.

They responded very differently. That did not seem to be because of their different situations — the suggested action was more appropriate for the Federal Government which refused it, and less appropriate for the State Government which nevertheless decided to give it a cautious trial. The responses seemed to be chiefly personal, reflecting the individual values and beliefs of the people concerned. In earlier years, I had written about the relations between values and technical beliefs in social science, and now the public servants' responses illustrated some of those relations vividly. So this report begins with a note about that earlier work.

It is written in a personal autobiographical way and describes conflicts in which I thought I was right and the rest of the world was wrong. Readers will allow for bias, self-righteousness, etc.; but I hope they will also allow for something else. Historically, it is very rare indeed for any broad set of social and economic troubles to arise from a single institutional mistake, or to be curable by a simple institutional trick. Nevertheless, the world teems with deluded people who think they have one-shot solutions to economic problems — governments have to brush off single-taxers and currency cranks every day. Unhappily, that fact of life makes desperate difficulties for anyone who *does* perceive the rare case of a simple malfunction with a genuinely workable cure.

Learning
I first met the modern social sciences quite early in their post-war career, at Princeton in 1948. As a history graduate looking for broader education, I took courses in economics, sociology, political science and international relations. It was a provoking experience. The economics was old-fashioned, perhaps wrong, but honestly meant. Large chunks of the other courses seemed to be simply fraudulent. Smart new operators were pointing the social sciences in smart new directions, trying to make them more abstract or more quantitative, more objective, more like physics — and whatever else, more profitable in the ordinary way of business. But on careful technical inspection, too much of the new business seemed to be strictly a sucker business, because too much of the new science was sterile, and certain to remain so. The models were inappropriate for their tasks, the theories were of types that could never deliver any new holds on the unknown, the objectivity was bogus, the jargon served chiefly to obscure the other shortcomings. Only the fund-hunting and sales approach were effective.

The intellectual pretension and trickery we were getting were fair samples of what rising numbers of students were beginning to get all over the affluent world; as the production of social scientists and their sale to business and government multiplied, and more and more of the ruling classes' recruits were put through six or eight years of undergraduate and postgraduate training, often within a single discipline or at least a single philosophy of science. Of course, education has to direct people to some degree, and these trainees were all supposed to have democratic and academic freedom to think as they pleased. But they were required to be scientific as their disciplines defined it, and many of the developing rules of 'discipline', 'objectivity' and 'science' were quite hostile to a genuinely observant, thoughtful, fruitful study of social life.

Such nasty-looking developments in the modes of conservatism, and in the selection and training of rich countries' ruling classes, seemed to be fit subjects for study by historians. But to study them usefully, a historian would need to understand the social sciences from inside. I spent the spare time of the next fifteen years learning to understand the main structures and directions of theory in contemporary economics, sociology and political science – also in history, because (contrary to what most of both parties were saying at the time) it struck me that the main methodological problems of the social sciences were very like the problems that historians faced in selecting and constructing historical explanations. In both cases, the problems were less technical than political – they were questions of scientific purpose, but in the social sciences those tend to be questions of social purpose too.

I eventually arrived at reasons for believing that most social theory and research *had* to differ according to the personal values of the theorists and researchers, and certainly *ought* to do so. It must do so not just from human bias or frailty, but for strictly technical reasons. The structure of natural-scientific theory is ultimately determined by its subject matter and the scientists' purposes. Social theory is the same, but its subject matter and purposes are inevitably more contentious and changeable. Therefore (unless society itself has no conflicts of interest) widely agreed, universally serviceable theories are not to be expected except where their use relies on shared values, or is enforced by political or academic coercion. Academic coercion is often associated with 'discipline', a portmanteau word whose meanings include rules and styles of work, and intellectual and administrative boundaries. Disciplines often define their boundaries and membership by the theories they elect to use, and the theories always incorporate somebody's values, however open or concealed.

Of course; the values may be more professional than social. For example, plenty of economists have thought their political opinions less important than their ambition to build an exact, unified science, as deductive and mathematical as possible. But it makes sense to build a science like that only to the extent that life is like that; that is, to the extent that reliably regular economic behaviour can be abstracted from the other social activity of which it is a part. If theory-builders push the exercise beyond those real-life limits, they get into two kinds of trouble. Theory becomes irrelevant, unreliable, unprovable, or all three. And in choosing their constants and variables, the theorists may develop a systematic bias in favour of social constants and economic variables. The effects of that bias are likely to be politically conservative.

An opposite response to social complexity has always come from a school of institutional economists whose twentieth-century leaders have included Wicksell, Myrdal, Paul Streeten and (in odd, uneasy ways) those political opposites Joseph Schumpeter and Paul Sweezy, both of them doctrinaires in principle but institutionalists in practice. Any economic system is a social and political creation. It will rarely be well understood without understanding many determinants of economic activity, which are themselves neither economic, nor stable. It may often include strands of repetitive behaviour which can be forecast by the use of local models and theories; but that is all, and even that is subject to historical change. It follows that useful economic understanding is always likely to depend in varying degrees on local knowledge. It will usually have to include a good deal of eclectic political, social and historical explanation. Most important of all, many technical beliefs about an economic system are part of it and affect its working; but they keep changing – so economists need to be able to step outside the going systems of technical belief (including their own) and observe *their* workings. Thinking through that last imperative, first Gunnar Myrdal and then Paul Streeten have contributed most of this century's best perceptions of the irreducible role of values in all the social sciences, not just in economics.

I had the extreme good fortune to be a fellow-student, then a colleague of Streeten's. Besides friendship, he and I have shared some common methodological interests and also the experience of living and working with Thomas Balogh, that most instinctive, original, flamboyant and warlike of Anglo-Hungarian economists and advisers to British Labour leaders. I began my academic life living in a flat in Balogh's house, followed some of his professional and political warfare, and shared some of his and Streeten's pupils at a time when the Balliol tutors were trying to give the school of philosophy, politics and economics some of its intended unity. While Streeten was writing his powerful first paper 'Programs and Prognoses',[1] he was also translating some of Myrdal's methodological work for publication in English. I was trying to follow suit, writing my first papers about social and historical explanation, and translating some of Balogh's manuscripts from actionable Hungarian English into libel-free English English. I was less successful than Streeten — my papers were not published, and Balogh had a regrettable tendency to translate his books back again. But by the time I moved from Oxford to Adelaide, I was equipped to follow the more general philosophical and theoretical developments in economics, as far as my studies of the social sciences required.

Those studies were a long time getting done. At various dates, there were short difficult papers which nobody would publish, then in 1966 a long book, which appeared three years later as *The Political Sciences: General principles of selection in social science and history*.[2] Most of it had been lonely work. In Australia through those years, some sophisticated methodologists emerged from the Melbourne history school, but the other social sciences either stayed old-fashioned, or adopted fairly mindless 'scientistic' ambitions.

If you questioned those ambitions in a technical way, you would usually be sneered at for persecuting Copernicus and wanting to restore religious censorship and a flat earth. Economists were calmer than sociologists, but no likelier to listen to 'outsiders'; and none of them seemed to have read Wicksell or Myrdal, or heard of Streeten. Meanwhile I had picked up one easy skill: if dealing with one of the unoriginal majority of the profession, knowing two of his or her opinions was enough to guess the rest of them and often also the textbooks they came from and the concealed values their owner didn't know they depended on. If we conversed at all, we were likely to irritate each other, and I learned to avoid it.

After *The Political Sciences,* I interviewed a great many town planners and administrators and wrote a more practical book called *Ideas for Australian Cities.* Unoriginally, its jacket blurb was headed *Women and children last*? That may have helped to get me appointed – I believe as token woman *and* token intellectual, a characteristic economy – to the board of the South Australian Housing Trust. It was then necessary to learn the housing business in a practical way, from the work of that frugal and efficient organisation and from Alex Ramsay, the general manager who keeps it so. Among the lessons: public housing performance has intricate relations with the behaviour of private housing and money markets, so it is necessary to understand those too. In Australian conditions, Housing Commissions (public housing authorities) that do nothing but build houses can easily do less good than they should, so the Trust was a town and community developer, a land dealer, a factory builder and the landlord of four hundred shops. Not by uses of 'government power', but by its business operations in the market, it had been expected since its foundation to exercise a State-wide influence on private land and housing prices and rents, and also on real wages, industrial investment, and the geographical distribution of work and community services. As a first principle of management, whatever else such an operation needs, it needs a number of the people engaged in it to be personally committed to its social purposes.

I spent 1973 overseas, part of the time studying British and Scandinavian housing developments for the Housing Trust. So I missed the first year of the Whitlam Labor Government, but arranged to work for it in a part-time way from 1974. How could I make myself useful to it? Max Neutze and Patrick Troy of the Australian National University's Urban Research Unit were succeeding with excellent urban and land policies, as far as the Constitution and some hostile State Governments allowed. Partly to complement those urban policies, and partly for other urgent reasons, the Federal Government needed a housing policy. So far it had no sign of one. Furthermore, it appeared to have no idea of the way in which some new distortions in the money and housing markets were contributing to its general economic problems of inflation and unemployment. So there seemed to be scope for a contribution to housing and banking policy.

One thing that helped Troy and Neutze was that urban policy was a new line for the Federal Government, so it had got a new department, with professionals recruited from outside as well as inside the public service, and chosen with as much attention to their values and commitments as to their skills. Housing policy, on the other hand, belonged to an old-established department, and of course depended on the co-operation of the Treasury, Commonwealth Banks and Cities Commission, whose professional personnel also survived from earlier regimes. In supposing that I could teach anything to that class of Canberra talent, I made my own capital mistake.

The Mistake in the Capital Market
In the 1970s, a general sickness seemed to be afflicting the Australian housing business. Less and less young households could buy houses — even the houses their parents had bought from lower real incomes. It was beginning to require an income above average, or two incomes in the household, or some inherited wealth, to get into the market at all. Young

families especially, if they depended on one breadwinner, were being steadily excluded. More of them therefore had to rent housing, share housing, put off buying it until later in life. But rents were rising. From 1973, private investment in new rental housing fell sharply; and contrary to orthodox expectations, *no* level of rent seemed able to attract new investment to restore the supply.

So housing, and the financial and other advantages of owning it, began to be redistributed from poorer to richer. While poorer households were excluded from housing choice and ownership, the richer households who could still achieve it did exceptionally well. They borrowed at negative real interest, built bigger houses than before, and made bigger capital gains than ever from the super-inflation of property prices, from lenders, and from tenants and tax concessions.

There was thus a paradox. Since the effective national housing performance of the 1950s, national productivity had increased by as much as half. Real building costs were still trending downward. But a richer and more productive population was now able to supply home ownership or cheap rental housing to a *falling* proportion of new households — although in real terms the houses were cheaper to build, and more households were willing and able to pay more for them than ever before.

Such an absurd contradiction had to conceal some basic mistake. It did. Except for the movement of land prices (which had independent causes), all those reversals of trend arose directly or indirectly from the 'capital mistake' of my title. In a sentence, this was the mistake: our financial institutions had responded to the new inflation in a way which lowered real interest but drastically shortened real credit, a combination which began to redistribute wealth and housing relentlessly in favour of the already-richer. As the main subject of this narrative, the mistake needs detailed explanation.

When money values are stable, debts maintain both nominal and real value over time. In unstable conditions, they cannot do that — 'money back' and 'real value back' are no longer the same thing. With the onset of significant inflation, lenders and borrowers therefore face a novel question. Should they go on specifying their debts in the old way, in nominal money terms? If they do that, they will have to cope with inflation by increasing nominal interest rates. Alternatively, they can decide to specify their capital debts in real terms, by linking the amounts lent to an appropriate price index. If they do that, it will still be possible to lend real value for long terms, and interest rates can go on behaving as they did in stable conditions.

With the onset of significant inflation, governments and banks and other financial institutions can therefore respond in one of three ways. They can continue to offer their customers the traditional nominal terms only, for all lending and borrowing. Or they can convert to offering indexed-capital terms only. Or they can offer facilities for both, and let market forces sort out the volumes and interest rates of the two flows. The third (dual flow) alternative is probably the efficient one. But in the 1970s, Australian institutions (in line with most of the capitalist world) continued to insist on the first; that is, on lending and borrowing in nominal money terms only.

If that policy persists under persistent inflation — even with 5% or so of inflation — it will lower most rates of real interest, shorten all long credit, change the structure of the national economy, reduce its efficiency, encourage additional inflation and unemployment, and make some steady net transfer of wealth and income from poorer to richer.

To explain how a single institutional mistake can have all those ill effects, it may be best to begin by defining 'real interest' and 'short credit' by an example. Suppose that in stable conditions you lend $1000 for ten years at 3% p.a. interest. You will be paid $30 interest each year for ten years, then you will get your $1000 capital back. Now compare what happens when you expect (say) 10% annual inflation, but still lend your money in the conventional way. You add the expected 10% of inflation to the interest rate, merely to protect your capital value from erosion by inflation. So you now lend $1000 for ten years at 13% interest. Call that nominal interest, because the first 10% of it merely maintains your capital value against shrinkage. Only the remaining 3% is genuine profit, or payment for the use of capital. That 3% is real interest, just as the 3% on your first loan was. Real interest is the difference between the rate of nominal interest and the rate of inflation.

Over their ten-year terms, both those loans will return the real value of the $1000 lent, plus interest. But there is a difference: the second loan will pay most of it back much earlier. In the first year, the 'stable' loan at 3% pays $30, but the 'inflated' loan at 13% pays $130; that is, the same $30 of real interest plus $100 *which is really an early return of capital.* That $100 used to be lent for ten years. Now it is only lent for one year. Similarly, the second annual payment will return some capital value which was only lent for two years; and so on. What has changed is not the rate of real interest, but the pattern of capital repayment. All long-term loans now have to make high early repayments of capital. That is what is meant by 'short credit'. It gets shorter, and the early repayments get steeper, as rates of inflation and nominal interest rise.

The critical economic effect is this: as the early repayment requirement rises higher, it excludes more and more classes of long-term borrowers whose private or business incomes cannot afford such early or uneven repayments. The reasons for excluding them have nothing whatever to do with the rate of real interest the borrowers could afford to pay over time, and the reasons have nothing to do with the efficiency or profit with which the excluded borrowers might have used the capital if they could have bid for it. With so many bidders excluded, those who can still borrow can usually do so at low or negative real interest, and are encouraged to borrow copiously, especially to buy property. So there are simultaneous contributions to unemployment and inflation. But most important, there is no longer fair competition, or rational adjustment, between short and long needs for capital. The central allocative mechanism of an efficient capital market has ceased to work.

Under these novel conditions, industries and firms begin to be sorted out as they never were before. They face new tests which never previously affected their capacities to compete. Industries and firms vary widely in their credit needs. Some need long credit for producers, some need it for their customers. Many depend on one another − plenty of cash of short-credit industries depends on business from long-credit industries, and vice versa. A main function of an efficient capital market is to adjust all those diverse credit needs to each other, at continuous prices for time, with competitive tests of efficiency. But when the wrong terms of debt persist under inflation, efficient adjustment ceases. Instead, industries begin to be sorted out simply according to their capacity to survive in a short-credit world.

If that test persists, its effects are bound to be destructive. It will cause structural unemployment. It will add to inflation, because those who can still afford to borrow will often still perceive the high early debt-repayments as 'interest' and build them into rents and product prices accordingly. That is violently inflationary pricing; it means that faster rates of amortisation and capital gain are built into prices. Above all, the new structure of industries will not serve real consumer preferences as well as the old one did.

These particular effects of inflation are curable. To correct the capital mistake, governments and financial institutions need to offer alternative, capital-indexed terms of debt to borrowers and lenders who want them. That allows genuine long-term credit again, for housing or anything else, with repayment requirements fitted to capacities to pay over time, and interest rates as they were in stable times. (From 1945 to 1972, *real* interest on long-term lending averaged between 1% and 2%.) The change has practical difficulties, but with care they can all be overcome.

In 1974, it was already obvious that the capital mistake created a general economic problem, not just a housing problem. But it was probably expedient to attack it first as a housing problem. Politicians would merely glaze over at technical talk of 'a slow-acting distortion in the capital market'. Housing was more understandable, politically sensitive, and the obvious place to begin reform. To conclude this section, this is how the capital mistake produced so many of the housing troubles of the 1970s:

Most housing has to be built or bought on long credit. A house typically costs about four times the annual income of its occupier. The occupier can afford to pay perhaps a quarter of his or her income in rent or repayment. Simple arithmetic shows that a household living on one modest wage can therefore pay, each year, up to about 7.5% of the whole value borrowed. That payment has to include some costs and capital repayment as well as interest, so the rate of interest needs to be well below 7.5%. Because three of four years' income have been borrowed, there is a relentless multiplier: each 1% of interest takes 4% or 5% of the occupier's income. A housing loan at 4% interest can typically be repaid from 20% of income; 7% interest takes 30% of income; 11% interest takes 45% of income; and so on.

Whole classes of borrowers begin to be excluded as nominal interest rises above 5% and the demand on income rises above 25%. Australian home ownership began to decline when interest rates passed 5% in the 1960s. When they reached 11% in 1974, the arithmetic of the multiplier hit every kind of housing. Rising numbers of would-be homebuyers were excluded because they could not afford the steep early capital repayments concealed in the interest rate. Private entrepreneurs would no longer put borrowed capital into rental housing, because their early debt repayments would similarly be beyond most tenants' rent-paying capacities. Public housing also suffered. Since its introduction in 1945, the public housing programme had run with little or no real subsidy — the tax-payers may even have made a nominal profit from it. But from 1974, governments had to borrow at 9% or more to finance housing which could still return only 4%, so Treasurers of both Liberal and Labor parties moved to reduce the volume of new housing. (Politicians meanwhile responded to public pressure by giving grants and tax exemptions to those who *could* still buy houses. That saved some middle-income buyers, but made most of the new inequalities worse.)

The effects on the population as a whole were slow but cumulative. More households would be hit each year, even if inflation subsided to 5% or 7%, which was the best that most people hoped for in the foreseeable future. As the numbers of frustrated citizens accumulated from year to year, politicians would have real cause for alarm. There did indeed seem to be scope for a true analysis of the trouble, and workable ways to put it right.

Canberra, 1974-75
From 1974, I tried with others to persuade the Australian Government to accept the above diagnosis of its housing troubles. The analysis of the perverse mechanism was not hard to understand. Many economists of all persuasions accepted it. So did some individual public servants in Canberra.[4] Austen Holmes directed one group with whom I worked. When he and I disagreed it was for reasons we both respected — he is not the subject of any of this chapter's complaints, and he accepted and improved the argument about the capital mistake. But most Canberra public servants and consultants rejected it, and so did Federal Governments of one political party after the other.

Early in 1974, the Ministers for Housing and for Urban and Regional Development had agreed to ask for an independent review of national housing policy. As one of the reviewers, I began some homework. But the Ministers' verbal agreement had first to be expressed in a letter requesting the review, and for most of the year their departments failed to agree a text for the letter. Waiting for it to come, I did enough work to arrive at the understanding of the capital mistake sketched above. (Also at a general set of housing policies for a national government, but those are not the subject of this chapter.) The months went by with no Ministerial letter and therefore no official use for all that homework. Then, in June, the Australian Broadcasting Commission rang up to ask for five half-hour radio lectures, with scripts fit to print as a short book. Having checked that my Federal employer didn't object, it was easy to decide that the talks should be about housing policy. It was much harder to choose the best 'tone of voice' for them.

Various things can help to sell a new idea to politicians: some awareness of trouble, some helpful public opinion, a workable project, and so on. It may also be necessary to convince departmental advisers, or to persuade politicians to override them. I bothered a lot about that last problem. Most of the relevant advisers, whether economists or not, had economic beliefs of a particular complexion. The mistake in the capital market could be explained to them in orthodox terms. But from personal conservatism, many of them still wouldn't want to do anything about it. Worse, they would certainly oppose many other desirable housing reforms (not described here) to which a capital reform would open the way; and in advising against those latter, they would use a lot of arguments which *did* derive authority from their orthodox theoretical beliefs. There was really no way — at least, no intellectual way — to attack those defences without attacking some of their theoretical foundations.

To persuade people to change course it is often hard to judge whether to adapt your projects to their existing assumptions or, on the other hand, to try to bring their assumptions and purposes into question. Rightly or wrongly, I decided that the radio talks should pick a deliberate, provocative fight with the hostile economic and housing ideologies, so as to draw as much attention as possible to their ramshackle nature. The scripts accordingly had two economic themes. First, housing is economic capital which can be fully productive only if it is rightly distributed. Second, for technical reasons, it cannot possibly be most productively distributed by open money-marketing. Capital markets are efficient when commercial production (in proportion to its competitive efficiency) earns the means of bidding for the capital it needs. But domestic or household production cannot compete for resources in that way, because its output does not bring direct money returns. It is the commercial wage-income of the household, *not its domestic productivity,* which has to bid for domestic capital. So there is no reason whatever why open capital-marketing should arrive at most productive allocations, either between the commercial and domestic economies, or between households within the domestic economy. That is a fundamental economic truth; but in 1974, few economists understood it, and most of the few who did were concerned with poor rather than rich countries.

The Canberra departments never did ask for the review of housing policy, but shortly before Christmas 1973, Prime Minister Gough Whitlam commissioned it. Thereupon, a group of Canberra economists, whom I did not know but with whom I must now work at the review, decided (helpfully) to clarify our opening differences by writing short responses to my broadcasts. Their papers were scornful, condescending and devastatingly informative. They appeared to know nothing of the history, philosophy or contemporary diversity of their own discipline — each had been drilled in one or another true faith, and appeared to know no others, even as 'error'. Their true faiths inclined more to the American than the English Cambridge, but most of all to Frank Knight and Milton Friedman. That really did spell death to our enterprise. Whatever light the Chicago economists may shed on other subjects, they are inevitably hopeless about housing. They won't interest themselves in the detailed 'imperfections' of land and housing markets, and they usually know little and care less about the mechanisms of housing finance and ownership through which banks, building societies, insurance companies, government agencies and other institutions distribute and redistribute among the citizens up to a third of affluent nations' capital and up to a quarter of many people's spendable income.

Predictably, if the institutional managers were doing

badly, these particular economists would want to 'free the market' to do what cannot possibly be done efficiently in a free-market way. If the housing industries were sick, they would want them to dwindle and die as sick industries should. If the capital mistake was putting houses beyond people's means, they would want to free the market for cheaper substitutes. (The institutional arrangements in Professor Friedman's country exclude forty million people from solid private housing of *any* kind, and the proportions who cannot afford housing of their own *rise* steadily as Americans get richer.) Though the institutional conditions of credit were prohibiting new private investment, Friedmanites would still want to leave the supply of housing to private investors. I also guessed (correctly) that these prospects of increasing inequality and unemployment would be so alluring that they wouldn't notice that Friedman himself (for different reasons) was proposing much the same remedy as I was for the capital mistake.

I should not have been so upset — that particular group turned out to be personally charming, and professionally there was worse to come from other quarters. In the course of the review of housing policy, we had six months of information-gathering, input papers from many sources inside and outside government, drafting and counter-drafting, and round-table meetings with experts from Housing and Construction, Urban and Regional Development, Cities Commission, Treasury, Reserve Bank, Repatriation, State Housing Commissions and private consultants. Philosophies collided every day — most of the modern history of economic thought showed up at one time or another, conscious or not, competent or not. There were even some leftish contributors. They and I should have been allies, but turned out to be enemies. They were hot against 'neo-classical orthodoxy' but rigid in their own orthodoxies. They refused to take the capital mistake seriously. Their opposition was decisive because their Minister trusted them and believed them when they assured him that I was a hopeless nut about housing finance. I forgave him — but not them,

CAPITAL MISTAKES 83

then or since.

Scarcely anyone, on left or right, would think of housing as productive capital, or consider how its distribution might affect its productivity. Nobody seemed to understand that the theorist's choice which defined it as 'capital' or 'consumer-durables' was a political choice, with drastic consequences if the categories and models of orthodox economic theory were then applied to it. Plenty of people knew that housing credit and ownership affected distributions of income. But they refused to see how the capital mistake was now affecting the distributions; and most of them thought (wrongly by a factor of 3 or 4) that all such distributive effects were caused by government taxes and subsidies, and none by the capitalist facts of access to credit and ownership.

There was much discussion of markets, dogmatic rather than practical. Many people wanted to force the States to charge 'economic' or 'market' rents and prices for public housing. Nobody would actually define what those terms meant (because it requires political as well as technical assumptions) and nobody would think through the problem of setting such prices in markets substantially influenced by the public dealers' pricing. (If you insist on being theoretical about it, it really requires a notion of just price. I didn't help my chances of being taken seriously by observing that the best theoretical discussions of that were still those of some mediaeval popes.) And they hopelessly misunderstood the likely effects of public price increases on the behaviour and prosperity of the private markets.

The debates were confused by at least six concepts of 'subsidy'. Some people confined the term to doles or revenue transfers. Others included the administrative costs of making the transfers. Others included notional opportunity costs of public investments. Others extended the term to include any abstention from taxing anything taxable, and any abstention from maximum monopoly pricing, or from any other workable extortion by public monopolies. All their concepts of subsidy had necessary moral premises, but most of their owners thought they were purely technical. And they had plenty of other moral/technical confusions. For example, if a prosperous private home-buyer could make fixed debt repayments in depreciating currency for an appreciating asset, and thus make fast capital gains, that was a market fact consistent with perfect social efficiency. But if a public tenant or borrower got exactly the same deal, he or she was perceived as getting a socially inefficient subsidy. If the Commonwealth Bank borrowed at negative interest and passed the benefit on in a loan to a private home-buyer, that was efficient money-marketing; if a State housing agency did exactly the same, that was bureaucratic, socially inefficient subsidising.

Most of these experts were as bad in practice as they were in theory, especially because they were armchair experts, very reluctant to study the markets they theorised about. They did not know and would not learn anything about the complex conditions which affect private investment in rental housing. So they were able to cling to absurdly ignorant expectations of the way in which private housing supply would respond to tax changes, demand subsidies, rent controls, public competition or other stimuli. I tried to get them to understand why private rents in Adelaide averaged a third lower than in other cities; but perhaps because the cause consisted of skilful public-sector activity, it remained invisible to them. With some difficulty I got a researcher assigned for some weeks to collect and summarise existing information about housing hardship. In a country in which some thousands were homeless every night (the national provision of women's shelters for 'battered wives' and children was then about thirty beds, and scores of thousands of households were put into poverty by the rents they paid), that highly qualified researcher reported *only* an estimate of the number of public tenants who were *not* in poverty, so ought to pay more rent. Another with first-class honours and a Ph. D. in economics said, only half in fun, 'My dear chap, I don't have to study the market out there, I can deduce it from here. You don't understand what science is *for*'.

And so on. But the incompetence and frivolity were not random, they were steadily reactionary in effect. They went with a curiously matched pair of prejudices: against public enterprise, but also against private home-ownership by the working and lower-middle classes. The bulk of the Canberra public service (all of them home-owners) favoured private landlording for the lower classes.

They would, of course, disclaim 'reaction'. Some of the younger members thought they were radical because they attacked the tax privileges enjoyed by affluent home-owners — but even that criticism, though just, was linked to the belief that most economic evils flowed from government. Older critics of government pointed to its poor record in trying to 'fine tune' the national economy — but that was scarcely relevant to the productive capacities of publicly owned businesses.

As advisers to any government, but specially to a Labor government, most of those people seemed technically and politically absurd. But it was marvellous to behold how they rationalised their prejudices. Day after day I sat around coffee tables and conference tables with public servants and private consultants who banked Commonwealth, flew Qantas and British Airways and TAA, enjoyed high-speed trains and geometrically designed superhighways, trusted the radio beams in the sky and the admiralty charts at sea and the ordnance maps in the bush, used government loans to buy government houses framed and lined with government softwood, preferred public to private superannuation, shot their children with Salk and Sabin, smoked Gauloises and fuelled their Leylands and Renaults with BP — but still knew in their bones as a fact of life, beyond any rational dispute whatever, that the private sector is the only productive sector, and that public ownership and management are always, everywhere and incurably inefficient.

That persistent doublethink mattered, because it helped to distort the whole discussion of national housing and banking policies. And the doublethink was proof against science, reason or anything else. At that time, the most ambitious and rigorous attempt in print to compare efficiencies in private and public management in Britain was Richard Pryke, *Public Enterprise in Practice*.[5] It had been out four years and reviewed in all relevant journals, but I couldn't find a Canberra economist who had heard of it. Trying to establish some common ground, I would agree that government should leave private industries as free as possible — with the corollary that it must do a good deal of productive business itself. It has generally been better at its own productions than at coercing private enterprises to act against their own view of their interests. For example, it can often influence prices more effectively by competing with them than by controlling them. When (as often in housing) 'intervention' and public enterprise are alternative means to social ends, the second can usually work better for both sectors of the industry. Or so I would argue, but I might as well have argued with brick walls. Those Renault-drivers just *knew*.

If ideology faltered, there was always straightforward bad behaviour. It would break rules to describe much of it. One public story can serve as a sample of plenty of unpublished equivalents. One department of the Federal Government moved to create an Australian Housing Corporation. A rival department believed in that sort of enterprise, but couldn't bear to see it in alien hands, so tried to kill it. They half-succeeded. In its final mangled form, the Act provided that the Australian Housing Corporation could not buy an acre, build a house or lend a dollar without six or nine months of bureaucratic preliminaries including the consent of the Treasury and both Houses of Parliament, with those procedures to be repeated for each new line of business. The day the Act was gazetted, the Prime Minister transferred responsibility for the new-born monster from the department that had created it to the department that had decisively crippled it. I saw many examples of that sort of malevolent mutual frustration or destruction. One permanent head assured me sadly that his status must always be measured by the fear and destruction he could inflict. Plenty of good people dislike the atmosphere and try to build co-operative networks within it; but I found the young, if anything, nastier than the old, and the prospects unpromising.

I have been depicting melodrama, or farce. It could have been dignified as tragedy if the housing problems had been genuinely intractable: in intractable predicaments, people naturally flail about. In this case, politicians, servants and consultants alike were deeply divided about the issues. So was the world outside, where the same divisions of opinion were being reiterated at conference after public conference, by disinterested reformers and self-interested lobbies alike. Broadly, three or four factions were contending for as many strategies, none of which in practice could possibly work as advertised. Tax reforms might improve tax justice, but they would not fix the housing troubles. Nor would industrialised system-building. Nor would a switch from solid housing to cheaper substitutes at higher densities. Nor would a general switch from public housing to private demand subsidies. Unpromising at the best of times, none of these lines of action could do any good at all, while the capital mistake continued to block or distort the provision of every kind of housing.

What the Federal departments did in those circumstances was to institutionalise their sterile debate and make it perpetual. As each new report appeared, it was made the subject of the next report or review, by one or another of the same group of useless people. Indecisive and unproductive, those repetitions continue into their fourth year as this is written.

Through most of those years I believe a solution to the capital mistake was available, and with it an effective set of housing policies, many already proven in practice in South Australia, all in line with the Whitlam Government's stated aspirations, but most quite capable of attracting bipartisan support. But for any of the warring Ministers to see through the confusion to that workable and politically rewarding option, they would have had to reject nine-tenths of the advice they were getting from their party and public services, *especially* from their economists and housing experts. By August 1975 it was clear that I could achieve nothing in Canberra, so I gave up trying.

Adelaide, 1975-76
The capital mistake ought to be put right by the Federal Government; but failing that, it should be possible for State and private institutions to do a good deal about it. Because of the general success of its land and housing management, South Australia had least immediate need of the reform, but for the same reason it had a government capable of attempting it. As far as university duties allowed, I spent September and October of 1975 licking my wounds and distilling all those discarded Canberra drafts into papers tailored to the State's powers and purposes. In case I really was mad, I also circulated a short analytical account of the capital mistake to some academic economists. Not everybody thought the proposed reforms would 'go', but nobody disputed the analysis of the trouble.

So I called on the State Minister for Housing, described the business, and asked him to read the papers himself. That was a tall order — they ran to sixty pages — but copies presently went to the head of the Treasury, the economist in charge of the Premier's policy unit and the Chairman and General Manager of the Housing Trust; and I was sent to confer with the Chairman of the State Bank. After the summer holiday, we all met the Minister. By then, a change of Federal Government had given more urgency to our business. South Australia had been avoiding the worst social and economic effects of the capital mistake by maintaining a big public housing programme, and also financing about a quarter of all new private home-buyers (mostly through its State Bank) at rates of nominal interest below 6.75%. But most of those services depended on making large allocations of State loan funds to attract Federal subsidy under the Commonwealth-State Housing Agreement, so the whole programme was dangerously vulnerable to the hostile action which might be expected from the new Federal Government. The State had twice before run its land and housing business without subsidy and independently of the Federal Government; it would be prudent to restore a standby capacity to do the same again. The current Housing Agreement had two years to run. That was little enough time to get alternative methods of financing developed and proven in the market, ready to replace or supplement the existing arrangements for low-income buyers and tenants if that should become necessary. Preparations ought to begin. The Minister agreed to two initiatives:

First, he would invite all banks, building societies and other institutions lending for housing within the State to constitute a regular conference on housing finance. If agreeable, its first business could be to explore the possibility of introducing capital-indexed facilities for borrowers and lenders who might want them. I wrote a short explanation of the business to go out with the invitations, and a longer one which the *National Times* printed to coincide with the first meeting.[6] Predictably, institutions governed from out-of-State were unwilling to experiment. But the local building societies were interested enough to commission the legal and technical work which would be required for the new type of business, and for final decisions about introducing it.

Second, we were to see if we could interest Life Insurance companies in bulk lending on an indexed basis, whether to agencies lending to individual home-buyers, or to independent charities providing non-profit rental housing. In the circumstances of 1976, quite modest levels of housing rents and repayments could give the Life companies much better fixed-interest returns than they had lately been getting. If such flows of lending could be established, they would add absolutely to the resources for low-cost housing; they would test an alternative way of financing public housing; they might diversify the ownership of public and other non-profit housing; and they would not offend against the Constitution or the national Loan Agreements. The Housing Trust began detailing projects that could be shopped around at firm prices.

Both these initiatives aimed to create facilities that lenders and borrowers could use if they wanted to. Government was improving rather than constraining the relevant markets, offering intermediary and managerial services, but not forcing them on anybody. Its reputation need not suffer (though mine might) if the market didn't respond at all.

Getting the business to that point took the South Australian Government about eight months. That included diagnosing the trouble, rejecting most of the strategies canvassed in the national debates, choosing two others for a cautious fail-safe trial, and creating machinery for the purpose. It went well partly because the Minister was an economist who took the trouble to understand and decide about the business for himself, but partly also because he had people in his department who understood it, sympathised with its aims, and could be trusted to develop and manage it competently.

Conclusions
Whoever was right about the issues, there was a striking contrast between the quality of the two government services — meaning only, of course, the bits of those services that are concerned with housing policy. The highly trained Federal social scientists tended to see themselves as experts with authority in their fields. The South Australians saw themselves variously as educated people or practical people or both, but committed to social values and political purposes rather than to specific scientific disciplines or dogma. They were also more co-operative, and felt more immediately responsible for the effects of policy — if there was trouble out in the market they would *care,* and also some of their heads would roll.

The Federal professionals outnumbered the South Australian professionals about twenty to one and tended to be younger, with higher academic qualifications and higher pay. Some of their sterility arose from their personal and political values. Some arose from the cliquish malice with which their service seems to be afflicted. But a disgraceful amount of their incapacity seemed to have been drummed into them at school. New science was usually worse than old, so the youngest minds tended to be the tightest shut. The reasons seemed to me to be as I alleged in *The Political Sciences*. I used to be decently modest about that work, but Canberra ruined my character (as it has that of others). I understand vividly why Balogh was always coming back from Whitehall and putting the libels back into his books.

But the South Australian performance discourages any *general* cynicism about government. Two broad conclusions suggest themselves, neither original. First, you can't expect progressive policy-making from conservative public servants, or vice versa. Plenty of policy researchers can serve successive governments, because governments share plenty of continuing and consensual purposes. But radical changes of direction will usually need some change of servants and advisers.

Second, a lot of teachers of social science have a lot to answer for. At the very least, their students should be taught to recognise their theories and methods as optional, controversial, value-structured instruments, and not as the accumulating dogma of the One True Science.

NOTES AND REFERENCES

1. Streeten, P. 'Programs and Prognoses', *The Quarterly Journal of Economics* LXVIII (1954).
2. Stretton, H. *The Political Sciences: General principles of selection in social science and history*, Routledge & Kegan Paul, 1969.
3. Stretton, H. *Ideas for Australian Cities*, an orphan book, 1970; republished by Georgian House, 1971.
4. Priorities Review Staff, *Report on Housing*, Australian Government Publishing Service, 1975, Ch.4 (for which Austen Holmes was responsible); Anderson, D.L., 'Indexation of Long-term Debt', *Shelter*, September/October 1975; Mahar, K.L., *Indexation of Financial Securities*, Australian Association of Permanent Building Societies, July 1976.

5. Pryke, R. *Public Enterprise in Practice: The British Experience*, McGibbon & Kee, 1971.
6. Stretton, H. 'An Answer to the Housing Crisis', *The National Times*, 7 June 1976.

REFLECTIONS ON AN AUSTRALIAN NEWTOWN

Lois Bryson & Faith Thompson

An Australian Newtown is subtitled 'Life and Leadership in a Working-class Suburb'.[1] When we started out, we certainly intended to study life in Newtown (a pseudonym for a suburban area in Melbourne, Australia) and we expected that this would include some consideration of leadership. It was our experience in the research situation, however, that led us to elevate the leadership theme to top billing and to consider specifically the local middle-class caretakers and their programmes for the largely working-class residents of the suburb. Because of this, the report of the study does reveal more of its own behind-the-scenes story than most, as some incidents that would normally be discarded became data. Nonetheless, in the final report we largely followed the convention of censoring the discussion of the backstage situation — the personal issues, the hassles and many of the problems with which we wrestled. Even at the time we thought this was a pity and were moved to write a journal article[2] which did discuss explicitly the problems involved in the relationship between us as researchers and those who requested the research. This relationship undoubtedly is the most distinctive aspect of the project and will provide a major focus of this article as well, though here for the first time we will present a far more personal discussion of the whole research process.

It is interesting to contemplate why researchers rarely say what really happened. There are obviously unwritten rules about how research should be packaged and we must assume that these serve to preserve the image of the competent 'scientific' researcher. They also prevent people from gaining any clear conception of what is involved in carrying out research. This mystification probably has the latent function of ensuring that the next generation of potential researchers is not put off by realising the detailed drudgery entailed for those who actually have to do the work. From *Inside the Whale* we get a more realistic picture.

Embarking on the Study
It all started in late 1965 when a number of leaders from a new Housing Commission (public housing authority) suburb on the outskirts of Melbourne approached Professor Marwick, then Chairman of the Department of Anthropology and Sociology at Monash University, Melbourne, to request assistance with research. At the time, the department was only in its second year of existence and was the first such department in Victoria. These local leaders were members of a group we called the Civic Group, which consisted almost entirely of what Halmos terms 'personal service professionals',[3] ministers of religion, social workers, teachers etc. They were generally concerned with community development in their suburb and felt that some social research would help them in their planning.

In the report of the research, we give three reasons for agreeing to the request of the local leaders.

> Firstly, sociology in Australia tends to be particularly lacking in studies with a broad basis which provide a picture of life of 'average citizens' ... Secondly the acceptance of such a request and the consequent co-operation of local leaders seemed partly to solve the problems that are often associated with access to research data. Thirdly investigation in an area of concern to local leaders gave the research dual value, that is direct practical value as well as theoretical value.[4]

This statement is certainly true, but it glosses over the difficulties involved in making the decision to undertake the study and the different personal emphases of the researchers who were involved.

For instance, we were dubious about doing a study in an area that was already stigmatised as a 'problem' area, as is the case with many newly established Housing Commission estates. We were well aware that our attentions could help to confirm the label. This problem was a constant source of worry in our contacts in the area. We were also nervous about publicity lest it sensationalise the research and identify the suburb. Perhaps because of our extreme caution, the few media reports that did emerge did not 'blow our cover' and did not reflect badly on Newtown.

As well as the ethical dilemmas in respect of the residents, we faced the technical problem that if we were to undertake a broad community study then it would be better undertaken in a less distinctive area and one with a greater cross-section of socio-economic status. Nevertheless, like many researchers we were anxious to co-operate with people in the 'real world' and to pull our weight, so the decision was made. As Dunphy has pointed out, we were probably flattered to be considered useful. However, we did not fall into the trap which he warns of when he suggests:

> it is a short step from seeing that we are needed, to uncritically accepting other's assumptions of what it is desirable for us to investigate, the ends to which our efforts should be directed and the guidelines for our activity ... we can readily become naive servants of power.[5]

In fact it was from our attempts to avoid serving the interests of those in power (albeit in a small local pond) that our most difficult problems arose.

In the initial stages, it was Professor Marwick who was principally concerned with the research. Though the project did not directly coincide with his own sociological interests, he saw it as providing the basis for a series of studies that might be undertaken by staff and postgraduate students in the future. Initially we were only peripherally involved, but gradually over the first few months of 1965 we took more responsibility as the professor became too absorbed in other matters and the project could not be stemmed because of the many obligations that had been incurred. Contrary to common belief, we did not take over the project when the professor left; well before this it had overtaken us. This effectively determined the topics we would work on for our higher degrees, as we had no time to pursue other research interests. We had to give up all ideas of the quite different and separate projects we had thought we would be doing when the year began. Instead we had a proposal accepted to present a joint MA thesis and this we duly prepared. In 1966 just before the extremely fat volume was bound, our supervisor suggested that we work further on the analysis and change our candidacy to Ph.D. A joint thesis for this degree was far too radical for the university's higher degrees committee and so we dismembered the report and presented separate theses. There is a good deal of irony in the fact that we put the two theses together again for publication.

For the first eighteen months we devoted almost all our waking time, seven days a week, to working on, thinking about and discussing the project. After that, our time commitment decreased, though it remained significant at most times and overwhelming at others until, six years (and three babies) later, Penguin published *An Australian Newtown* in 1972.

There were others involved in the project at various stages and for varying lengths of time.[6] It would have been interesting to have had their versions, but at best these would have been fragmentary. During the six years of the project, the longest involvement of anyone else was less than a year.

The fact that there were two of us working together, both with a high level of involvement in the project, was of undoubted importance. We were able to provide mutual support, and the constant discussion of problems that was possible proved invaluable. Our experiences left us with a firm belief in the advantages of joint projects. It seems a pity that traditional attitudes to higher degrees tend to discourage or even entirely prevent this in the social sciences.

Funding also played a part in the course of events, but in our case its influence was at one remove from that usually experienced by research workers. As we have indicated, the project developed round the professor's interest and involvement and it was Professor Marwick who applied for and received a research grant. The money was used primarily to employ a full-time research assistant for ten months in 1965, for other part-time assistance as required and also for travelling expenses of staff and students which was a significant item. From our point of view, the more important effect of the Australian Research Grants Committee giving a grant to support the project was the contribution this made to our motivation to finish the study. This was by no means the only factor, but we did feel obliged to produce a report and at times when personal circumstances made continuing problematic, this obligation did take on some importance. We did not want to let down the Department.

Carrying Out the Study
There were four distinct sections of the study; two that used fairly conventional methods and were planned from the outset, and two that were less conventional and developed in the course of the interaction with the local leaders. The first of the planned sections consisted of a household survey; the second involved participant observation and other broad-ranging techniques for getting to know the area and understanding ongoing events. The two less conventional and more problematic methods we used involved a community self-survey of local groups, and a welfare survey that involved welfare personnel and organisations. The difficulties encountered here were that the surveys were suggested largely as forms of social action; they were not embarked on primarily for the purpose of research. The projects were not entirely successful, either in providing solid research data or in achieving the practical goals for which they were undertaken. It was in this situation that we learned that our

conception of an effective way of planning for the area was at variance with that of the local leaders. At this point it is worth looking at each of the four stages of the study separately.

Collection of Background Information
The collection of background information is often not explicitly seen as a research technique, particularly in projects involving surveys. We were skeptical about how much one can understand about a group of people without the benefit of a broad spectrum of information, including as much historical material as possible. We sought out local newspapers, census data, interviews with people active in the area and also undertook participant observation. Part of this was carried out by one of the researchers during a short period of residence in the area. This raised a minor problem, that of obtaining appropriate accommodation. It was hoped that the researcher would live with a typical family, but because of the relatively small size of the houses, combined with the Housing Commission policy that offers houses to people with a large number of children, we were not able to achieve this. After some difficulty in finding any accommodation at all, the researcher finally went to stay with one of the members of the Civic Group, a widow with one daughter. This had the problem of not providing a typical domestic situation but was the best that could be arranged.

Because we were working with the Civic Group while at the same time seeing them as part of the 'community study', all our dealings with them took on the guise of participant observation. This created difficulties because, despite our explanations to the members that the Group and its activities were part of our subject matter, the process of working together created a situation in which friendly relationships developed and we were treated as colleagues. When we came to write up the research, this left us with acute ethical problems which we shall discuss later.

The decision to do participant observation must be seen as one influenced by our anthropological leanings and also as resulting from our ideological position. After the initial meeting during which the Civic Group members explained their interest in research, we were moved to wonder to what extent they in fact represented the views of the working-class residents. Thus we were theoretically disposed to see the situation as one involving different interests and views and to expect that these would be linked to class situations. We basically adopted a conflict model of society. Had we adopted a consensual model, and expected essential similarity of interests and views, we might not have seen a need to study the leadership and its goals as well as the led.

The Household Survey
Our reasons for doing a household survey were fairly conventional. The members of the Civic Group had requested one and indeed, like many people, tended to see the social survey as *the* sociological research technique. Although we did not similarly anticipate the use only of a survey, we did want to obtain data about the characteristics and attitudes of the residents and wanted this information to be as representative as possible. An approach to randomly selected residents seemed the obvious way to do this. We also had a departmental policy that students learning research methods should, where possible, be involved in a research project. It was feasible to involve a fairly substantial number of students, 90 in all, in the task of interviewing, whereas some other research techniques were not adaptable to mass effort. There has been a great deal of discussion in recent years about the ethics of student participation in staff projects and we have heard it said of this project that we were 'just using' students for the purpose of getting higher degrees. This was not the case, because initially the project was not intended for use towards postgraduate degrees and, more importantly, the teaching policy had been adopted because staff members believed in the efficacy of learning by experience. After taking part in the projects, the majority of students did feel they had learned a lot. Nonetheless, today we would recommend that students be given a choice of research task.

In 1966, even the most reasonable tertiary training schemes were basically authoritarian.

The involvement of students in the interview programme created its own difficulties. In the nature of things, most students are inexperienced at interviewing, yet given the time constraints within the university, it is impossible to embark on a programme that will turn them into experienced interviewers, though we did organise briefing sessions. Thus the quality of the completed interviews was very varied — some were first class, others reflected the students' uncertainties, unfamiliarity and, in certain instances, lack of commitment.

In those cases in which households refused to be interviewed when approached by a student, they were subsequently called on by one of the staff interviewers. In many instances, the people then agreed to answer the survey questions. These staff interviewers were trained social workers with experience in both research and clinical interviewing, and their relative success seems to suggest that experience, and perhaps commitment, are important factors in obtaining co-operation.

With a large number of interviewers, some of whom needing support, it was decided to mount Sunday and Wednesday interviewing drives with headquarters in a local school and the local hall, respectively. The interviewers used the school and hall as bases for discussion of their experiences with us and their fellow students. Also, as the interviewers returned, their schedules were checked and ambiguities and gaps were corrected on the spot. One of the consequences of this group project was an increase in the depth of students' relationships with each other and with the staff. Similar organisation in other projects has proved equally successful.

The perennial problem of what to exclude from our interview schedule was exacerbated in our case by two factors. First was the limitation set by students, who would be lacking in confidence, doing the interviewing. But more particularly, we were trying to meet the needs of the local leaders. These were diverse and not always tempered by an understanding of what one can hope to achieve in a relatively brief interview.

Before designing the interview schedule, we asked members of the Civic Group to provide lists of issues they thought it would be profitable to investigate. As most members were concerned with some form of welfare activity, this meant that on the whole each was interested in his or her own, usually specialised, field. The questions submitted for possible inclusion in the survey covered a vast range of topics, including family relationships, finance, employment, housing, health, education, leisure, social class, religious affiliations, attitudes to community facilities, migrants, youth, the aged, delinquency, alcoholism, gambling, marital disharmony and psychiatric disorders. Patently one survey could not cover all these topics, so priorities were set in collaboration with a research subcommittee of the Civic Group, which had been formed to liaise with us. It was agreed that apart from general social characteristics of the residents, the Group members were primarily concerned with questions of financial status and the opinions of residents about living in the area, existing services and services that should be developed in the future. This left us very little room to indulge our own 'purely sociological' interests, a limitation that certainly proved a restriction on the final analysis.

In carrying out the household survey, we faced the expected problems such as wording of questions, possible interviewee bias etc. One problem we did feel we solved satisfactorily, if in a somewhat unorthodox manner, was that of obtaining a representative sample. We sampled from all the houses in the area, using random number tables; but on inspection found the sample to be unevenly distributed throughout the area in terms of those factors we knew about, such as household composition, ethnicity and the age of the houses. It was not until the third randomly selected sample that we found a distribution that seemed adequately to represent these factors. We could not see that the third random sample should be any less acceptable statistically and from a 'rational sampling' point of view, it was far preferable.

When we did compare the characteristics of our sample with the Census data for the whole area, they proved very similar in almost all respects. This was true for the sample actually seen as well as the sample drawn. Unlike many researchers, we were able to check some of the characteristics of those households that refused with those that participated in the study. We were able to do this by combining information, from a card index of all addresses in Newtown that we had compiled from a variety of sources, with data that we collected through informal sources and contacts. Overall, we found no systematic bias among those who had refused in terms of such factors as tenancy or ownership, length of residency, occupation as recorded on the electoral roll, ethnic background or family size.

To avoid giving an unrealistic picture of the process involved in collecting data, it seems worthwhile to give a chronological list of all the tasks undertaken in the household survey, even though some of these have already been mentioned. A similar list could be made out for the other three stages of the project and for the analysis. We have opted to do this only for the household survey, because of the popularity of the survey method and because it would be too boring to do this for all the stages. Even so, those familiar with the process of carrying out a survey might be well advised to skip the following tedious list of tasks (or should that be list of tedious tasks!).

As far as we can remember, the sequence of events was roughly as follows; discussion with local researchers who had undertaken projects of any relevance; collection of interview schedules from relevant local and overseas research; culling the literature for discussion of topics that might be touched on in the interview, including first obtaining copies of books (at times from interstate or overseas sources); discussion with the whole Civic Group (membership about 20) on basic priorities; numerous meetings with the Group-appointed liaison subcommittee, and continuous collaboration face to face and by phone with members of this subcommittee; drafting and many times redrafting the schedule (including typing and retyping) to deal with problems of theoretical and practical relevance, wording, order, layout for ease of recording, layout for ease of analysis, length etc; carrying out a pilot study by taking the draft schedule to the area and interviewing about a dozen householders; final redrafting in the light of experiences in the pilot study; typing and production of 500 copies of the schedule; obtaining maps from the local government offices and recording as much detail as was available from local records, electoral rolls, directories etc.; checking the location of recently built private housing by driving around the area; drawing a random sample, preparation of a card for each of the 400 or so addresses in the sample; liaison with the Henderson poverty research team[7] who had a sample in the area for their research, to avoid interviewing the same families; preparing and disseminating pre-publicity for the survey by giving information to local papers and leaders; introduction of student interviewers to the project; arranging and carrying out briefing sessions; organising interview drives, arranging for central venues with appropriate facilities and arranging transport for interviewers; preparation of kits for interviewers with a letter of introduction, a map, addresses and schedules; on the interview days, supervising the interviewing and discussing problems; vetting of completed interview schedules; completing contact of sample through 'mopping-up' activities, revisiting refusals, calling back on people who were not at home, arranging interpreters where necessary; sending out letters of thanks to all interviewees.

Having collected the information, the task of analysing it could begin.

The Group Study

As already pointed out, we attended meetings of the Civic Group as participant observers. In the early stages we observed only, while the members attempted to thrash out the purpose of their organisation, its structure and future goals. When this problem seemed to have been clarified and they were looking round for ways to promote development in Newtown, we suggested to them a survey of all the formal groups in the area by using a 'community self-survey' technique. This process was to involve members of the Civic Group going out to do the interviewing themselves. We felt that such a survey would provide a detailed picture of activities already existing and bring the Group into contact with the members and leaders of other groups, thereby enabling them to gauge local opinion about what their future role should be.

Some members of the Civic Group had already been involved in something that was a good preliminary for such a study. They had worked on collecting information and finding local backing for the publication of a Newtown Community Directory, which was provided for each household. They took up the idea of a study of local groups with alacrity and decided to take an active part in designing and implementing it.

All formal adult and youth groups in Newtown were the target population. The survey was so organised that the groups had a choice as to whether they only provided basic factual data on the history, aims and membership of the group, or became more involved and spent some time in discussing what members felt about living in Newtown, and what changes, if any, they wanted. To gain the co-operation of the group and to record the data, an observer was made responsible for each group.

Members of the Civic Group acting as observers put a considerable effort into the study. Where they felt unable to act themselves, they recruited others, finally involving about fifty people from in and around the suburb. In practice, the Civic Group members infrequently collected information from groups with which they were not already associated in some way, either through direct participation or friendships with members.

Overall, 128 groups took part in the study and of these, 42 elected to provide both facts about their group and opinions about Newtown. There was considerable variability in the quality of the information collected. This variability was due principally to the large number of observers involved and the impossibility of our exercising greater control over them when our resources were already strained in trying to complete our primary commitment, namely to finalise the household survey as quickly as possible.

The presence of observers who were not members of the Civic Group brought other limitations. It drastically reduced the effectiveness of the 'self-survey' as a technique to promote the goals of the Group. However, the effectiveness was also limited by the Civic Group members themselves. Even when they acted as observers, the information was collected as a routine matter and no apparent attempt was made to use the opportunity for liaison purposes and thereby to lay a foundation for future social action. Overall, the study may, however, have improved the climate in and among groups and perhaps contributed to the unprecedented success of the Youth Seminar held in late 1966 and sponsored by some Civic Group members. On the other hand, in the case of some local groups for which observers were not found and in which the leaders were critical of the activities of the Civic Group, it seems unlikely that contact would have been made at all had we not pursued this ourselves. In the long run, the information was handed over to the university and construed as something the university 'needed'. Before considering the message to be gleaned from this experience, we shall outline stage 4 of the study — as with only variations in detail, much the same process occurred.

The Welfare Study
Welfare problems had always been of key concern to a number of members of the Civic Group. Indeed, it was in an attempt to co-ordinate local welfare services and to develop special programmes for families with many problems that the group had been formed originally. However, as the group's interests broadened, the members decided that a welfare subcommittee was needed to cater for these more specific interests.

From its inception, this subcommittee had a slightly clearer function than its parent body but there was a good deal of uncertainty about what their next steps should be. In an attempt to assist the members, we pointed out that the household survey would not answer a lot of the questions they wanted answered. We reminded them that they already had, at their fingertips, much of the information required to identify the most urgent tasks for the subcommittee. What seemed to be necessary was a way of pooling their knowledge and looking at it systematically.

For this to happen, some conflicting requirements of practice and research had to be faced. The subcommittee members felt blocked in pooling their information by the ethical consideration of a possible breach of confidentiality. We shared their concern over this. We also recognised that there would be an important flaw in the results if, during the analysis, it was not possible to tell how often different workers recorded the same problem in regard to the same family.

A number of possible ways of proceeding were suggested, which took into account the requirements of anonymity and accuracy. The scheme that we tended to favour involved us in an initial collation and allocation of case numbers to avoid duplication in the figures; removal of residential area identification from the questionnaires; and handing them to the welfare subcommittee for analysis and, hopefully, more informed action.

We also suggested obtaining information from other agencies not represented in the Civic Group to complete the picture. As an independent organisation we could undertake this task, whereas the involved agencies could not. All this was greeted with enthusiasm. The welfare personnel helped to design case history questionnaires and then filled these in for their own cases during the two months of the welfare study.

So far, so good; but again we were left 'holding the baby'. In the end, all the material was handed over to us for analysis; and indeed, by this stage the purpose of the exercise had been reconstrued as offering information to 'help the university'. We in fact did oblige by undertaking an analysis and presenting a special report, though there seems little evidence that it was acted on.

There are certainly lessons to be learned from our experiences in these two parts of the study. Lest we seem even more naive than we undoubtedly were, we should point out that the group study and the welfare study occurred at much the same time, so that we were not in a position to learn from our mistakes.

Nevertheless, at the time we began the group and welfare studies, we definitely underestimated the relative importance that the Civic Group attached to having 'expert researchers' on the job, as compared with benefiting from the group study research processes or obtaining the research results themselves. Had we fully comprehended this, there is no way that we could have expected that they would be satisfied with themselves in roles of primary responsibility for the results of the two studies.

We did learn again, finally, an important lesson which we temporarily neglected in the initial stages of these two studies. Simply, this lesson is that even if people ask for suggestions, and then appear to accept them eagerly, this is no guarantee that they are committed to act on these suggestions. We should have generalised this lesson from our social work training and practice. In social work, practitioners are taught to be alert to the traps and limitations of giving advice, even when it is solicited. It is an axiom that good practice requires the worker to facilitate people in arriving at their own solutions and must resist the temptation of championing remedies that they themselves might prefer. In our defence, we submit that in a colleague type of situation, there is a tendency towards assuming that discussion is taking place within a shared frame of reference. If we had perceived ourselves as being in a therapeutic relationship to the group, it is unlikely that we would have made this misjudgement.

When considering involving people inexperienced in research in such tasks, it is also as well to remember that probably very few realise the concerted effort required to carry through a project. It may be overambitious to expect that they will. When one relies on voluntary labour, not all of whom have an intensive commitment, it is difficult to control the quality of the data collected, so that it is not surprising that for both the group and the welfare studies, we found that the data finally available for analysis were patchy in quality and coverage.

Analysis
And so to the analysis. Inside our whale at this time there was mostly paper. There were hundreds of schedules from the three surveys, cards, coding instructions, coding sheets, lists and letters of thanks to all who had helped in various capacities and at different stages. Later these papers were joined by stacks of computer print-outs from the household survey tabulations. The group and welfare data we did by hand.

Each stage of the analysis had its problems, large and small; they were all-absorbing at the time, but mercifully many of the details have faded now. Only the more intransigent or tediously time-consuming ones can be recalled readily.

This was a period of intense attention to detail; coding and recoding, grouping and regrouping of data, runs and reruns and some new programming. Even in retrospect, it seems a protracted period, high in frustrations and low in psychological and data returns. As we plodded on, we told each other we would know how to avoid some of these pitfalls next time. Privately, we vowed to ourselves never to get caught up in anything like this again. (Such is the frailty of human memory that we must admit that we have both, severally and at different times, broken these wise promises to ourselves.)

In February 1967, a year after the collection of background data had begun, we were set to start grappling with the results. By this time, we were the only people working on the research: one of us lived in an inner urban area of the city and had a full-time university teaching commitment, the other lived in the bush on the urban fringe and had a brand-new baby. Distance, energy and what to do first were all problems then.

Other problems in analysing the data stemmed from our relationship with the local leaders. A major one was the time factor. Understandably, and like many people concerned with practical matters, the Civic Group members were constantly aware of an urgency about finding solutions. They were anxious for us to produce findings and seemed to have little understanding of the impossibility of making good sociological sense of data at great speed. To take the heat off the situation, we produced an interim report, though it is not clear that it was used and certainly we could not feel satisfied with it.

In analysing the data, we were constantly confronted with gaps caused by trying to cover too much for a range of different purposes. The most important gap was in relation to the values of the residents of the suburb. This means that our data were unbalanced. Through working with the leaders, we managed to gain a considerable amount of detail about their views and values. We did not have the same amount of information about the views and values of the rank-and-file residents. This can be seen as a ramification of the fact that the study was not designed primarily around a sociological problem and that the main thesis was thrown up in the course of the study, rather than developing from the study's basic hypotheses. We would maintain, however, that the development of insights in ongoing situations has its own value. For example, the process of having the research problem developed during the course of fieldwork allows the researchers to be sure that they are studying something that is a real issue within the context they have chosen. In much more colourful circumstances and with infinitely more inspiring results, Whyte appears to have gone through a similar process before he eventually focussed on the gang life of Cornerville as the central theme of his study of a slum area. He started off to study a relatively orthodox problem connected with economic structure and only after a considerable time in the field, and several false starts, did his attention turn to the *Street Corner Society*.[8]

Another problem that militated against rigorous conceptual and theoretical development was our casting of the project as an exploratory study. This is an easy trap to fall into, but how often does one do the follow-up study? Partly because we were overwhelmed by the range of problems of interest to the leaders and partly because of the urgency they felt, we launched very quickly into the data collection, promising ourselves to take up specific issues in depth later. We designed the interview schedule and completed interviewing 344 householders within the first five months of the study. This did not allow time for extensive reading and careful, critical theoretical development. Not that this always achieves its purpose, but we did find ourselves fighting a rearguard action in respect of our theoretical interpretation.

Haste, however, was only part of the problem; the other part was largely unavoidable. In research with an action component, issues must be pursued as they arise and therefore forward planning cannot be comprehensive. To this extent, such projects must always remain 'exploratory'.

Relationship with Sponsor

By this stage, it should be abundantly clear that our relationship with our sponsoring body, the Civic Group, was a critical one. The relationship had the advantage of not involving a money obligation as the research was financed by the Australian Universities Grants Commission. However, this only slightly lessened our obligation, and then only noticeably in relation to publication, as our freedom to publish as we thought fit was never at issue.

The research, as requested, did not really coincide with the sociological interests of any members of the department at the time, but was agreed to largely because of the attraction of providing a practical service. The local leaders were energetic, intelligent and enthusiastic, and it seemed the practical pay-off would be worthwhile. The many objections we recognised tended to be rationalised in the light of this. Also, the request was quite open-ended and therefore apparently offered scope for the pursuit of a range of topics of sociological interest. Nonetheless, throughout the study we continued to have difficulty reconciling sociological and practical aims, and the situation was compounded by the fact that the leaders' practical aims turned out to be based on different premises from our own. Indeed, the Group seemed to have a community development programme largely worked out before approaching us and was often unprepared or unable to make use of the research findings.

On reflection, we concluded that what they required was some means of validating the activities the members were undertaking and would undertake in the future. Social research is a fashionable means for achieving such legitimation. Research also has the attraction, provided it comes up with the expected answers, of removing responsibility for action onto the shoulders of more distant and apparently impartial experts. Not that we are suggesting that this motivation was conscious, although some members of the Group did at times come close to verbalising such a position. As convinced professional people who identified their mode of thinking as the 'informed' position, they initially did not doubt that 'systematic' academic study would confirm their views. Like most of the community, including many scientists, they had a fairly simplistic view of 'scientific research techniques' and did not understand the role value judgements play in research itself and in social action. We tried to make clear our own view that the most that can be expected from research is information, which can then be used to inform the value judgements that ultimately must be made with regard to action.

We may have taught too well, since we found that eventually the members of the Group lost interest in the results. This was highlighted by their decision to establish a part-time fee-paying counselling service without consulting the results of the welfare study. The public statement that preceded the opening of the service inferred that the decision had arisen from research findings. However, while such a service would prove of value to some families, our evidence suggested that it would not alleviate the main areas of need for which the residents sought assistance. Consequently, in opting for a counselling service, the members were following their personal preconceptions and perhaps the line of least resistance, since sponsorship was available for such a service.

The evidence from the surveys suggested that measures to assist with economic matters would have been more appropriate than a counselling service, but such services are more difficult to establish, although a credit union was one of the obvious suggestions we made. Undoubtedly these practical considerations were important but also, as was true of most professional helpers at the time, the social philosophy of the members of the Group predisposed them to favour remedies that aimed to modify the adjustment of individuals to their circumstances, rather than remedies that would alter a person's life chances through social and economic changes. The crux of the problem was that our social philosophy did not favour remedies similar to those favoured by the Group.

In addition, there are certain tensions between social action and social research which are not easily reconciled. It may well be that people of action, being people of strong convictions, are not open to being swayed by research findings unless they are in line with their preconceptions. The attitude of 'don't confuse me with the facts' is probably fairly general; in fact, commitment to being 'open minded' can be seen as just one among the many intellectual positions that people may adopt.

Although McNaul is writing primarily of science and technology, much of what he has to say is pertinent to social and behavioural scientists and it gives some support, from a systematic analysis, to the line of argument that we have just outlined. In his view there is no doubt that researchers and practitioners evaluate knowledge differently, and from his analysis we should expect that there will be at least six areas of potential conflict whenever researchers and practitioners come together over a problem.[9] To this extent, then, it seems fair to say that many of our problems could be experienced by other researchers undertaking work for practitioners, particularly if they are involved in an ongoing action programme.

For example, McNaul considers it to be generally true that researchers tend to have a longer time perspective than practitioners. Unfortunately, we are not altogether convinced that in our case, discussion and agreement on a more detailed timetable at the outset would have entirely overcome this difficulty and the mutual frustrations that this disparity entailed.

It is probably unrealistic to expect people such as those in the Civic Group, and others like them, to mark time until a mass of research material is collected and analysed. Perhaps they should be persuaded that research is not what they need.

It can be inferred also from what McNaul says that many personal service professionals (in his terms 'non-experimental practitioners'), partly because of the requirements of practice, will view knowledge as having greater finality than would be acceptable to people primarily oriented towards research. He contends that skepticism, which is considered a virtue in a research worker, is less likely to be highly valued in a practitioner since performance, in such areas as counselling, teaching and social action, can be affected adversely if the practitioner is not confident about the premises on which he or she is acting. Thus, to an extent, practitioners are likely to have a set towards consolidating their knowledge along lines already internalised.

In addition, it is to be noted that when practitioners are influenced by information, it is more usually that obtained through a personal interchange, especially that between associates who consider themselves to be professional peers. Published material, at best, plays a very subsidiary role.

This suggests that our emphasis on report writing was misguided if our main aim was to have the Civic Group heed our results.

Ethical Issues

Publication raised acute ethical issues. We were anxious about the possibility of adverse publicity for the area and the 'fish bowl' effect if there was media coverage of the findings, but our fears in this respect proved groundless. To our knowledge only one report of the research has identified the suburb. This was an article entitled '... (Newtown) warts and all' which was published in the local paper in 1974. It was written by a journalist who obviously knew the suburb well, and liked and respected its people.

The major problem was in relation to the leaders. They were all recognisable by virtue of their offices and some of them were bound to be upset by our interpretation of their activities and their relation to the working-class residents. Although, as sociologists, we were primarily concerned with ubiquitous processes of social interaction, inevitably they were likely to see the issues in personalised terms and thus at times to believe our interpretation to be personally critical of them.

Things were complicated by the friendly relationships which had developed during the course of the study. Members of the Civic Group treated us as colleagues and the implications of our protestations that we were studying them as well were never really heard or assimilated. We agonised about our interpretation of the situation, about the breach of trust that might seem to be involved, and long and hard over whether or not we were justified in publishing.

When we had completed our joint thesis, we circulated this to key members of the Civic Group. We discussed their reactions fully with some members, but with others the report had so complicated our relationship that this could not be done extensively. Their reactions were varied. One member who presented us with written notes on the report found the interpretation of the Group as 'external caretakers' illuminating, saying 'Yes, that's exactly what we were doing'. Others rejected our interpretation, and for some there was undoubtedly a feeling of a breach of trust and personal affront. One member saw as conservative our recommendations which emphasised, when setting out to meet people's needs, that you should do so in terms of these people's own perceptions. His interpretation was one we had not contemplated and it did lead us to attempt to express our basic philosophy more clearly in the final publication.

Such was our anxiety about the possible adverse effects on these people that in a version of the report that we made available (without the cover of its pseudonym 'Newtown') to the local library, we omitted the analysis of the activities of the Civic Group. We now wonder how justified such censorship was, although in this case, it may not have mattered much as very few locals showed interest in the report.

By the time we were contemplating the publication by Penguin Books, almost all the Civic Group members had left the district and, since we believed our message was a general one of some importance, we decided to go ahead. In fact we recognised an obligation not to protect the positions of the middle-class activists at the expense of information that might have value for working-class people. A few members, who are now in fields in which sociological literature is read, apparently found the publication irritating and possibly even embarrassing. We know of two articles published in Melbourne magazines by caretakers from Newtown which were aimed at refuting our interpretation.

On the other hand, when we circulated complementary copies of *An Australian Newtown* to key people in the Civic Group, several members responded favourably to it. One member, who was by then working on a funded research project in another district, subsequently requested one of us to participate in the project.

Other Reflections
We believe that it is worth recording that we do not think either of us separately could have completed this project,

or at least, not as it now stands. There is the obvious fact that there was too much work for one person. There is the less obvious fact that, without our partnership and resultant peer group support, it is unlikely that either of us could have developed, and sustained, a frame of reference that was divergent from the one favoured by the Civic Group.

We also think that it may be of interest to make explicit that we were ambivalent to the project when we began, and that we remained so. This ambivalence had its origins in the fact that we were largely 'conscripted' to the task and somewhat reluctantly drawn further and further into a web of responsibilities and loyalties, which effectively committed us to the completion of the research. We would wish to distinguish between our undoubtedly great involvement in the project and the degree of personal identification we felt with it. Because of our ambivalence, we remained in our minds at least one psychological step removed and this had important implications for the way in which the research finally evolved.

If our ambivalence had been greater, it could have been crippling to our progress. As it was, it was just sufficient to stand us in good stead. It did more than act as a good defence mechanism against the possibility of it all being a dismal failure. It also helped us to escape that degree of identification which, although an excellent source of motivation, is likely to be a stumbling block when trying to distance yourself psychologically from your material in order to appraise it. In particular, the small degree of detachment this ambivalence was able to sustain, almost at all times, was crucial for us when we were groping to detail how and why our frame of reference differed from that held by the members of the Civic Group. For us, at least, ambivalence proved to have more positive uses than we had been led to expect.

There is not space to explore the many problems that attend participant observation, but it seems desirable to make at least a few comments on our experiences.

It is often said that participant observation is an underused method and we feel that we understand why. It has many taxing aspects and ethical complexities. Not least among its difficulties are the contradictory demands of participation and observation. If you are observing well, you are probably not participating enough, and vice versa.

The technique requires constant auditory, psychological and visual vigilance; we were fortunate to be two since, hopefully, our attention did not always flag at the same moments or in the same ways.

Under the conditions of our study, participant observation did involve a flexibility to other people's timetables; this was exhausting and demanding. Probably these particular problems would not impinge in quite the same way on someone living full-time in the field, as would be the case in a fully fledged anthropological study.

Ambiguities in relationships are probably unavoidable under conditions of participant observation, and we would argue that this places a special responsibility on the observers' shoulders, as the 'observed' have not asked to be bedevilled by this unprecedented type of relationship, for which there are no conventions on which to fall back. We acknowledge that unfortunately we were not always as skilful in discharging these responsibilities as we would have wished.

Was It All Worth It?

It is difficult to assess whether or not the project was worthwhile. The local residents, whom we naively wished to assist, seem to have been supremely unaffected by the work.

The results may have had some influence on practical affairs, although we cannot assess what part, if any, our recommendations have played in the subsequent initiatives by local government and other agencies that have led to the extension and consolidation of a range of services within Newtown. One unintended consequence, of which we know, is that some real estate agents and land developers have found the information useful.

The members of the Civic Group are now widely

dispersed and we believe that there would be considerable variations in the degree of positive and negative feelings with which they would recall the Newtown study on which they expended so much time, talent and enthusiasm. For those we have seen, or heard of, in recent years we are pleased to be able to say that by all outward signs, they continue to be active in public life and successful in their careers.

Strange as it may seem, we do not have a clear-cut view as to whether or not it was personally worthwhile. Sometimes we were definitely convinced that it was not; at others we were ready to persuade ourselves otherwise. In retrospect, it is perhaps easier to record a 'yes' vote. Clearly we benefited in academic terms; we were lucky to have a stimulating partnership to sustain us through the roughest periods and it was undoubtedly a period rich in experience. It was also one heavy in its demands on our private lives. In the final account, it is probably for others to say whether it was worth completing, as we are in a very bad position from which to judge the results.

We know, however, that the book has been bought (though not necessarily read) by a substantial number of people, as recently it was necessary to have it reprinted. Probably the most extensive use of the report has been by academics and people in the welfare field, some of whom have told us that reading the book has led them to question some assumptions which they had previously taken for granted.

We cannot claim that our work was necessarily influential, but it is clear that in recent years in Australia, the notion that there is likely to be a disparity between the values of professionals and the majority of their clients has now moved into the realm of conventional wisdom.

Whether such understanding leads to changes in practice is more difficult to know, and it is to be borne in mind that we might not approve of all the changes that might conceivably be generated by caretakers reading the book. As we have stressed all along, whether the insights are used for conservative or radical purposes is not inherent in the results, but will depend on the values of the practitioner who chooses to use them.

Because of the success and prestige of the natural sciences we, in the social sciences, have sometimes tended to take over their procedures and trappings without sufficient reflection. Perhaps it is time to stop and think hard about the values we are enshrining when we adopt consultancy roles. Do we in fact want to develop this mechanism further, which directly confirms the schism between research and practice, and would seem to be more appropriate to a day and age that did not have the reservations about the possibilities of 'value-free' research which exist today?

A fascinating chapter is waiting to be written on the latent functions of consultancy; but for the here and now, we believe that no one should embark on problem-focussed contract research without first posing to themselves the questions which Maurice Stein[10] suggested should be mandatory in this situation. His questions were 'Who wants the problems solved?', 'Who wants them left alone?', and we would add, 'And why?'.

NOTES AND REFERENCES

1. Bryson, L. & Thompson, F. *An Australian Newtown: Life and Leadership in a Working Class Suburb*, Kibble Books, 1972.
2. Bryson L. & Thompson, F. 'Research and Social Planning: A Case Study of Conflict of Values', *The Australian and New Zealand Journal of Sociology* 6, 1 (1970).
3. Halmos, P. 'The Personal Service Society', *British Journal of Sociology* XVIII, 1 (1967), p.13.
4. Bryson & Thompson, *An Australian Newtown*, p.319.
5. Dunphy, D. 'Putting Sociology to Work — The Social Relevance of Sociology — An Immediate Issue', *The Australian and New Zealand Journal of Sociology* 10, 1 (1974) p.6.
6. Apart from Professor Marwick's involvement in the early stages, the other staff members were Oscar Roberts who acted as consultant statistician, and Rosemary Otto who was research assistant for the project for ten months. Numerous other people worked part-time for short periods on such

activities as coding, computer programming, typing, drafting maps and diagrams, etc.
7. A series of related studies, under the overall supervision of Professor R Henderson of the University of Melbourne, that was investigating the extent and causes of poverty in Australia.
8. Whyte, W. F. *Street Corner Society,* Chicago University Press, 1943; and 'The Slum: On the Evolution of Street Corner Society', in A. J. Vidich, J. Bensman & M. Stein (eds), *Reflections on Community Studies,* Wiley, 1964.
9. McNaul, J. P. 'Relations between Researchers and Practitioners', in S. Z. Nagi & R. G. Corwin (eds), *The Social Contexts of Research,* Wiley-Interscience, 1972. The six areas of potential conflict that he identifies are in relation to evaluation of knowledge, methods of communication, time frame, uniqueness versus patterns, the degree of finality of knowledge and the use of environmental controls.
10. Stein, M. R. *The Eclipse of Community: An Interpretation of American Studies,* Princeton University Press, 1960, p.332.

TAKING THE QUEEN'S SHILLING
Accepting Social Research Consultancies in the 1970s

Eva Cox, Fran Hausfeld & Sue Wills[*]

With the election of the Labor Government under Gough Whitlam in 1972, a startling change overtook Australian Federal politics. It also changed the relationship between the Federal Government and academic researchers (especially social scientists). For the previous decade or more, a long-established government had tended to maintain customary policies and to avoid new researches which could have provided the impetus for demands for policy changes. However, 1972 saw a new government installed, one which welcomed, invited, demanded and financed a multitude of research projects which were to serve as guides for, and/or legitimators of, policy initiatives. In the 1960s there had been relatively few opportunities for social scientists outside the bureaucracy to gain experience of government-sponsored policy research; in the early 1970s there were suddenly more research opportunities than either experienced researchers to carry them out or experienced bureaucrats to oversee them. Problems inevitably arose: problems for the civil servants and government appointees in defining, controlling and assessing researchers and their contributions; problems for social scientists committed, on the one hand, to their professional standards and often, on the other, to specific social changes they hoped would follow from their recommendations.

[*] Conceptualised by Eva Cox, interpolated by Sue Wills, reinterpreted by Fran Hausfeld. A feminist collective enterprise.

The relationship between government and research is complex: the role of research in policy formation is seldom clearly articulated; and government involvement in research may constitute either a commitment or an alternative to action. Where governments are committed to needs-based polices, data on needs and informed speculation on policy outcomes are prerequisites for policy initiatives. However, when public problems incite a general outcry, public (and perhaps governmental and bureaucratic) unease may be defused by the initiation of an enquiry which legitimates inaction while 'the facts' are sought. The latter case does not necessarily constitute deliberate avoidance of governmental action, but may allow publication of a series of reports and recommendations which, over time, can be used as a sounding-board for the assessment of public opinion – or even its redirection.

In Australia in the early 1970s, there was a genuine shortage of information on which new governmental programmes could be based. Thus there was a recognised need for policy-related research *before* policy changes could be formulated. There was no need for a new government to defuse public demands for policy changes or to fear the outcome of enquiries.

If the enquiries criticised previous action or inaction, they could be used for political advantage over the preceding government, now in opposition. Thus government-sponsored research could only benefit the government: first, because it needed the data and recommendations on which sound and attractive policies depended; and second, because, as a newcomer to power, it was not threatened by enquiries which could in no way reflect on its own past performances.

Out of this situation came a rapid explosion of research funding, through government departments and specially mounted enquiries and commissions, intended both to provide information and to act as legitimators of decisions which could be presented as responses to proven needs. Among these enquiries were: the Social Welfare Commission, whose role was to recommend a range of changes to the provision and delivery of social welfare; the Schools Commission; the Interim Children's Commission; an extension of the Commonwealth Commission of Enquiry into Poverty (a legacy of the previous government), adding four million dollars to the original grant; the Royal Commission into Australian Government Administration; and the Royal Commission on Human Relationships.

With so great and so sudden an expansion of funds available for empirical research, it was difficult to find sufficient suitably qualified and experienced personnel to undertake the projects now made possible. Most State and Federal Government departments already had research subsections (or divisions) but, without adequate staffing and funding, they tended to collate existing data rather than to design and execute autonomous research projects for the collection of new information. Department-based research, when it did occur, tended to be slow and costly: one highly paid professional, hampered by the absence of trained subordinates, would be backed by only a small clerical or secretarial staff and lacked sufficient funds to commission outside helpers, so would be forced to become interviewer and collator as well as designer and director. Prior to 1972, limited funding had been available, primarily for academics, through the universities and certain government grants for social research. In addition, there was the usual structure of commercial research organisations serving the needs of marketers and advertisers. These were occasionally able to provide skilled staff for social research, but had limited resources for expansion. When the new call for research came, there was little hope that it could be answered adequately, either from within the existing bureaucracy or by outside commercial organisations, despite the provision of extra funds. Great number of academics 'took the Queen's shilling', although not always with the same rank.

Many of the projects were 'oncers' which had to be completed in a relatively short time. With the funding problem eased, but with little possibility of a permanent increase in the numbers of professional research staff, the solution for most department-based projects was to use outside consultants whose other commitments would not allow them to take up full-time positions, but who would be able to provide the needed skills on a part-time, consultative basis. *Ad hoc* bodies of enquiry also used consultants, but sometimes employed a few full-time researchers on short-term contracts, an arrangement particularly suitable for academics contemplating permanent governmental work or for those 'resting' between academic appointments. Whatever the method of recruitment, it resulted in academics, bureaucrats and heads of *ad hoc* bodies being brought together for a common task, but lacking both agreed definitions of their various roles and a common understanding of how those roles interrelated.

Because the research task can be subdivided into several phases, each demanding different skills, consultants can be used in various capacities. The consultant who is seen as an expert in the subject area is usually someone whose expertise is attested by publications in the field and, possibly, a previous history of research grants in that area. The expert in techniques, on the other hand, does not necessarily have any special subject area of expertise, but is seen as an expert in devising the research machinery and strategies best suited to the collection of data in any designated subject area. Similarly, contract researchers may be seen as either subject experts or technique experts; further, they may be employed either to carry out research themselves, or to coordinate and oversee researches carried out by others. Obviously, conflicts and problems can arise when different members of the research team have different definitions of their own and others' roles.

Cox and Wills were both involved in a project to explore Australian Attitudes to Sexuality and Sex Roles for the Royal Commission on Human Relationships. Whether they were employed as consultants with subject expertise or as consultants with expertise in research techniques (or even as both, together or severally) is as unclear to them today as it was during their contact with the Commission. They now feel that this lack of clarity in role definition was probably the cause of many of the difficulties they encountered, as well as of many of the problems they no doubt presented to their clients and temporary colleagues. Cox was also involved in the Inquiry into Poverty; in research funded by various grants under the Child Care Act (1972); in the Schools Commission; in the Royal Commission into Australian Government Administration; and in a study on Women and the Workforce for the Royal Commission on Human Relationships. In these research consultancies, her role was sometimes explicitly defined and limited, sometimes vague and contradictory. She found a positive relationship between the degree of explicitness of role definition, on the one hand, and the number of work-based problems and difficulties, on the other. The account that follows is based upon experiences undergone by Cox and Wills during this period when each 'took the Queen's shilling', acting as consultant for governmental enquiries set up to provide information on which policy decisions could (and allegedly would) be made.

Both commonsense and experience suggests that clients of research consultants may vary in many ways: in the clarity and explicitness of their research aims; in the extent to which they will allow prior policy commitments to take precedence over research-based recommendations; in their own sense of competence to deal with experts; in the extent to which they are prepared, or able, to listen to the consultant's advice when there may be a multiplicity of advisers; in their vulnerability to political pressures because of the political sensitivity of their task; and in their willingness to take rather than to avoid action. The consultant may become embroiled, unwittingly, in problems which, while not inherent in an apparently straightforward research task, emanate from such 'hidden agendas'.

On the other hand, consultants may themselves be responding to different and potentially conflicting pressures. They have long-term professional reputations to consider;

they may have personal commitments to certain kinds of actions rather than others; they may doubt the ability of the client to understand the subtleties of their interpretations and recommendations; they may become apprehensive about the uses to which their work will be put. The government, avowedly committed to social reforms *via* soundly based initiatives in social policy, was calling for large numbers of competent, socially responsible academic researchers to carry out designated research projects and to submit proposals for funded research into areas of their own choice. In this political climate, it can be anticipated that self-selection processes will lead to a number of already committed consultants moving into a number of politically sensitive research areas. Pressures on both consultants and clients will differ markedly from the pressures usually encountered by researchers in pursuit of the academic life.

A client with a clear and limited task, who can give an explicit role to the consultant, causes few problems for the researcher. For example, Cox was employed for a substudy in the legal section of the Poverty Enquiry, in which she was asked to assist in the adaptation of an overseas interview schedule, in the drawing of a sample and in the training of interviewers. Here her role was clearly that of an expert in technique, her tasks were explicit and her involvement with the vast and complex Enquiry itself was minimal. There was no role conflict with her immediate clients. Similarly, her relations with the Schools Commission were limited, explicit and unambiguous: the Commission had a section reporting on the problems encountered by girls in the education process and her task was the preparation of certain retabulations, together with their interpretations, of Census data. She also served as a research consultant to the Royal Commission into Australian Government Administration and worked with the Commission's own research staff. Once again, her role was clearly that of a technician, her expertise was in research techniques rather than in the substantive issues of the structure of the service. She designed questionnaires and advised on other issues of data collection. The relationship was clearly defined and presented no problems.

However, when the terms of involvement are less clearly defined, when client expectations are ambiguous and when client commitments are ambivalent, problems occur. For example, the Social Welfare Commission employed Cox as a research consultant, using her skills for the collection and interpretation of data on social work educators. Not being a member of the social work profession, she was not employed as an area or subject expert. Unfortunately, a 'hidden agenda' operated: some social work educators, who preferred self-evaluation to outside evaluation, tried to organise a boycott of the postal questionnaire distributed to various institutions concerned with welfare training. Although they were relatively unsuccessful in the boycott (the response rate exceeded 50%), they did manage to embarrass the Commission and devalue the report, partly because the dissidents could successfully (but irrelevantly) show that the researcher was not an expert in the area. Had the Commission been more certain of the research role and its legitimacy, the report may have been put forward more confidently.

Peculiar and new difficulties may arise when research is not merely contracted, but is actually solicited by the allocation of research funds on a submission basis. This is especially so when the area of research is politically sensitive (so that the call for submissions attracts adherents of competing points of view) and when the government has no strong commitment to a specific policy proposal (a state of affairs usually prompting the request for submissions in the first place). An example is the funding of various research projects under the Advisory Committee on Child Care Research (which was later subsumed under the Interim Children's Commission). Here, governmental indecision, sensitivity to political controversy and the involvement of competing policy proponents caused serious problems for all concerned.

When Federal funds were committed to extend the very limited provision of early childhood services offering surrogate care for children under school age, considerable public debate (between professionals, experts and lay persons) on the advisability of the provision and extension of such services ensued. The depth of the ideological gulf between opposing groups is apparent in the rhetoric used. There was talk of the vital importance of 'mothering', of a denial of the woman's right to work, of the subjugation of women to the needs of their children, of the dangers to the well-being of children, of 'maternal deprivation', and of 'selfish women callously avoiding their responsibilities'. The government's decision to fund research (including research on the basis of solicited submissions) reflected the pressures being exerted by this controversy: the government needed to justify both its involvement in child care and the limited nature of this involvement. It sought such justification in research findings which could be used to demonstrate the responsibility of its actions.

Advertisements appeared in the daily press, inviting applications for funds to do research into a wide variety of issues concerning the needs of children. This provided an avenue of funding for both those in favour of, and those who opposed, such services. It also allowed some groups to dust off old projects and adapt them to new guidelines. Other applications came from a variety of organisations who saw research as a source of funding for an expansion of their other activities. Various 'experts' evaluated the submissions and advised on which grants should be awarded. Unfortunately, the relevance of many of these projects as aids to the government in the formulation of policy cannot be determined since, at the time of writing (four years later, 1977), few of the reports have been published, and those few by the authors, not by the government.

Cox had been actively involved in the extension of child care services and in research into child/parent needs; she took part in three grants. In two of these, she was part of a research team in which autonomy and agreement meant that no problems relevant to the discussion in this chapter arose. There were many conflicts, however, with the third.

A small social welfare agency, in conjunction with a local

school, applied for a grant to investigate the reasons for parental noninvolvement with the school, tying it loosely to child care by associating it with the provision of after-school activities. Inexperience led to gross undercosting so that although the full sum requested was granted, there was only sufficient money for one part-time salary and little else. A voluntary research committee was formed, to advise the part-time research assistant, who admitted limitations in the field of survey research. Cox offered her services to the committee because of personal interest in the project: she helped with questionnaire design, interviewer training and data handling. Together with another sociologist, she also accepted the responsibility of working through the data and presenting the material in such a way that it could be included in the report. Here serious conflicts arose.

The two sociologists, widely read in the problems of disadvantaged schools, interpreted the material in the light of their sociological expertise. In discussions with the staff of both the school and the agency, however, it emerged that the staffs saw themselves not as part of the research, but as its interpreters. In fact, the staffs had defined the problem, before beginning the research, as resting in the parents and their attitudes. The sociologists, on the other hand, took the school staff as part of the research universe and interpreted the data as showing that the problem lay in the interaction of parents with teachers. Naturally these different perspectives led to different recommendations: the two sociologists agreed that there should be changes in the school's attitudes to parents as well as in parents' attitudes to the school. The staffs, however, rejected this interpretation and omitted it from the final report, recommending instead the provision of more social workers for the area.

The greatest and most frustrating problems associated with 'taking the Queen's shilling' arose for both Cox and Wills, in their relationships with the Royal Commission on Human Relationships. The curious circumstances surrounding the setting-up of this Commission, the complexity and indeterminacy of its task and the politically sensitive nature of its investigations are unusual, and illustrate the confusion of research and politics that exists in the minds of politicians and the public.

When an attempt to make abortion legal in the Australian Federal territories was lost on a free vote in Federal Parliament, a bipartisan motion was passed to set up an enquiry into what were described as 'human relationships'. The motives for the move are difficult to determine. The abortion issue was controversial, but its failure to pass the House was also controversial; although Parliament was unwilling to take the proposed action on abortion, it may have felt obliged, in the face of public demand, to take *some* action. Some members may have hoped that the public, taking the intention for the deed, would forget the whole issue in favour of something more readily solved by parliamentary action. In August 1974, the Royal Commission on Human Relationships was established with three Commissioners: a judge, a journalist and a bishop. Its terms of reference were dauntingly wide:

'To enquire into and report upon the family, social, educational, legal and sexual aspects of male and female relationships...'

It was to gather its information from written submissions, from statements at informal hearings, from oral evidence given in formal public hearings, from existing literature and from 'research done by and on behalf of the Commission'. The budget was $1.5 million.

Four factors probably made the major contribution to the wariness of the Commissioners, both in their perceptions of what they would be able to do and their concern about what they would be seen to be doing. First, there were the circumstances that led to the inception of the Commission. Second, there was the media publicity surrounding its establishment which, at times, treated the whole idea of such a Commission with levity. Third, there was the awkward fact that the Commission's terms of reference dealt with what are traditionally seen as private matters, not public issues. Fourth, there was the Commissioners' subjection, from the outset, to suspicion from and lobbying by radicals and conservatives alike, including some groups with a certain political importance.

The role of Royal Commissioners is often ambiguous; and in such an enquiry as this, it is inevitably and essentially ambiguous. Are they appointed as experts with special knowledge in the area? Or as enquirers with specific investigative skills, to find out what others cannot? Or as representatives of the general public, as lay persons of prestige and probity who will sift the evidence of experts and arrive at their own 'considered opinion', the informed opinion of Everyman and Everywoman? Clearly, with this Commission, the Commissioners were appointed neither as experts nor as skilled investigators. Rather, representing the judiciary, the Church and the media, they appeared to be the government's attempt to reach a balance of informed, lay opinion. None of the three had experience in professional research in the social sciences, the disciplines most closely related to the Commission's areas of concern.

Human relationships as a subject for research, particularly in the context of possible governmental initiatives, presents even the most experienced researchers with problems. This was compounded by the need to placate the political figures funding the research, the public servants from the Treasury approving expenditure, the media seeking startling stories, and the public being both for and against particular kinds of research and possible recommendations. The proliferation of actual and possible conflicts is then easily seen to be formidable. How should the Commission choose projects to be funded? How should it select the personnel to staff them? What criteria should be used to assess the value of projects and the competence of researchers?

The Commission tried, in good faith, to solve these problems. It failed in many ways, perhaps inevitably. In building up their research staff, the Commissioners appeared undecided as to whether they should hire experts in techniques or experts in subject areas. Indeed, it is not clear that they recognised this question sufficiently to make an informed decision. In its full-time contract appointments, the Commission appears to have compromised, hiring people with different experience in the subject areas and with varying levels of research experience. Possibly because of this type of compromise, together with the controversial nature of the subject of enquiry, the Commissioners themselves initially attempted to maintain a high degree of involvement in and control over the actual research projects. It is at least questionable that they were, in fact, appointed to act in this way, rather than as wise lay members of the community leavening the results and recommendations of experts.

The kind of role that the Commissioners seem to have decided to adopt *vis-à-vis* Commission-originated research and those assigned to carry it out raised serious communication problems and caused professional consultants serious professional misgivings in some cases. What the Commissioners no doubt saw as the proper and conscientious exercise of their responsibility could be interpreted, by professional workers, as unproductive interference in a sound research design. What the Commissioners no doubt saw as the judicious balancing of competing interest groups, the professionals could see as the distortion of a cherished project. And when the Commission first requested and then greatly altered a specific project — hedging the researcher around with conditions and personnel uncongenial to the kind of academic autonomy and professional prestige to which he or she was accustomed — then it was easy for the professional to interpret as vacillation and indecision that which the Commissioners no doubt saw as the careful protection of the Commission and the government from unwanted political conflicts and pressures.

For example, as a result of a conversation with one Commissioner, Cox submitted a one-page note suggesting that the stress of women coping with housework and outside employment may be relevant to the Commission's enquiries. She suggested a study of the time-budgetting problems facing the younger, working mother. Such studies have been done overseas, but no local data were available. Subsequently, Cox was invited to attend a meeting in which the Commissioners suggested she might like to take part in a study of young mothers' attitudes to work, particularly the question of their continuing to work if given a choice, as Cox had already done research in this field. The Commission, based in Sydney, was funding a Melbourne study, and offered Cox a complementary Sydney study. In making the offer, the Commissioners seemed to be asking for both her research skills and her special knowledge of the particular subject area to incorporate some of her original research interest (the younger, working mother) in the Melbourne study.

Conceptual and methodological differences between Cox and the Melbourne researcher slowed the project suggested by the Commission. Neither researcher was permitted to prevail but, unfortunately, the Commission's own research officer, with little or no experience of field research, was unable to arbitrate. The political sensitivity of the research concepts (such as the problems of individual choice versus problems of economic reality) exacerbated the situation. While these conceptual problems caused difficulties, the methodological ones were more serious: Cox tried four times to resign because she felt the status of the research was being jeopardised and, with it, her own professional standing. Although both her skills and her subject expertise were being sought by the Commission, she was not given the authority to use them. The Commission's own tendency to vacillate between seeing her as an expert in technique, for some purposes, and as an expert in the subject for other purposes, and occasionally just as an employee, made effective research difficult.

An even more unsatisfactory research experience with the Commission was that of Wills and Cox who, together with a colleague (Antolovich), conceived a study of attitudes towards homosexuals and homosexuality. In this research team, which proposed (rather than solicited) a research project by means of a submission to the Commission, Wills was the subject-area expert, Cox the expert in technique and Antolovich the administrator. This combination seemed appropriate.

A detailed submission on the reasons for the research, its utility, method and probable cost, was submitted. It was explained that it would be necessary for any scientifically adequate study first to ascertain the range and variety of attitudes towards homosexuals and homosexuality in the community, and then to attempt to measure the proportions of the public holding these attitudes. For this reason, the study was to be a two-part exercise, consisting of first a qualitative and then a quantitative element, each using its own appropriate techniques. The first part was to involve holding taped, unstructured discussions in groups controlled for age, sex and socio-economic background. From these discussions, a questionnaire would be constructed, incorporating the range and variety of attitudes uncovered. This would be administered to as large and varied a sample of the population as possible.

This project was submitted to the Commission on 15 April 1975. They expressed immediate interest in funding it. On 2 May 1975, the researchers were called to a meeting with two of the Royal Commissioners, together with the research officer assigned as the liaison person with the Commission. At this meeting, the difficulties the Commission saw in this research team undertaking an investigation of attitudes to homosexuality became apparent. The problem was that two of the team were publicly known as homosexuals and all three were women. The Commission expressed fears that some unspecified people were bound to see bias in the results because of the nature of the research team, and they reminded the research team that the credibility of the Commission, as sponsor and funder of the research, must be taken into consideration.

The fact that the biases of heterosexuals studying homosexuals (or of men studying women, or of white people studying blacks) were seldom questioned was not relevant to the issue, which arose solely because of the political sensitivity of the Commission itself and its brief. Nor were the Commission's doubts indicative of a lack of confidence in the research team, whose academic and other backgrounds were appreciated. The Commission was reacting to the almost impossible task set by the government that was made no easier by the Commission's own intention to carry out the assignment to the best of its ability.

The team was asked to redraft the submission, expanding it to include an investigation of attitudes towards sexuality in general; and in addition, to accept a fourth member into the team: a male heterosexual minister living and working in Melbourne. Thus the project was to be split into two components, and altered to take account of the Commission's fears of public hostility or derision. The broadening of the scope of the project was welcomed: there would be advantages in viewing attitudes towards homosexuality within the broader context of attitudes towards sexuality in general. The revised proposal was resubmitted (by the original research team of three Sydney women) on 14 May 1975 and agreement was given to the inclusion of the Melbourne researcher in order to ensure approval of the project. Treasury approval for funding was long-delayed and it was not until March 1976 that funding was finally approved.

In the meantime, attempts to co-ordinate research with the Melbourne member proceeded and, to this end, he was flown to Sydney for a discussion of the equivalence of research design in order to ensure comparability of data. Unfortunately, during this period, staff changes within the Commission made continuity of liaison impossible. The Commission's recently appointed research director was finally assigned to undertake this task, but agreement on comparability of research design between Melbourne and Sydney proved impossible, and the Commission finally agreed, reluctantly, to the execution of two different projects on the one general topic. The Melbourne project was to consist of structured group discussions which were not taped, but noted; and the same groups would be given a questionnaire. The Sydney project would consist of unstructured, group discussions which would be taped; and a different population comparable in sex, age and socio-economic background, would answer the questionnaire.

The continuing closeness of the Commission's scrutiny was irksome to Cox, Wills and Antolovich; they had expected to make a submission, have it approved after discussion and agreed modification, and then be left to carry out the research and submit the findings to the Commission. They expected the Commission research officers to act as clients: to determine the relevance of the research to their overall programme, to purchase the team's skills and expertise and to deal with the results as they saw fit. Instead, the Commission staff insisted on participation even in the determination of minor details, such as the wording of particular questions. However, in failing to insist on having their role *vis-à-vis* the Commission explicitly defined, the team contributed to the resulting confusions and frustrations. What compounded the situation was the Commission's marrying of incompatible personnel in the interests of credibility in the eyes of some unspecified 'other', a marriage which led to compromises desired by neither part and incapable of solving the original problems.

Difficulties associated with questionnaire design illustrate the types of problems that continued to occur and were not resolved. First, there was a basic disagreement regarding open-ended as compared with forced-choice questions. This is a technical problem and its solution depends upon methodological assumptions. There were also arguments about the wording of certain questions because of ambiguities. This is a delicate task, demanding considerable experience in even a noncontroversial and well-researched area. Although the Commission's research director sat in on these discussions, he provided no adjudication; nor did he set up any mechanisms for reaching compromise. On an even more fundamental level, the Sydney team's judgement that the Melbourne draft questionnaire failed to conform with the original research brief (because the Melbourne questionnaire canvassed issues of morality rather than of attitudes and their formation) was not assessed by the Commission officer, let alone supported or refuted. Although Cox, Wills and Antolovich were the original researchers and their proposal, despite amendment, was the basis of the research, they found themselves on the defensive, having to justify their attempts to match the research tools to the research objectives.

Unresolved conflicts dragged on without the protagonists being able to agree and without any firm action from the Commission. The Sydney team was finally reduced in status from independent, specialist consultants to the category of naughty and obstructionist children by the letter that each of them received from the Director of Research on 19 February 1976, which included the following paragraph:

> The project will continue to be co-operative and comparative. This means that an agreed format must be reached if the study is to proceed. Agreement is therefore the key issue, not the achievement of a solution satisfactory to any one person or group in the project. If a comparative study cannot proceed, I can see no justification in expending public money on two more or less similar projects. You must therefore decide if the integrity of your approach to the project will be violated to an unacceptable extent by achieving agreement on the technical and procedural issues. If you decide that this is the case, I must make my judgement about the future of the project with this in mind...

From this letter two things became apparent: first, that the Commission officer saw himself as the team's boss, rather than as acting for the clients of specialist consultants; and second, that the conflicts were to be reduced not by examination of the issues, but in terms of personalities and ultimata. Since it was precisely the integrity of the team's approach to the project that was (amongst other things) being violated, first Cox, and then Antolovich and Wills, resigned. The latter, in their letter of resignation, pointed out that

For some considerable time the relations of the Sydney research team with the Commission have been deteriorating and have now reached the point of driving away one member (Cox) of our research team...
We are also concerned not to lend our names to nor participate in a research project with which we are not entirely satisfied. The 'final version' of the questionnaire which we received is not to our satisfaction. It contains omissions of questions which we feel are essential to properly carry out the research commissioned under the brief and it contains question wording which is simply ludicrous – for example, question 23 – how anyone could answer that their 'childhood background' was 'hypocritical' is rather difficult to imagine...

The Sydney team, in resigning, forced a resolution of the research deadlock. The Commissioners invited the Sydney team to withdraw their resignation and allow the project to be completely split, each team submitting its own report, but retaining some level of comparability. This solution was not an effective research strategy, but an attempt to salvage an important part of the programme. In part, the Commission, by proposing and endorsing this 'solution', negated their attempt at balance (which had given rise to the deadlock in the first place), because the resulting projects were only partially comparable and, had results differed markedly, would have put the Commissioners in an embarrassing position in deciding the relative legitimacy of the two different projects.

These experiences of working for the government or its contractors are included here as examples of the types of problems that people are likely to encounter when they move from the academic world of autonomous research and recognised consultancy expertise into government-funded, politically sensitive policy research overseen by bureaucrats and other lay persons. Good experiences, like good news, do not make for interesting experience – or for useful insights into many problems of social research. Many other experiences of the writers in doing social research have therefore been omitted. This chapter has concentrated on the relationship of research to social science in the context of practical field experience and, particularly, in the context of governmental research.

In most of the illustrations presented here, the conflicts and frustrations affected the researchers, personally, more adversely than they affected the research itself. The level of remuneration was based on costings provided in the original submissions when research was solicited; and the time spent in attempting to resolve issues, together with the expected government delays on approvals and payments, meant that the financial rewards finally worked out to only a few cents an hour. Without commitment to the necessity for the kinds of research undertaken and a belief in the importance of adequate reporting, the researchers would not have perservered. Once the decision to continue is taken, the professional academic researcher is committed to the provision of academically sound results for personal professional reasons.

The issue of the committed researcher/social scientist and his or her possible relationship with government-funded research is both complex and important. Although fewer social scientists today, especially those in academic fields, will talk about objectivity or lack of bias in research, both governments and civil servants wish to appear impartial (even when they are not). Thus their inclination is to commission research and researchers who are above suspicion. If the research is to be the basis of policy decisions, particularly in areas of possible conflicts of values and ideology, the problems tend to increase dramatically. Here, the politicians must appear to make their decisions on scientific grounds rather than on political expediency. The setting-up of research can be either a genuine attempt to find a solution to a vexed question, or an exercise in defusing a situation by appearing to take judicious and informed action by initiating research.

The situation of the researcher is affected by the political input when devising research strategies. Projects such as the Royal Commission into Australian Government Administration (RCAGA) appeared, both internally and externally, confident of both its legitimacy and its potential efficacy as an agent of change. For these reasons, working for it presented no problems. In contrast, the Royal Commission into Human Relationships (RCHR) was, from the start, in the political limelight. Unlike the RCAGA, it faced doubts about and problems associated with both its legitimacy and its ultimate efficacy. The RCAGA set up a programme of research, then sought people to assist in its implementation under the supervision of research staff, and employing outsiders with an interest in, but no great commitment to, the issue it was investigating. The RCHR, on the other hand, found itself deluged with pressure groups and carpet-baggers touting issues and proposals. In an attempt to appear uncommitted, the Commissioners therefore increased their difficulties (and those of their staff) by not allowing their commissioned researchers to operate within the context of experts in techniques or experts in issues, or both.

Had Cox and Wills not had existing interests in the issues involved, they would not have initiated discussion or made submissions. Had the Commission not recognised their professional skills, they would not have commissioned the research. Had the writers not been involved in the projects, they would not have accepted and tried to work through the problems engendered by the work situation. But had the Commissioners not been so anxious about known biases, and the need for the apparent objectivity and credibility of the Commission, they would not have constrained the research in an attempt to forestall possible charges of bias.

One important lesson seems to be that the working social scientist, particularly one working as a contract researcher outside the academic institution, must define his or her role in relation to the client. This problem of role definition probably decreases as the individual researcher moves up the status ladder of his or her own profession: professors and readers are eminent enough for them to define their own role in relation to projects without being questioned.

But if the research consultant is small fry, not someone whose publications have established his or her expertise and reputation, but someone who has experience as a researcher and an area of professional or personal interest, there are problems. For the government or hiring body, dependent on the consultant's skills, also wants to be able to assure the public that they are getting value for money and facts, not opinions, when the consultant specialist is not yet prestigious enough for the two to be accepted as equivalent. In sum, therefore, *caveat vendor*!

NOTES AND REFERENCES

1. 'The Queen's shilling': a shilling formerly given to a recruit on enlisting.

WORKING IT OUT TOGETHER
Reflections on Research on Women Academics

B. Cass, M. Dawson, H. Radi, D. Temple, S. Wills & A. Winkler

Initially five, and then six women, all working in universities in Sydney, set out to investigate the position of women working in universities. From this intimate connection between our daily activities (and our source of income) and the object of our research, it is clear that we did not enter our study in a spirit of disinterested detachment. With collective experience in the fields of education, biomedical science, history, politics, psychology and sociology, and collective experience of different positions on the academic ladder (ranging from senior lecturer to part-time tutor and postgraduate student), we were intensely *interested* in the status of women in the academic labour market.

We were interested in the ways in which women are recruited into the university workforce; the family, educational and workforce experiences which predate their university jobs; their distribution in the academic hierarchy; their work, community and household experiences; their social and political attitudes. As consciously feminist researchers, we were committed to asking the basic questions about women in a profession: why are they so few, and why are they even scarcer at the top of the hierarchy where decisions are made and control is exercised?[1]

In retrospect, our research techniques were fruitful because:
1. We were *immersed* in the social situation that we were

researching. We were not strangers in alien territory; middle-class sociologists in the 'underprivileged' suburb, or white Western anthropologists in a small-scale society in which the researcher needs to acquire a sympathetic understanding of language and lore before he or she can begin. The written and unwritten codes of the university social system were part of our daily experience, and we could work within their universe of meanings. As a result, we won the co-operation of those sections of the university workforce who shared some of our assumptions, and the hostility of other sections who understood our language, but were opposed to our intentions. We generated co-operation and hostility, just as we would if we were involved in any other political activity, because social research, is, acknowledged or unacknowledged, a political activity.

Social research is political because the researcher has interests which may coincide with or contradict the interests of the researched.[2] All social research has an end: the formulation of policy; the conservation; reform, or radical transformation of the social situation being studied; or, in the case of 'disinterested' research, the pursuit of knowledge and the enhancement of the researcher's professional status. Even research with no express policy orientation may have unintended consequences — since social knowledge is used by different groups in the pursuit of their own interests. We were aware of the political nature of our research: to alert women and men to the existence of sexual segmentation and sexual stratification in the university workforce, as in the general workforce.[3]

2. We were a *multidisciplinary* research group. Multidisciplinary research, when it takes the form of people from different disciplines constituting themselves into a special group to investigate a particular area of concern, can be both stimulating and nerve-wracking. Within the broad concern to investigate the position of women in

universities, we all had special areas of interest and we had different views on how best to find out what we wanted to find out. Take; Temple, a pharmacologist (trained in the natural sciences); Dawson, an educationist; Radi, an historian; Cass, a sociologist; Winkler, a psychologist; and Wills, a political scientist — and at times the pharmacologist is bound to feel the odd one out, especially when it comes to the adequacy or otherwise of a 68% response rate to a questionnaire:

> In my work, supposing I did an experiment with 100 mice and 40 got away. I'd say that experiment had failed and I'd start again. But you can't do that with people.

As far as collecting the data was concerned, the differences of opinion within the group over special areas of interest and ways of collecting information were incorporated rather than resolved. Our methods were both qualitative and quantitative: we used a very long questionnaire, which was sent to every woman working in a teaching/research capacity in the three universities in Sydney and the NSW Institute of Technology. A shorter version with some questions reworded according to gender was sent to a randomly selected sample of male academics. We conducted in-depth interviews with self-selected female respondents. We examined statistics from the year 1891 onwards of university staff and students, compiled by both the Commonwealth Statistician and the universities themselves. While the use of different methods to collect the data may be applauded by those who advocate multiple approaches to the research field,[4] it presented us with the later problem of handling the great mass of information we had collected. Because of these varied techniques, and the varied data that they produced, we are never able to lapse into complacency about the meaning of our research findings. We continue to explore ways of meshing the cross-tabulations of variables produced by questionnaires with the accounts of lived experience produced by oral histories, against a background of statistics that chart the historical patterns of women's involvement in universities as staff and students. In some ways we are following C. Wright Mills' ambitious formula for social research: meshing social structure, history and biography,[5] but the project is not an easy one.

3. In the course of the study, the research group established itself as an informal support system: a focus for collegiate relations and the sharing of work experiences, which was itself informative about the nature of the academic enterprise. Cynthia Fuchs Epstein's analysis of women in the professions shows that professions function like small, relatively closed and homogeneous communities — anxious to control recruitment of personnel, to exercise exclusion practices, to exercise social control over their members, and to protect the interests and privileges of their members, *vis-à-vis* their clients, the State and employing bodies.[6] In the academic profession, men predominate in these moral communities, not only because they constitute the majority of the absolute numbers in the university workforce, but also because they are, even for their absolute numbers, highly overrepresented in positions of authority.[7] Our research group, having been established to investigate this phenomenon, eventually became itself an alternative community, with much less power than those communities that exercise control, but nevertheless, a significant reference group composed of women.

The History of the Project

The initial idea for a study of women university teachers was conceived ten years ago by Madge Dawson and Diana Temple, who were active in the Sydney University Staff Association. With the promise of some funding from Sydney University Research funds and from the Department of Adult Education, the project was set in motion in 1973, when Dawson and Temple invited a group of women who were full-time and part-time university teachers and post-graduate students to lunchtime meetings. Three years later, those of us who remained, self-selected from the original group, asked each other why we had come and why we had stayed to carry out the research, particularly when that work had to be fitted into the interstices of already crowded days and nights.

Our motives (reconstructed) ranged from the scientific pursuit of knowledge — 'No figures existed; we needed to know' — to the desire to validate quantitatively hitherto unsystematised observations and experiences of women's place in university life, their contributions, advantages and disadvantages, their underrepresentation on most committees, their difficulties with promotion. Winkler, who came from recent experiences of the politically energetic women's movement in the United States, believed that we needed information not only for the confirmation of previous observations, but also as a basis for social action.

Our initial research strategy was immediately fruitful; group discussions generated a file of written autobiographies, life histories of childhood/schooling/university/workforce experiences — comprehensive material generously provided. If we had stopped there, we would have been using the techniques of a fifty-year-old tradition of social science research,[8] more recently resurrected by feminist researchers eschewing quantitative empirical methods for the rich immediacy of the personal document.[9]

However, we followed the tenets of a more 'scientifically' acceptable empiricism that suspects the validity of generalisations founded on personal document material, because of the unrepresentativeness or small size of the sample from which it is drawn.[10] We used the insights gained from the life histories to construct a pilot and a final questionnaire; so that we could broaden the research field, gain representative material from women in the sciences, the humanities, the social sciences, law, medicine, architecture, social work, and from women in all positions in the university teaching workforce. We decided to use the mass survey, plus interviews, plus background statistics, in order to compile a research report that could not be criticised for its unrepresentativeness, nor found to be lacking in rigour.

In using a survey, we enlisted the interest and enthusiasm of a large number of women (430, who needed enthusiasm in order to complete 40 pages of questionnaire), and the hostility of others. We followed the tradition, established in the nineteenth century by researchers and publicists like Mayhew and Booth,[11] of using the social survey as a fact-finding expedition, a preliminary to social action, and as itself a form of social action. Recent feminist research has continued the tradition.[12] Parts of the questionnaire have since been taken up and used again by the group studying the status of women in the Australian National University,[13] and by a joint staff associations' committee investigating discrimination by sex.

The questionnaire is not merely a cut-and-dried set of questions of the fixed-choice type. We left ample space for open-ended questions which ask 'why?' or 'please comment', or 'how did this affect you?'. This allowed our 430 respondents to express themselves freely, often with enthusiasm, sometimes with passion. In effect, the questionnaire duplicated the life-history technique, but in a more structured way. The open-ended questions have provided us with a wealth of material about our respondents' feelings, beliefs and experiences, a personal construction of their past and present reality. These responses cannot be coded and quantified (they defy such manipulation); they survive in their immediacy as testimonies of women's experience.

What about the non-response rate, the 32% who got away? That worried us, even though we read the books and found that all mailed questionnaires are fraught with the problem of non-response.[14] We found a close match between our respondents and the general population of women university teachers, in terms of their positions, their departments and their universities — who, then, are the women who did not reply?

We have made various guesses about the reasons for non-response: lack of time, lack of interest, initial interest turned sour by the length of the questionnaire, protection against invasion of privacy, and doubts about the maintenance of respondents' anonymity. Even though we sent a covering letter ensuring anonymity, it is understandable that some women (and men) would wish to protect their privacy in a matter as close to the bone as their occupation. But the most interesting supposition for our purposes is lack of sympathy with the project itself. Perhaps women who are unsympathetic to a study of the status of women in their own occupation have had different patterns of life experience from women who are sympathetic. Such problems associated with non-response are built into the nature of survey research, and are intensified when the research has a strong hint of the controversial or the polemical.

One woman, who later volunteered to be interviewed, told us that she had not filled out the questionnaire, but she was willing to provide countervailing evidence, the other side of the picture. She was unsympathetic to the project because she sees women university teachers as a privileged group, while there are women in much less privileged circumstances who could become the focus of our research energies. She went on to reply at length to interview questions, generously sharing her own life history.

(The question of why we studied a supposedly 'privileged' group is one that we explore in our research report. We ask: in what ways are tertiary-educated women, employed in a profession, privileged? This question must be asked in relation to inequality of educational opportunities, determined by class and sex, in Australia.[15] In what ways are women in the academic occupation disadvantaged? Clearly, the question is a matter of reference group: Privileged in relation to whom? Disadvantaged in relation to whom?[16]).

We gave our respondents the opportunity at the end of the questionnaire to comment on the questionnaire itself. Unlike mice, people can answer back. From a sample of their comments, we can gain some impression of the variety of responses that the questionnaire elicited.

From our female respondents we received comments which ranged from

> Thank you for the opportunity — an excellent questionnaire

to

> As far as questionnaires go, it is O.K., but like all questionnaires doesn't allow for enough subtlety and gradation of answers. Nor does it allow for the different answers that applied at different times to a question being asked in general about a long time span.

and

> Questionnaires of this nature, and the whole women's movement, however well intentioned, are pointless and harmful, creating dissidence and dissatisfaction by constructing and postulating enmity where there is none. Almost every question here shows its compilers to be suffering seriously from a desperate lack of confidence in themselves as people.

From our male respondents we received comments such as:

> No trouble; most interesting questionnaire. One cannot help noting the absence of males from your panel of five. Were there no volunteers?

> I assume your interest in all this is political as well as academic. I hope so. Give the results a lot of publicity. So much needs to be done.

> I find the questionnaire somewhat distasteful because of its feminist bias.

> Generally, I think questionnaires are atrocious and this one is pretty good. I do feel it is a crusade, however, I guess it's like Black Racism — understandable.

When we were reading, coding and making tentative interpretations of the women's questionnaires, it became apparent that we needed a control group of men in university teaching, in order to compare the backgrounds, attitudes, rates of promotion, and domestic responsibilities of the two groups. We produced a shorter version of the questionnaire for men, because we knew which questions had not been useful. As a result, the two research tools were not identical; the questionnaire for men came into the field several months after the first, which went only to women. Male university staff were probably aware of the first survey, and therefore aware that they constituted a control group, not the primary research interest. We drew a random sample of men, which contained a higher proportion of men in the upper ranks of the university hierarchy, and a higher proportion in science, engineering and the professional faculties, than pertained for the female group of respondents. The male sample's proportions are a close fit with the distribution of men on the academic ladder (skewed towards the top); and the female sample's proportions are a close fit with the distribution of women (skewed towards the ranks of tutor, senior tutor and lecturer). This must lead to caution in making comparisons between the two groups taken as a whole, but there are statistical and computer techniques which enable us to make comparisons between subgroups of men and women.

In retrospect, we would have created fewer problems of comparability if we had sent the same questionnaire to men and women at the outset. In the beginning, our primary project was to investigate the experience of women entering and remaining in the university workforce. The need to compare rates of progression, contributions and attitudes of men and women only became clear when we had already accumulated data and read research reports from England, the United States and New Zealand which were published after we had begun, or were well under way.[17] Again, there is a major comparison between men's and women's income which we were unable to make because we did not ask the women about their income. Because our project began as a study of *women* in an occupation, not as a comparative study, we designed our research instrument for this purpose.

In the course of the study, however, the emphasis shifted slightly, as often happens in research work. Research on women is particularly prone to this sort of ambivalence: researchers focus on women as their object of study, but then are usually made aware by their findings, by their colleagues and by their reading that statements about women require comparable statements about men, if conclusions are to be drawn about unequal or discriminatory treatment. There is irony here: before feminist social scientists began to analyse critically the research and theory of their male colleagues, it was usually taken for granted that a study of occupations, professions or, more generally, 'work' would not consider the presence of women, and would certainly not enquire into the comparability of male and female status in the workplace.[18] Feminist researchers constructing a new paradigm have two options: they can concentrate on the position of women — bringing the previously invisible sharply into focus — or they can compare the positions of men and women on a number of points: such as occupational security, income, rates of promotion, responsibility for child care. We attempted both — with major emphasis on the former.

We also conducted twenty-five in-depth interviews with women who had been asked to participate, or who had indicated their willingness. These long, frank and generous interviews ranged over: life histories; experiences of educational struggle or opportunity; opportunities blocked by stereotyped views of women's field of learning; encouragement by mothers, fathers and teachers; current attitudes to teaching and research, to university politics, to relations with colleagues; perceptions of discrimination; perceptions of equal or favourable treatment; and attitudes to the women's movement. These oral histories show us some of the ways in which a particular group of women broke out of the boundaries that narrowly circumscribe women's place in Australian society. Like the material derived from the written life histories and the open-ended questions, we cannot make statistical generalisations from these data, but such testimonies of lived experience possess a human validity which transcends the narrow limits of 'scientific' validity.[19]

The questionnaires, however, *were* quantifiable, they required coding, counting, correlation techniques — in short, transformation into a form acceptable to the computer. In order to do this, we required some mastery of computer technology — some of us had to acquire the skills to crack the code and understand the rituals of the technology of quantification. Like most people using computers to count and correlate their data, we experienced delays and frustrations. Some of us began to suspect that we might have gained equally significant research outcomes if we had done 200 in-depth interviews and searched for similar patterns of experience without the aid of the computer abacus. However, we would then have missed out on the experience of demystifying computer technology by the simple procedures of reading the manual, asking questions of the computer terminal staff, making mistakes, asking questions of colleagues with more computing experience, being persistent, becoming confident.

The questionnaire survey, and the use of a computer to count and correlate replies, are far from being essential skills in the researcher's kit-bag. However, when the decision is made, for whatever reasons, to use the questionnaire technique and the sample is large, it becomes virtually impossible to analyse, compare and make patterns from people's replies without the use of technological aids. As a group, we had varying levels of computing skills, but enough understanding of the sexual differentiation of knowledge to make a determined bid to master the technology. In a number of industrial societies, including Australia, women are much less likely than men to specialise in mathematics and the physical sciences in their senior secondary and tertiary education.[20] A minority of determined women do enter and remain in physical science-based fields of study and occupation,[21] but because they are few, certain areas of science and technology have developed a 'masculine' countenance. The product of our interaction with the computer was not only a room-full of print-out requiring interpretation, but also the discovery that computer technology is not impenetrable and is, on the contrary, quite accessible, with practice.

Why Have We Taken So Long to Complete the Project?
Firstly, we undertook a very large project with small funding. A very welcome Australian Research Grants Committee grant covered the salary of a research assistant for one year, and small grants from Sydney University and the University of New South Wales helped with typing, card-punching and computer-time; but we spent a considerable amount of time wondering how and where to find the next dollar, and how to stretch the dollars that we had. This put constraints on our ability to hire the part-time labour and the expert consultants who might have completed some of the tasks much more quickly.

Secondly, we were all involved in other areas of paid work, research and family commitments. This means that a very comprehensive and underfunded research project was being carried out by people committed to it, but with different degrees of commitment at different times, depending on other work loads.

Thirdly, our involvement in research on women generated new interests, new ideas, new contacts and new projects. Some of us began new courses or new research studies on women's issues before the project was complete. There was an impetus set in motion by the original research project, which gave birth to new projects and so deprived the parent of some of the time and energy that it still needed. However, these additional activities are themselves significant for a feminist understanding of research as a political activity. Some of us participated in a national conference (Australian Frontier Consultation, Sydney, November 1975) on women in the workforce, adding some experiences of women in the university workforce to the experiences of women in the public service, in business and in the professions, as particular instances of the general position of women in the labour market. Some of us discussed our research findings at a University Staff Association seminar on women in the workforce and the trade union movement. One of us helped to produce the first Australian national feminist newspaper, *Mabel*. Two of us helped to produce several editions of the women's studies journal, *Refractory Girl*. Time became a scarcer and scarcer resource.

The completion of our report, which is happening as we write this chapter, gained impetus not only from our own urgent desire to 'put it all together', but also from expressions of interest from colleagues, particularly those who participated in the study as respondents, and who are eager to read our research findings.

What Outcomes Might the Research Have?
By way of conclusion, we reproduce a discussion that we taped when we met to organise the writing of this chapter. This discussion brings forward some of the questions well worth asking about the reasons for doing research about women. Although we don't make the links systematically, it is clear that we believe that a theory of women's place in economy and society, and a study to test that theory, and ideas about appropriate strategies for change are all interrelated elements in the research enterprise. Our individual views on these issues are far from identical; in fact, we are remarkably pluralistic.

Cass:
    Why did we study a so-called privileged group of women?
Dawson:
    Yesterday, I heard Gintis give a lecture, pointing out that capitalist society is structured so that men have preference over women, whites have preference over blacks in the labour market. This is built into the structure of the workforce be-

cause it has its source in beliefs and prejudices which are dominant in the society generally. Our group of women are very much like most employed women because the hierarchy in which they work functions for them like the work hierarchies in which most women are involved.

Wills:

Given the opportunity to do a similar piece of research with other groups of women, would you investigate the position of women in universities again? Given the same resources and equal access, do you think anything would bother you about researching a 'privileged' group rather than a less privileged group? Is this an issue because people feel that perhaps some good might come out of the research for the women who were studied? There are dilemmas in looking at a group of women as sociological objects. What happens to the group after you've researched it? The consequences may *not* be beneficial, they may be unpleasant, which is an issue which worried Eva and Jeanie about their research on migrant women.[22] Academic women may be more immune to ill effects. But once you've done the study, and have pushed for improvements in women's position in universities, it seems to be giving support to the whole hierarchical system, as it now stands, by trying to push women up into it. That's another dilemma.

Temple:

I was about to agree with you that academic women may be more immune to ill effects from research; but we forget about the positive effects. We heard about a colleague in Canberra who said that the Australian National University survey made her do some research quickly, because she did not want to add fuel to any misconception that women don't do research. And I know of a close friend who applied for promotion after she became aware that some women do not have the confidence to apply for promotion. Awareness of the processes which are operating to keep women in lower ranks made her determined to counteract those processes.

Radi:

We encouraged each other to do things. This has been one

of the reasons for the delay in writing up our research — I started a new course on women in history, and another research project which has women in it.

Cass:
What about the other level of research experience that Heather is talking about — the relationship between the research enterprise and the effect it had on us, on our own understanding of the social situation. I once gave a talk on our study and I started off by saying: 'Why carry out a study of women who work in universities; how do we justify our interest in the educated and the articulate?' And I went on to discover, in the course of reading the British, American, Canadian, New Zealand, East and West German material, and the Australian statistics, that women's position in the university workforce is a microcosm of the position of women in most other occupations. I hadn't realised this at all before. I started reading about women in the labour market in general, after I'd met Margaret Power, and went on to read her research.[23] The connections between the positions of women in different occupations, which became clear when I compared her work with ours, were a revelation to me. The ideas which I had explored previously about university teaching as an avenue for social mobility became insignificant in the light of this new perspective.

But if we *had* found that university women were privileged, or some of them at any rate — why is that an argument against research? Should we only do research on the 'underprivileged'?

Dawson:
The university teaching occupation is a sort of test of the limits really. How far can a woman go — she can't go very far.

Wills:
We are apologising for doing research on women in universities because we think we are going to *do* something for them by studying them — that they are going to *get* something. We are just producing information. Presuming that someone will take action to better their position relative to men is

a load of codswallop.

Dawson:
In our application for a research grant we said that we hoped to influence policies.

Wills:
You can hope to all you like. You can't assume that you will.

Winkler:
Our research is a good example of the lack of gap between researcher and the experience of the researched. We didn't use our subjects in an odious sense. I think you can only have good social research when your experience isn't alien to the group you are studying.

Dawson:
But some people said that we were looking for discrimination against women, and so imposed categories on them which didn't fit. I don't accept that.

Radi:
We fell over backwards not to appear to be looking for discrimination, didn't we?

Dawson:
But there were several obvious questions. Like the one about 'feeling that you did not belong to the club' and the one about assessing your chances of promotion.

Wills:
You wouldn't expect a survey not to have those questions.

Dawson:
You would have, ten to fifteen years ago. A survey about women didn't ask about discrimination. Do you think that our objective was to help women join the male hierarchical system? Are you suggesting that such motives impelled us?

Wills:
No — I'm saying that if you assume the result of your survey will be used to improve existing conditions, you are giving tacit approval to the existing structure. Do you want to do that?

Dawson:
That's the fundamental question: will the position of women

be changed only by the transformation of the total system, or do women have to be assimilated into the system in order to be able to change things?
I like Alice Rossi's three models of sexual equality:
In the first model: men and women, like blacks and whites, are considered to be theoretically equal but different, and these differences are ineradicable. In this pluralist model, men and women are not equal at all, but their separate spheres of life, and women's dependence are justified by pointing to the physiological differences between the sexes.
In the second model: society rejects the idea that a boundary exists between men's and women's potential. Women accept the existing structures and move into positions in the economy and in politics, theoretically to reach 50% representation. But they do not mount a critique of these structures which men, as the dominant group, have formed. Rossi calls this the 'assimilationist' model.[24]
I see this as the stage before true sexual equality can be achieved. How can women achieve a new society without experience of the male economic and political order?
Cass:
You are saying that when women move into power structures; that move is, in itself, an enormous change — likely to promote other changes. But Sue is saying that some women may simply be co-opted, taken up into the hierarchy which they accept and reinforce.

We don't pretend to have resolved these questions. We note only that all research is located in political/ethical issues, although often these issues are hidden by the guise of value-freedom.[25]

What Did We Learn?
1. Commitment to a particular way of seeing and interpreting the social world is an inevitable position from which researchers start.
2. We were immersed in our research field — and this was fruitful.

3. It is hard to do quantitative research without adequate funding.
4. And — of greatest significance — research starts with *theory*. None of us went into the field merely to gather facts. We all held fairly coherent theories about women's place in society before we began, and we checked out these theories against our own and other women's experience. It would also be true to say that these theories were *grounded* in our own experience.

The research techniques we used, the questions we asked and the issues that we thought it necessary to explore were constructed out of these theories, and out of these collective experiences. Our research started with theory and ended with it: the conversation cited is an example of our ongoing attempts to locate our study within a coherent theory of the position of women in the workforce of an advanced industrial society. Over three years, the books we read, the conversations we had about our data, about what was happening in the survey and what to do next, were all basically concerned with creating a systematic interpretation of the diversity of human experiences that we had tapped.

We found, very early, that we had data specific to three universities in Sydney and the Institute of Technology — but the situation is remarkably similar in Melbourne, New Zealand, United States, Britain, East and West Germany.[26] We were actually investigating a phenomenon grounded in the workforce conditions and sex-role structures of advanced industrial societies — in which men and women occupy particular positions in the division of labour and of authority in the university, as in other labour markets. Why? How is this maintained? How might it be changed? These are the central issues of our research.

NOTES AND REFERENCES

1. Fuchs Epstein, C. 'Encountering the male establishment: sex status limits on women's careers in the professions', in A. Theodore, *The Professional Woman*, Shenkman, 1971, pp.52-73; Astin, H. & Bayer, A. 'Sex discrimination in

Academe', in A. Rossi & A. Calderwood (eds), *Academic Women on the Move*, Russell Sage Foundation, 1973, pp.333-356; Blackstone, T. & Fulton, O. 'Sex discrimination among university teachers: A British American comparison', *British Journal of Sociology* 26, 3 (1975), pp.261-275; Cass, B. 'Women in Academic Institutions', in Australian Frontier Consultation, *Adapting to meet the changing role of women in society*, Sydney, November 1975, pp.22-31; Wills, S. 'Women at University. 2. Some Preliminary considerations', in *Refractory Girl* 10 (1976), pp.13-19.
2. For a useful and critical discussion of this issue, see Gouldner, A. W. 'The Sociologist as Partisan', in *For Sociology. Renewal and Critique in Sociology Today*, Penguin, 1973, pp.27-68.
3. See ref. 1. For the position of women in the Australian labour market generally, see Power, M. 'Woman's Work is never done — by men: a socio-economic model of sex-typing in occupations', *Journal of Industrial Relations* 17, 3 (1975), pp.225-239. Also see Riach, P. 'Women and the Australian Labour Market: Problems and policies', in J. Mercer (ed.), *The Other Half. Women in Australian Society*, Penguin, 1975, pp.63-93.
4. Denzin, N. K. *The Research Act in Sociology*, Butterworth, 1970, p.308. This discusses the value of multiple research methods.
5. Mills, C. W. *The Sociological Imagination*, Penguin, 1971, pp.11-14.
6. Fuchs Epstein, 'Encountering the male establishment'.
7. For articles on 'Women and the Workplace, see *Signs, Journal of Women in Culture and Society* 1, 3, 2 (1976). Also see Roper, T. 'Inequalities in the Australian Education System: Women in the Professions', in Mercer, *The Other Half*, pp.139-154.
8. See Madge, J. *The Tools of Social Science*, Longmans, 1967. Discussion of the 'Personal Document', Ch.2, pp.81-91.
9. For Australian examples of writing using personal histories, see Brophy, V. 'An Australian Housewife: A Disillusioning Experience', in Mercer, *The Other Half*, pp.323-332. Also see Wesson, G. *Brian's Wife, Jenny's Man*, Dove, 1975.

10. Madge, *The Tools of Social Science,* p.90.
11. Thompson, E. P. & Yeo, E. *The Unknown Mayhew. Selections From the Morning Chronicle: 1849–1850,* Penguin, 1973. Also see Booth, C. *Labour & Life of the People of London,* MacMillan, 1889–1902.
12. For a representative Australian example, see Cox, E., Jobson D. & Martin, J. *We Cannot Talk our Rights. Migrant Woman, 1975,* NSW Council of Social Services, and School of Sociology, University of NSW, 1976. The report of a survey organised and devised by women in the women's movement, carried out by migrant women, to gain knowledge of the situation of migrant women in Sydney.
13. Bramley, G. M. & Ward, M. W. *The Role of Women in the Australian National University,* Australian National University, 1976.
14. Moser, C. A. *Survey Methods in Social Investigation,* Heinemann, 1967, pp.127–144.
15. *Girls, School and Society,* Report by a study group to the Schools Commission, Schools Commission, 1975.
16. See Long Laws J., 'A Feminist Analysis of Relative Deprivation in Academic Women', *The Review of Radical Political Economics* IV, 3 (1972); and Wills, S., 'Women at University'.
17. Astin & Bayer, 'Sex discrimination in Academe'; Blackstone & Fulton, 'Sex discrimination among university teachers'; Lodge, J. 'New Zealand Women Academics: Some Observations on Their Status, Aspirations and Professional Achievement', *Political Science* 28, 1 (1976), pp.23–40.
18. For discussions of women's invisibility in social science research, see Oakley, A. *The Sociology of Housework,* Martin Robertson, 1974; and Daniels, A. K. 'Feminist Perspectives in Sociological Research', in M. Millman & R. Kanter, *Another Voice,* Anchor, 1975, pp.340–380.
19. For a similar approach to the study of work, see Terkel, S. *Working,* Avon, 1974.
20. *Girls, School and Society,* pp.79–91.
21. Encel, S., MacKenzie, N. & Tebbutt, M. *Women and Society. An Australian Study,* Cheshire, 1974, pp.130–131.

22. Cox, E. and Martin, J. 'Factory Fodder or Breeding Cows'. Paper presented to 47th ANZAAS Conference, Hobart, 1976.
23. Power, 'Woman's Work is never done'; and Power, M. 'Adapting to Meet the Changing Role of Women in Society', in Australian Frontier Consultation, Sydney, November 1975, pp.7–21.
24. Rossi, 'Sex Equality: The Beginnings of Ideology', in C. Safilios-Rothschild, *Towards a Sociology of Women*, Xerox, 1972, pp.344–353.
25. Gouldner, A. 'Anti-Minotaur: The Myth of a Value-Free Sociology', in Gouldner, *For Sociology*, see ref. 2.
26. See ref. 1. Also see Lodge, 'New Zealand Women Academics', for New Zealand data; and University of Melbourne University Assembly, *Women's Working Group Report*, July 1975. For East and West Germany data, see Sommerkorn, I. *et al. Women's Careers*, P.E.P., 1970.

APPENDIX
Women as a Proportion of All Full-time Teaching Staff in Australian Universities: 1971–75*

Rank	1971	1972	1973	1974	1975
Professors	1.8%	1.6%	1.5%	1.3%	1.2%
Associate Professors, Readers	2.6%	2.7%	2.9%	3.6%	4.0%
Senior Lecturers	6.6%	5.5%	6.9%	6.9%	7.0%
Lectures and Teaching Registrars	15.0%	13.0%	14.0%	14.6%	14.9%
Senior Tutors/Demonstrators/Assistant Lecturers	33.8%	31.3%	37.7%	36.2%	36.1%
Demonstrators, Tutors, Teaching Fellows	32.5%	36.1%	34.3%	35.7%	34.8%
All Staff	13.8%	14.0%	14.8%	15.1%	15.1%

*Adapted from *University Statistics 1975, Part 2, Staff and Libraries,* Australian Bureau of Statistics, p.13.

Notes:
1. There has been almost no change in the representation of women in the total university workforce, or in the various ranks, over the five-year period.
2. Women are more than doubly overrepresented in the ranks below lecturer: in 1975, 15.1% of the total staff yielded 35% (approx) of sublecturer staff.
3. Women are highly underrepresented in all ranks above lecturer: in 1975, 15.1% of the total staff yielded 1.2% of professors and 4% of associate professors.

NATIONALISM, RACE-CLASS CONSCIOUSNESS AND SOCIAL RESEARCH ON BOUGAINVILLE ISLAND, PAPUA NEW GUINEA*

Alexander F. Mamak

Introduction

In recent years, research in the South Pacific region has tended to focus more and more on social change as a consequence of capital-intensive development. South Pacific nations have very limited resources to allocate to this type of research and much of it is being funded by multinational companies engaged in extensive mineral extraction in the region. Can multinational company-financed research be directed towards serving the felt needs of the research population? Is it possible for company-sponsored researchers to develop meaningful research techniques and a sense of responsibility to people subjected to a type of development that involves large-scale foreign investment?

The writer, an anthropologist, has recently completed a detailed assessment of social change on Bougainville Island, Papua New Guinea, with research funds provided by the copper mining company through the University of Hawaii. The purpose of this essay is to provide a highly personal

---

*I am grateful to Dr Richard Bedford for his friendship and co-participation in the Bougainville research project, on which this chapter is based; to Professor Orlando Fals Borda and the organising committee of the Cartagena Symposium on Action Research and Scientific Analysis for inviting me to present an earlier version of this paper; and to Professor Douglas Oliver for supporting me in many ways during my period of fieldwork.

account of the conceptual, practical and moral issues surrounding the research project. It explores several facets of my role as a researcher among a disadvantaged population, and discusses the problems and frustrations I encountered while in the field. It is not my intention to make this essay a justification of my involvement in the project. This would be too easy, even for less conventional and more dubious types of research.[1] Nor is it my intention to respond directly to intellectual critics of company-sponsored research.[2] Rather, I hope to utilise this essay to describe some social relations and events, to raise suggestions and criticisms, and to encourage sensitivity to some problems I encountered in doing research on Bougainville.

The Research Project
Bougainville (recently renamed the North Solomons) is one of twenty provinces in Papua New Guinea. It includes the islands of Bougainville and Buka, and a number of smaller coral island groups. In June 1971, the total population of the province was estimated at 90 000, with an indigenous component of 84 000 or 3.5% of the total indigenous population of Papua New Guinea. There are nineteen distinct language groups on Bougainville. The *lingua franca* for all of these groups is Melanesian Pidgin.

Europeans comprise the bulk of Bougainville's non-indigenous population. European influence in this area increased from around the middle of the nineteenth century when many Bougainvilleans were recruited as labourers for plantations in Queensland and other parts of the Pacific. Following a brief period of German control, the islands became a part of the Australian Mandated Territory of New Guinea in 1921. Except for the period of Japanese occupation during the Second World War, Australian administration continued uninterrupted until late 1974 when Papua New Guinea was granted self-government, and independence a year later.

Economic development in Bougainville over the twenty year period following the Second World War was reflected in gradual increases in plantation primary produce and some minor commercial growth in urban areas. Other economic and political changes were also slow to develop and in sharp contrast to abrupt changes initiated in the late 1960s.

In 1964 Bougainville was found to be rich in mineral concentrates; copper, gold and silver. The subsequent exploitation of the ore body, located 26 kilometres inland from the south-east coast of Bougainville Island, stimulated rapid changes in the social, economic and political life of the people. Astounding rates of change are clearly visible in the area of mining operations. For example, the number of persons licensed to drive a motor car increased from 45 in 1966 to 3 953 in 1970; cargo tonnages at the local port increased from 35 000 in 1968 to 460 000 in 1971; and the urban population increased from around 750 in 1966 to over 14 000 in 1971 – the peak of the construction phase. Most of the new inhabitants were 'outsiders', both European and Papua New Guinean, drawn to the mining complex and housed in two new towns and surrounding areas on a temporary basis.

The copper mining company, after consultation with several foreign academics, was interested in monitoring these changes. A major interdisciplinary research programme was initiated under sponsorship of the University of Hawaii's Research Corporation; and as part of this programme, my colleague (a social geographer) and I commenced research in the growing urban complex on the east coast of Bougainville in early 1973.

Perhaps the two most important factors facilitating my activist concerns at a later stage of research were: firstly, the assurance given by the chief organiser of the research programme that all reports were to be published and distributed publicly; and secondly, the very broad terms of reference for the urbanisation study. For example, when I asked the chief organiser what specific objectives he had in mind for the project, he replied 'Do what you want'.

A number of basic objectives were drawn up by my colleague and I after several weeks in the field. These were, in the following order of priority:

1. To establish characteristics of a range of social, economic and demographic changes, and problems which owe their origins to copper mining.
2. To assess the nature of indigenous participation in and reactions to the emerging urban society.
3. To suggest ways by which urban development in this area can be directed to benefit all sectors of the population.

These objectives are not unique in urban research. However, when combined with developing solidarity and nationalistic tendencies of the research population, they take on more practical significance as their utility for immediate political purposes becomes increasingly evident.

Nationalism and Social Research

The new-found social and political salience of Bougainvillean identity was expressed on the scene very shortly after our arrival. In order to defend their common interests and to exert greater control over their affairs, Bougainvilleans began to direct a great deal of activity towards encouraging Bougainvillean solidarity. Not surprisingly, the central government, which has a substantial stake in the exploitation of Bougainville's mineral deposits, began to attach considerable importance not only to the economics of the project but also to the political orientation of the Province. We gradually began to realise that these activities were influencing the nature and direction of social change, and promised to be of considerable significance to an understanding of Bougainvillean participation in the emerging urban economy and society. We therefore decided to record the major political developments and changes taking place to provide a wider frame of reference for our major study. This brings me to say something about the way in which these issues were approached and defined.

Let me turn briefly to the attitudes, values and beliefs I brought with me to the field. I am now certain that my views on social processes in Bougainville were conditioned just as much, if not more, by my colonial past as my previous fieldwork experiences and the academic training I received in several American universities. My perception of society and of the world in general is influenced in part by the twenty years I spent growing up in the British Crown Colony of Hong Kong, and being socialised by a Eurasian mother and a father of East Indian descent.

Sharing the same skin colour, environment, colonial status and experiences of many low and middle-income non-Westerners living under colonial rule helped me to establish symbolic identification with many of the people in the communities I was to study later. But all the frustrations, sense of alienation, oppression and discrimination I experienced as a non-white member of a racist society were largely taken for granted at the time, and did not begin to have an impact on my role as a researcher until I undertook a study of a colonial city for a thesis in anthropology. In Fiji, where I conducted most of my previous investigations on urbanisation, I found that my academic training in the methodological views of Western social science and its emphasis on 'scientific objectivity' conflicted with the experiences of my colonial past. The traditional way in which social science research is conducted proved inadequate for an understanding of the reality, needs and desires of the people I was researching. It was during this period that I began to learn about the all-encompassing nature of scientific enquiry to include the possibility of making social research more relevant to the needs of the researched, and to concentrate on the causes of oppression and exploitation as opposed to a study of the oppressed.

In retrospect, coming from a non-Western culture and having grown up under a colonial umbrella facilitated my entrée into Bougainvillean society. Despite the fact that most Bougainvillean leaders and informants were aware that our research was being financed by the company, I was permitted to attend a large number of important political meetings, the purpose of which was to discuss plans for making Bougainville a paradigm case for the development of an autonomous political entity within Papua New Guinea. In the end, Bougainvilleans succeeded in this objective; a record of these events and frustrations, and an identification of the source of these frustrations, were described in our book *Bougainvillean Nationalism: Aspects of Unity and Discord.*[3]

Although we did not take an active part in politics, our work gave further publicity to Bougainvillean objectives. The purposes in writing the book, in collaboration with several Bougainvillean leaders, were twofold. Firstly, to document a crucial period in the Island's political history; and secondly, to emphasise the ability of Bougainvilleans to organise themselves and to act as a dynamic and viable force against all forms of oppression. All copies were sold in Bougainville within a few months, and the proceeds were returned to the people on the Island.

By the summer of 1973, I not only did standard data-collecting work, but also chauffeured people to meetings, drafted and typed reports and minutes for leaders, met informally with them to discuss possible strategies for achieving desired objectives, and encouraged them to make decisions. These activities proved valuable to the research and I hope to the political cause of the Bougainville people.

In retrospect, the political events of 1973-74 modified our theoretical approach to the subject of development. Initially we had set out to describe the disruptive effects of rapid urban-industrial development, but later decided instead to emphasise the role of self-determination in social change, and to examine in a political context the organised responses, adjustments and adaptiveness of an essentially nonindustrial people to new situations of change. Like Franz Fanon, we became convinced that 'The people who take their destiny into their own hands assimilate the most modern forms of technology at an extraordinary rate'.[4] This should not be taken to mean technical change can provide an alternative to institutional reform and political change. Social scientists interested in the study of change are becoming more and more conscious of the need to explain and perhaps to try and alter the nature of exploitative systems, as opposed to a theoretical preoccupation with systems maintenance. Two anthropologists whom I met recently looked at each other with unconcealed horror when I mentioned the adaptability of the Bougainvillean research population to change introduced by the copper mining complex. I went on to say I was using the term 'adaptability' in the context of nationalism and organised as opposed to disorganised responses to change. I suggested that much of the recent literature on the impact of capitalist development on traditional societies has tended to emphasise this type of development as an all-pervasive force which compels the affected population to yield to its pressures.[5]

The research perspective that derives from the above assumption, and which we carried with us to the field, is addressed by O.H.K. Spate, a former Director of the Research School of Pacific Studies at the Australian National University, Canberra. In an article confirming the School's acceptance of funds from the copper mining company to carry out research on Bougainville, Spate noted 'the effects [of mining operations] on Bougainville society will be so dramatic, even traumatic, that intensive study of the resulting social and economic problems is absolutely essential'.[6]

The trouble with a strictly problems approach, we found out soon enough, was that it restricted our role as researchers to one of note-takers and recorders of social problems that were said to exist on Bougainville. (Note that in the absence of mining operations, many of these problems would not have existed in the first place.) It also encouraged us to direct our attention to manifestations of the problems, and to intellectualise rather than to confront them. Hence, our attention was initially diverted away from the fundamental source of these problems. Furthermore, this approach conflicted with the objective knowledge of Bougainville society we were slowly gaining in the field. Unlike many other nonindustrial peoples who tend to be disorganised and therefore powerless, Bougainvilleans gradually developed into an organised force to overcome some of the unhealthy conditions associated with capital-intensive development, and catch up with some of the privileges and advantages of industrialisation.

Gradually, as our initial perspective became modified, we began to see nationalism on Bougainville as the result of efforts by an underprivileged group to improve its lot through collective mobilisation. As previously mentioned, the process of collective mobilisation was in its embryonic stage at the time of our study and our major concern then was to develop an objective definition of the movement, and to describe it as a quality that others should commend. The adaptability of the people was based on several facts, which stand out clearly from a consideration of their nationalism. The first was the resistance to control and domination. This led Bougainvilleans to reconsider their relationship with the central government and the copper mining company. The second was the determination to unite. And the third, and perhaps the most significant in terms of liberation from exploitative systems, was the desire of Bougainvilleans to exercise control over their futures, to make their own decisions and to gain the necessary power to effect them.

Our attempt to define objectively Bougainvillean nationalism may have been not only of practical value to Bougainvilleans, but also of theoretical significance. The study describes how capital-intensive development can stimulate rapid general social change, and suggests that the emergence of a new political power and social structure in the change process can lead to further alterations in the society and the creation of a new socio-economic system.[7] In terms of meaningful development, nationalism helped to overcome internal discord, stimulated Bougainvilleans to work towards commonly defined universal goals, and provided the foundation for a more broadly based type of nationalism and sense of unity with Papua New Guinea. The study also provides additional case material that serves to correct some prevalent notions about nationalism from the point of view of modernisation theory; namely, that traditional societies are generally resistant to change, that modernising elites are the main forces of change, and that the masses are not involved in nationalist movements.[8]

Race-Class Consciousness and Social Research

Data collected during the next stage of fieldwork came mainly from months of participant observation among urban residents and low-income industrial workers in the mine site. This period of fieldwork showed me once again the importance of actually living with people in order to understand them. I not only slept in worker's camps that summer; I ate and drank with the local workers, played volley ball, went to the picture show, helped them to organise into groups and associations, and attended all important meetings of the trade union and other voluntary organisations. These personal experiences, combined with instances of injustice on the mine site, brought home to me the difficulty of serving the interests of the sponsor while serving the interests of the research population whose expectations were often conflicting and diverse. It was also during this period that I developed from an unconscious agent of change to a conscious activist.

Lacking a concrete theoretical framework to work with encouraged me to emphasise the viewpoint of the insider, and gave me the flexibility to allow informants themselves to dictate the problems that should be researched. In the end, such an approach proved theoretically useful as it encouraged a more balanced investigation, and provided more complete understanding of the problems under investigation. By attempting to seek knowledge of the people's own views of the local situation, I was led into areas of investigation that have traditionally been of little concern to anthropologists. To describe the meaning of work for the research population led me to examine the effects of capital-intensive development and the implications of the resulting structure of inequality in the mine site. My informants concern with low pay and poor working conditions, and their attempts to organise collectively, led me to re-examine the usefulness of a Marxian perspective and the possibility of looking at the situation in both race and class terms.

By a Marxian perspective, I mean identification of the major source of conflict existing between privileged and underprivileged groups in their struggle for control of the means of production and/or power.[9] I began to see race as an expression of specific, mainly economic interests, and in relation to questions of material well-being, standard of living, income and occupation. My approach and argument runs as follows: The mining community is stratified by race and class. An approach that emphasises one type of differentiation will express only a partial truth. In the earlier period of industrial relations in Papua New Guinea, stratification by race and class tended to coincide, but the tendency for writers to focus on race to explain behaviour diverted attention from the underlying class structure. At the time of our study, social relations in the mine site were defined in both race and class terms. This is partly because local mine workers were experiencing upward occupational mobility, and a few were in almost an identical class position as whites. In the latter case, the boundaries existing between blacks and whites are obviously racial.

My attention began to focus on trade union activity, the exploitative and unequal relationship existing between management and an organised but weak labour force, and how workers can bargain more effectively.

The Role of Participant Observation

I have already mentioned the use of participant observation as a research method in our study. Gradually, I discovered that participant observation, the method of social enquiry most used by anthropologists, involves reciprocity and an ongoing dynamic relationship between the researcher and his or her informants. As workers increasingly shared their experiences with me, and as I became sensitised to some of their problems, I saw the need for direct research towards helping them to understand the implications of oppressive power relationships and how these can be changed. To some extent, then, my research presence acted as a catalyst, encouraging workers to act in opposition to the powerful.

Let me elaborate on this point by describing my views on the method of participant observation and how I attempted to refine it in the field. In my opinion, to be a participant observer means, in general, to take an active part in the way of life of the people you are studying while being sufficiently detached so as not to lose sight of your original scientific objectives. Junker has identified four possible social roles played by the researcher using the method of participant observation.[10] Two of these roles — complete participant and participant as observer — imply an element of subjectivity, sympathy and comparative involvement in the lives of the research population. By contrast, the two remaining roles — observer as participant and complete observer — imply objectivity and comparative detachment. The above roles match and enable the researcher to collect and analyse four categories of information — private, secret, confidential and public. While my choice of roles shifted from one to another during the course of fieldwork, depending on the individuals and groups I was working with, towards the end of my research I found myself cast more and more in the role of participant as observer; that is, my observer activities were at times subordinated to my activities as participant.

My choice of roles was largely determined by the fact that the people who co-operated in my research project saw me as a person of influence and knowledge, and expected me to assist them in overcoming some of the problems they were experiencing. How each researcher resolves the dilemma that arises when he or she is forced to choose between being a neutral observer and a friend is perhaps largely a personal matter. My position on this issue is summed up by the anthropologist Bernard Gallin in describing a similar predicament:

> I was in a situation of being given the opportunity to do something in return for those who were doing so much for me by their cooperation. To refuse to help would have seemed to me immoral.[11]

I have so far suggested that at times the method of participant observation involves a decision as to whose side the researcher is on. I shall now describe some problems involved in putting the role of participant as observer into action.

Up to this point, the sponsor did not try to influence our work despite the fact that *Bougainvillean Nationalism* and other reports published in the field contain passages highly critical of the mining company.[12] But as my research presence and activist concerns became more obvious, I was brought into open conflict with some representatives of company management. Two specific examples are described here and both concern the dissemination of research information to the public.

The first was concerned with my making available to the Papua New Guinea Minimum Wages Board a report (later published in the country's newspaper), which concluded with an argument for immediate and substantial increases in the rates of pay for local mine workers. The report emphasised another major facet of black-white socio-economic differences in the new towns of Bougainville, and was based on my survey analysis of urban family income and expenditure. It reinforced and documented the belief, already held by many local mine workers, that they were becoming less equal to the white population.

The second example was related to my making available to the local trade union (and the sponsor) some results from research, such as the steep increase in the urban cost of living, which assisted the union in its negotiations with management.

The trade union was struggling to develop at the time and I wanted to study its successes and failures, and the difficulties it faced in getting itself established. In March 1974, I sought and obtained permission from management to sit in on wage negotiations between the union and management for a new award, the first in two years. I did not want to prejudice the negotiations and decided intitially to play the role of complete observer.

As the struggle unfolded, however, and as I became increasingly aware of the unequal relationship existing between management and the union, I found myself becoming more and more emotionally involved in the proceedings. I do not believe this reaction is unusual since, in the words of the well-known black sociologist Nathan Hare, 'If one is truly cognizant of adverse circumstances, he would be expected, through the process of reason, to experience some emotional response'.[13]

After many weeks of silent observation I became convinced that intervention was necessary to help the union overcome its feeling of dependency, and to encourage them to express their frustration over the way the negotiations were proceeding. I have elsewhere described the callous and spiteful attitude of the management towards the union, and the range of tactics used by the company's representative during the negotiations, but it may help to summarise a few examples of these here. They included: threatening union officials with dismissal if they used a hard-line approach; conducting the meetings in a foreign language (English); forcing the union to reach a quick decision by threatening to withdraw all existing benefits; providing the union with a false sense of accomplishment by taking a hard-line approach on every item in the union's log of claims, then agreeing to some of the union's less important demands; and attempting to get the union to accept a complicated package scheme that would effectively lead to a decrease rather than an increase in pay.[14]

On the day when negotiations for a new wage structure began, I presented a great deal of research evidence which lent support to the union's case. The evidence was challenged by the company's representative and eventually contributed to a breakdown in communication between the union and management. While I continued to systematically record my observations, my activist concerns during this period won me acceptance as a participant in the union's affairs, provided me with a great deal of information that the union allowed me to obtain, and enhanced my understanding of the day-to-day activities of the union and its members. The rate of worker participation in the union increased rapidly as workers became more aware of the external sources of their dissatisfaction. In the end, support for the union developed to such a point that management was forced to concede to many of the union's demands.

I have described the incident in some detail to show what may be involved when a researcher approaches a social situation as observer-*cum*-participant. In the process, I saw the need to redefine my research role, and to be actively involved with workers in their struggle for better wages and working conditions. Studies of staff civil rights activity in the southern United States show how the participant-observer role may be interpreted to serve the felt needs of the research population. Three phases of action are recommended:
1. Engaging in direct confrontation with the dominant group in the presence of the powerless.
2. Actively supporting the powerless as they begin to confront the dominant group.
3. Retreating to the background and assuming the role of observer as the oppressed group confronts the dominant group directly.[15]

The words of psychologist Kenneth B. Clark,[16] as he describes himself as an 'involved observer' in his study of urban black Americans, also typify this approach:

> The role of the 'involved observer' ... demands participation not only in rituals and customs but in the social competition with the hierarchy in dealing with the problems of the people he is seeking to understand.[17]

As it became increasingly evident to management that I was allying myself with the workers in their struggle against inequality, the chief project organiser was notified, and steps were taken to redirect my research activities in the mine area. By now, convinced that activist concerns are a normal part of the research process and that I had fulfilled my obligations to the sponsor by telling the truth as I saw it and by advising them of the consequences of their decisions I was unable to continue my work under conditions that made me feel accountable to the company for my actions. I informed the chief organiser of this and offered to withdraw from the project. He was sympathetic and was able to convince company personnel that I was acting under terms of reference they had previously agreed to, and which guaranteed independent thought and action. Fortunately, these incidents occurred towards the end of my research and I was able to complete it successfully.

Summary and Conclusions
Anthropology has acquired a bad image in Third World countries and I do not want to give the impression that there was no opposition to anthropological research in Bougainville at the time of our investigations. But to the best of my knowledge, at no time during our two years in the field were we aware of any local opposition to our study. By contrast, several representatives of lower-management, who believed their positions in the company could be adversely affected by the study, were openly opposed to it. I do not doubt that our study can produce negative effects, such as the possible misuse of data on informants. However, anthropology is a two-edged sword and the publication of our study may be more harmful to the interests of the company; as company sponsorship provided us with many opportunities to gain insight into the workings of a large multinational company. One way of redressing any imbalance caused by research among a disadvantaged group is to make such knowledge available to the latter and to all interested persons.

This essay describes how the anthropological perspective in development research funded by multinational companies can be made relevant to the research population. In the present case, the problematical nature of multinational company-financed research was minimised in part by a flexible research design, a refinement of the method of participant-observation, and by undertaking research from the viewpoint of the peoples being studied.

To introduce more reality into our studies, we must not be afraid to tackle controversial problems. This entails a move from the study of what interests us professionally to a study of the experiences and interests of the research population. Empirical and theoretical relevance are synonymous and involve a shift from an almost exclusive emphasis on theory to a focus on theory developing out of solutions to practical problems. The theories we develop in sociology and anthropology must come to terms with the reality, needs and desires of the research population. Only in this way can more adequate theories of society in general, and social change in particular, be developed so as to provide a useful guide to action as well as further research.

The exchange between the researcher and informants should be characterised by recriprocity. In acting as a catalyst for beneficial change, the researcher's participation in the lives of his or her informants is legitimised. In the present case, the importance of nationalistic tendencies and developing solidarity among mine workers in Bougainville not only influenced our decision to record it but also emphasised the practical relevance of research results and facilitated rapport between researcher and informants.

In all types of research, the degree of honesty and freedom of the researcher are relative and depend to a large extent on the circumstances. While there is a certain amount of difficulty and tension inherent in a nontraditional research situation like the Bougainville research project, the outcome of such projects depends on a number of complex factors, including the researcher's own political beliefs and convictions, shaped by previous experiences and personal background, perhaps more than on the policies and beliefs of the company, or on 'invisible knots' that supposedly bind researchers to the sponsor.

NOTES AND REFERENCES

1. For example, at least five valid reasons for accepting a United States Army-sponsored study of insurgency and potential revolution in Latin America were shared by the social scientists

involved in the project. See Horowitz, I.L. *The Rise and Fall of Project Camelot*, MIT Press, 1967. In the Bougainville case, some interesting points were raised by Spate, O.H.K. 'A.N.U. on Bougainville', *A.N.U. News*, July 1972, pp.16-18. This article attempts to justify the Australian National University's acceptance of research funds from the copper mining company.
2. See, for example, *Arena* 31 (1973); 38 (1975); and 41 (1976).
3. Mamak, A. & Bedford, R. (with the assistance of Hannett, L. & Havini, M.) *Bougainvillean Nationalism: Aspects of Unity and Discord*, University of Canterbury, 1974.
4. Fanon, F. *A Dying Colonialism*, Grove Press, 1965, p.9.
5. Compare Bodley, J.H. *Victims of Progress*, Cummings, 1975.
6. Spate, 'A.N.U. on Bougainville', p.16.
7. The Bougainville provincial development plan of 1974-75 was designed to initiate a long-term programme of rural improvement and mobilisation, community education and involvement, integrated development projects and the use of intermediate technology.
8. Omvedt, G. 'Towards a Theory of Colonialism', *The Insurgent Sociologist*, 1972, pp.1-24.
9. Galeski, B. 'Conflict and Change as Aspects of Development', in D. C. Pitt (ed.), *Development from Below: Anthropologists and Development Situations*, Mouton, 1976, pp.158-61.
10. Junker, B. H. *Field Work: An Introduction to the Social Sciences*, University of Chicago Press, 1960, pp.35-36.
11. Gallin, B. 'A Case of Intervention in the Field', in T. Weaver (ed.), *To See Ourselves: Anthropologists and Modern Social Issues*, Scott, Foresman & Co., 1973, p.39.
12. A public affairs officer employed by the company at the time made several unsuccessful attempts to gain advanced information on political developments from us; but except for our published work, the sponsor received very little feedback on information concerning our research.
13. Hare, N. 'The Challenge of a Black Scholar', in J. A. Ladner (ed.), *The Death of White Sociology*, Vintage Books, 1973,

p.68.
14. See Mamak, A. & Bedford R. *Bougainville Copper and Trade Unionism,* in preparation.
15. Rothman, J. *Planning and Organizing for Social Change: Action Principles from Social Science Research,* Columbia, 1974, pp.39-40.
16. Clark, K. B. 'Introduction to an Epilogue', in Ladner, *The Death of White Sociology,* p.403.
17. Mills, C. W., in *The Sociological Imagination* (Evergreen, 1961, pp.185-86), has described a way in which social scientists can exercise their 'means of power': by addressing their work firstly, to the powerful to show the responsibility of their decisions or lack of it; secondly, to those who are unaware of the consequences of their actions; and thirdly, to the powerless to help them understand the implications of unequal power relationships and to inform them of the actions of the powerful.

THE BACKGROUND TO *BRADSTOW*

Reflections and Reactions

Ron Wild

Reflections

Community studies have been criticised as idiosyncratic, subjective, atheoretical and noncumulative. Ruth Glass once wrote that they were 'the poor sociologist's substitute for the novel'.[1] This is an exaggerated and unfair criticism, as many of these studies have contributed greatly to empirical knowledge and the development of theoretical models. At the same time, they are often vivid and fresh to read and provide a fascinating account of everyday social relationships. They enable us to see behind the facade of social life, and therefore to demystify the world in which we live.

Community sociologists have tried 'to capture some segment of an elusive reality which would be true to the world of the observed as seen by the particular perspective of the observer'.[2] Consequently, there is an intimate connection between the research workers, their methods of investigation, their results and their own intellectual development. The data gathered partly depend on the experiences, the abilities and the personality of the fieldworker. For this reason it is important to understand how such studies originated, what made their authors do them, how the projects were formulated and carried out, and what difficulties were encountered in collecting and analysing the data. Since William Foote Whyte wrote his impressive essay on the background to

Street Corner Society, other community sociologists and anthropologists have followed suit and attempted to place their work in its personal context.³ In this paper I shall discuss the background to my community study, *Bradstow,* and some of the reactions to the publication of the book.

Bradstow was not designed as a project in three weeks or even three months. It was rather the result of a slow ten to twelve years' growth of interest in different cultures, especially at a localised level, and in social inequality.

My interest in other cultures developed first. I was born and raised in a cotton and linoleum manufacturing town in north Lancashire, my grandfather and father worked in the local factory, and we lived in a small house built by a Victorian magnate for his workers. I attended a small Junior Technical School and developed special interests in geography and art. I remember one day talking to the mathematics teacher about a geography essay and he said he had a book at home that would interest me. The following day he presented to me as a gift Daryll Forde's *Habitat, Economy, and Society.* This was my first contact with anthropology and it generated a powerful interest in other cultures. On completing the General Certificate of Education at 'O' level, I was accepted into the Sixth Form of the Grammar School where I continued to study geography and art. During those three years, three events further consolidated my interest in localised populations of various cultures.

First, I spent three months with an Exploration Group studying glacial movements in the Jostedalsbre mountains of Norway. I spent as much time getting to know the Norwegian hill farmers as I did measuring the rate of ice flow. Second, I was awarded a scholarship provided by a shipping company which sponsored exchange tours between English and West African schoolboys. Third, on a geography excursion we visited a field centre in the Welsh borderlands. I was intrigued by the nature of Welsh village life.

In 1962 I won a Drapers' Company scholarship to study in any university of the Commonwealth. I arrived at Sydney university in February 1963, ready to study Geography and

Anthropology. I had, by this stage, a well-developed curiosity about different peoples but was not fully aware of the nature and importance of social inequality.

In the middle years of my undergraduate course in Anthropology, I was profoundly influenced by honours seminars on sociological theory which discussed the writings of Marx, Weber, Simmel, Durkheim and Pareto, and the contemporary interpretations of them from Parsons, Dahrendorf and Aron. As Dahrendorf has pointed out, it was questions about 'The Origin of Inequality among Men'[4] that were the first to be asked by sociology and were the primary concern of these early writers. This theme of social inequality, of social stratification and differentiation, was important to me because for the first time it made me fully aware of my own social situation during my upbringing.

I was brought up to accept the social structure with its inherent inequalities as being right and given, and to believe that one must do one's best to rise within this system. In other words, it is possible to be almost totally unaware of gross social inequalities because they are accepted as the natural order of things. The sociological theory, particularly of Marx and Weber, came to life for me in the ethnography of my own background.

Two further factors helped to formulate my interest in localised populations. First, anthropologists have always been concerned with small groups or categories of people, whether it be a family, a horde, a tribe or a village. In my undergraduate courses, such units were always the object of analysis, and anthropologists who had turned their interests to modern industrial societies had studied such things as a small Welsh village or a slum area of a metropolis. Second, I was influenced by honours seminars on community studies and I was attracted by the ethnography of the well-known studies of Middletown, Gosforth and Springdale, as well as their implications for wider theoretical issues.

With a theoretical interest in social stratification and an empirical interest in small towns, I went into my final honours year and wrote a thesis called 'Social stratification:

An examination of the theories of social stratification and of its manifestations in the United States of America and Australia'. I was further stimulated in this direction by three seminar courses on sociological theory, elite theory and community studies. I felt that there was a need for a closer relationship between some central theoretical issues and the ethnography, and Stein's book *The Eclipse of Community* assured me that this was possible.

With a vague idea of centering a study around some theoretical propositions concerning social stratification, I started to look at a number of small towns. For practical purposes,[5] I wanted a town that was a political unit at a local level rather than part of a wider entity such as a shire. As the smallest municipality in New South Wales has an approximate population of 2500, I was limited to places with a greater number of people. I also wanted a place where I could get to know and talk to a large proportion of the inhabitants. As a single fieldworker with few resources, this limited me to towns with a population less than 10 000. A member of the Anthropology Department was mid-way through a study of a predominantly working-class, single-industry town and we thought it would be useful, for comparative purposes, to select a different type of locality. I listed several towns in New South Wales that fitted these criteria and went to visit them. Many people have asked me why I did not select a typical country town. I must admit that I still do not know what constitutes a typical country town. In a country with no tradition in community studies, the only measure of typicality is in terms of average statistics. Some towns in America have been selected for study on the basis that their occupation, income and education statistics correspond closely with the average figures for the State. At the intensive level of anthropological research, and at the level necessary to understand the core features of stratification phenomena, this sort of typicality is hardly relevant. I selected Bradstow because I felt an empathy with the place I had not experienced elsewhere. Perhaps it was because the area reminded me of parts of England or because I met a friendly historian who told me about former times. It was probably a combination of many of these sorts of things but whatever it was, I felt that I could do some valuable research in this town.

This occurred during my final honours year. I visited the town occasionally and read widely on the history and economic activities of the Bradstow District. Somewhat unconsciously, this was the first specific preparation for my research project.

After completing my undergraduate course, I was awarded a postgraduate scholarship and I enrolled for a Ph.D. This scholarship, like many others, was provided by the Department of Education of the Australian Government and channelled through the University of Sydney. I had complete freedom of choice in my research topic. I did not have to supply the Government or the University with interim research reports, and the only requirement for annual renewal for four years was my supervisor's recommendation that my work was progressing satisfactorily. Consequently, I had few ethical problems to cope with concerning my financial support. The ethical problems with which I did have to deal were of a different kind and I discuss these here.

After catching up on some reading and organising accommodation, I moved to Bradstow, with my wife of several months, in March 1967. One of the first things I did was to write an article for the local paper saying that I was a postgraduate student conducting an anthropological/ sociological research project on various aspects of town life. I spelt out the areas in which I was interested and mentioned that at a later stage I would be doing a random sample household survey. Being chronically short of copy, the Bradstow Press ran this article on the front page with a photograph. Consequently, most people in the area knew what I was doing although there were different levels of understanding. For some people I was 'just writing a book on the town', but others had a much more accurate perception of what I was doing. When I first met one of the solicitors he said to me, 'I know what you are doing. I did Anthropology at Sydney University and I can tell you they would have made your job a lot easier if they had sent you to the Trobriand Islands. You will have a difficult job finding out how this town works'.

Initial contacts were important because they introduced me to different sections of the social structure. I shall restrict my remarks to the status system, because this dimension of stratification emphasises the many different types of social situations that can occur. My first informant was the Real Estate and Stock and Station Agent who arranged my accommodation. Where the research worker lives can be important for determining people's initial reactions. There were two houses available for rent. One was a small cottage near the railway line and the other was a two-storey gatekeeper's lodge about one and a half kilometres out of town on the south-eastern outskirts. We took the latter, a National Trust classified building on an acre of land which had been subdivided and sold when the main house and property were taken over by a convent. The house was close to Grange, but sufficiently marginal so as to be able to avoid close identification with that exclusive residential area.

Our agent was regarded as a professional man (because he charged fees), as against the local businessmen who are seen as being in trade: an important distinction in Bradstow because it determines who is eligible for membership of the exclusive Bradstow Golf Club. As a professional, this agent mixed socially with the people from Grange, primarily retired professionals or businessmen from Sydney, retired Colonial service personnel, and wealthy Sydney folk with weekend villas and grazing properties.[6] In the first two or three weeks, the agent invited us to various cocktail parties and I met a wide range of people from this status group.

During this period, I had several long conversations with the Deputy Town Clerk, a local historian, whom I had met on one of my earlier visits. As well as being able to clarify aspects of local history, he knew all the municipal council aldermen, and almost all the businessmen and tradesmen. He introduced me to many of these people and invited me along to the council meetings and to functions of such organisations as the historical society, the gardening club, and the senior citizens homes committee. The contacts I made through him; particularly the Mayor and a number of aldermen, invited me to Rotary, Lions and Apex meetings, and I arranged through these people to sit in on the town's biggest committees, the Flower Festival and the Swimming Pool.

I have played the game of soccer for the greater part of my life and I now had an opportunity to let this game help my research. I joined the Bradstow Soccer Club and made many friends among unskilled, skilled and clerical workers. The status of my educational background, which had provided acceptance among the Grange-ites, could have gone against me in this situation; but this did not happen and I was accepted into their social circle on the basis of my playing ability and, perhaps partly on my obvious pleasure in drinking at the pub after the match. I became secretary of the club and the coach of a junior team.

During the first few weeks, my wife and I met a small number of people who became and remain close personal friends. These folk were primarily artists and potters who were living in the district because it was a pleasant place. Most lived outside the town, took little or no part in town affairs, and formed a fringe group. Some were referred to as 'weirdos' by the townspeople because they 'had beards', 'did not work', and 'refused to have their children christened'.

The Bradstow District Hospital is large for a small town but serves a wide area. My wife, a nursing sister, had arranged a job there helping to deliver the town's babies. Coming from a big Sydney hospital, she was highly valued by the general practitioners who run the hospital, as she was conversant with all the latest techniques and drugs. Consequently, she established good relationships with the doctors. Through these contacts I had an easy entry into their social circle and was able to establish the important position that the doctors and solicitors held within the social structure.

These professionals are among the small number of people who can cross the central status cleavage between the Grange-ites and the townspeople.[7]

During the first few weeks I made contact with, and was collecting data from, a wide range of status levels. But there were two further status groups that had eluded my first impressions, and these were at the very top and bottom of the status hierarchy.

At the beginning I associated such terms as the aristocracy, the 'blue-bloods', the Golf Club crowd, the 'Grange-ites', the old family group, the landed gentry, the wealthy elite, the 'silvertails', the better class of people, the 'poo-bahs', the snobs, and others as synonyms, and by some people they were used as such. But there was an important distinction here, which first struck me when I was standing in the main street on a busy Saturday morning talking to the owner of a junk shop. An old lady walked past and climbed into a vintage Daimler which was parked at an odd angle with its bonnet pushed into a small parking space and the back section protruding onto the road. He turned and said to me, 'that's Mrs Legge-Smith'. I asked who she was. He replied in hushed tones, 'She's one of the old families, she's real aristocracy. This crowd out here (nodding his head towards Grange) are just nouveau riche who have come to live here to pretend to be landed gentry. And what's more, that car never gets booked.' This casual conversation outlined the distinction between the Grange-ite nouveau riche and the gentry. This enabled me to ask further probing questions about this cleavage and I was able to isolate a small core group of long-established gentry families, most of them having three to five generation connections with the district.

In the first weeks no one mentioned the existence of what one informant later called 'the low ones who are really low' and who are generally referred to as the 'no hopers'. I was aware by looking at the housing conditions near the railway and in Stone Valley, a shanty area reclaimed from swamp land on the extreme eastern edge, that there were some poor people, but on first impressions I thought they were probably the poorer fringe of the manual workers. Several families living in these areas turned out to be in this position, but there was a small category of families who were generally despised by the rest. One particular incident made me fully aware of this distinction.

A businessman challenged a man leaving his shop. The man produced a packet of biscuits from his pocket, apologised, put some money on the table and ran from the shop. The owner called the police and charged him with stealing. As it was a repeated offence, he was gaoled for six months. The man and his wife were both invalid pensioners and had several children. This incident received wide publicity in the Bradstow Press, including a photograph. The businessman cut out several of these press reports and pasted them over the front of his shop window. When I discussed this incident with two other businessmen, one said to me,

> Oh, there are a few no hopers like him in Bradstow. They are just lazy bastards. They'll never do a day's hard work. There are about a dozen families like that. Most of them have been in prison and some are prostitutes. I can tell you I'd like to kick them all out of town.

One of the main problems after the initial two months was to gain entry and acceptance by such disparate status groups. Some were easier than others. I was collecting data almost straightaway from the blue and white collar workers with whom I played soccer. An interest in art, music, drama, history and gardening was essential for any rapport with the Grange-ites, especially the women. My keen interest in local politics and service club activities provided me with an entry into the businessmen's circle and the political cliques. My boyhood and adolescent experience as a boy scout enabled me to fill in as a scoutmaster for a period and provided immediate entry into a number of tradesmen's, businessmen's and schoolteachers' homes. However, it was difficult to obtain information from the gentry and the no hopers.

I solved the first problem quite by chance. One afternoon, I met a distinguished-looking old gentleman taking a stroll close to my house on the outskirts of town and we started talking. I eventually found out that he was the owner of a very big shipping and retail business and that his family had moved onto the land in Grange when they had become wealthy after the turn of the century. After this chance encounter I used to join him for afternoon tea on the sun verandah of his twenty-odd room house which overlooked some three acres of immaculately kept gardens. At other times I was invited for drinks; always the best scotch whisky served promptly at five-forty every evening in the library. This contact became perhaps my closest link with the gentry.[8]

I did not have the same success with the no hopers and at one stage it was only a wife's restraining arm that stopped her husband from hitting me for 'asking damn fool questions about my private life'. It soon became obvious that I was not going to get much information just by trying to talk with them at home or even in the pub. In the public bars, they were sometimes ostracised by the other workers. I struck on the idea of trying to get some information from their children. I knew one boy in the soccer club who mixed with some of the no hopers' children, some of whom played rugby league. I got him to take me along to a particular hotel where they monopolise the lounge with a pop band and dancing on Friday and Saturday nights.[9] I attended for several weeks, at the end of which I had gained sufficient acceptance to obtain general information on such things as style of life, leisure activities, how a typical week was organised, attitudes to local politics, and so forth.

One further major difficulty I had with gaining acceptance was with a small crowd of people about my own age (twenty-four at the time) who had established their own businesses as painters and decorators, plumbers, welders and builders. This group drank regularly at the Bradstow Hotel and one evening I introduced myself to them in the saloon bar. A painter and decorator, who was their main spokesman said,

'You are the bloke who is writing the book are you? What's it all about?'. I replied, 'Well I am writing a book partly about local history and partly about how the town is run and organised today, local politics and things like that'. He answered, 'And you get paid to do that by the University? What a bloody waste of time. And anyway, who sees that you get up at eight o'clock and start work on time? I think all this bloody education is overrated. Look at me, I left school before my Intermediate and I employ seven blokes now and make a fair crust.' I replied cautiously and pointed out that people are interested in different things and he had obviously done well in the area he had chosen. But it was clear I was not making any headway. I could not get them to answer any probing questions.

I went to the same bar of the hotel for almost two weeks. I drank with them and eventually got to play in their games of darts, but I was still not getting the information I required. Finally, one Friday night I was invited to join them at the Country Club after the hotel closed. At the Club we played snooker and table tennis as we drank on until after one in the morning. Before we were about to leave, the painter and decorator came up to me and said, 'We all thought you were a prick when we saw you. We didn't like your hair, and the way you talked, but you've had a few beers with us (over eighty middies in the past two weeks in fact) and you're not bad at darts, so we think you're not a bad sort of bloke.' He then extended his arm and we shook hands. On leaving the Club, the youngest member of this crowd whom I knew through the Soccer Club turned round and remarked to me, 'They've accepted you now. It's a sort of initiation that goes on for a while but you're in now and you won't have any more trouble.' He was right: a few weeks later I interviewed in depth two members of this group.

Another difficulty for the sole researcher can be his or her sex. One of my female students working in a small town has experienced difficulties in obtaining acceptance from the male political elite. The usual argument is that the female researcher is perceived first as a female and second as a sociologist. Not only does this situation make it hard for her to break into a male political scene; it may also create problems in her relationship with the wives of politicians. The male sociologist is not supposed to suffer from these difficulties and this may well be true in the sphere of male-dominated politics. But it is not accurate in all situations. One afternoon I was interviewing a wealthy Grange-ite lady. Before the interview, she insisted on showing me her extensive garden, during the interview she plied me with sherry as she stretched out her answers, and afterwards she gave me a conducted tour of her gracious house. We eventually arrived at her painting studio. She invited me to relax on her large couch and suggested that we 'get to know each other a little better'. I hurriedly left. Certainly the male sociologist has the distinct advantage of being able to operate more easily within the normative order, but the sex of the single research worker, whether it be male or female, can produce some difficult situations in intensive fieldwork.

It should be clear by now that to gain acceptance and obtain information from disparate status groups entails the playing of many different roles. Trying to prevent clashes occurring between one's normal behaviour and one's role expectations in a particular social situation can be difficult, and the investigator may have to become almost devious in avoiding such incidents. The observer may also, in some situations of conflict for example, have to avoid being seen by the members of one group when he or she is mixing with those of another.

In such situations as these, personal relationships have to be developed, established and kept up for instrumental purposes. This is one of the more difficult and least attractive aspects of this type of research. Such situations develop even more tension when the status gap between the investigator and the respondent is particularly great. Two social dramas, one centred on the Golf Club and the other on the teenagers' pop lounge, indicate the types of social situations at vastly different status levels with which a participant-observer has to cope.[10] In the former situation, I was dressed in a dark three-piece suit, white shirt and University tie. I drank double scotches and the conversation centred on politics and business. In the latter context, I wore corduroy jeans, desert boots and a purple floral shirt. I drank schooners of old beer and talked about sport, cars and women. The more researchers can equalise the status differences between themselves and their respondent, the more (and better quality) data they will obtain.

Gans has suggested that the researcher plays at least three roles: total researcher, researcher participant and total participant.[11] I played the first role on very few occasions. My attendance at the Municipal Council meetings, for example, took this form but after the meeting over drinks in the Mayoral Room, I took on the second role. I played the role of researcher participant in most situations. I became a total participant with several close personal friends, and also when I was playing soccer, running the scout troop, and helping with various projects. What may begin as a researcher-participant situation can become a total participant one. As total participants, investigators must exercise particular care because they become less observant and their own biases intrude in a more forthright manner. Further, as a total participant — that is, when the researcher has forgotten his or her research role and is acting as a normal person — it is easy to offend people. Once this has been done, it rebounds on the research role and makes future interviewing and participant observation more difficult. I found that in most participant observation and interviewing situations, it paid me to take a neutral stance and to act as though I knew nothing about the topic. In these circumstances, most respondents keep on talking to avoid the silences. A similar technique is used by the Australian Broadcasting Commission's in-depth interview television programme, 'Chequerboard'. Essentially, participant observers have to sell themselves to the respondent or group in order to obtain the type of information they require and they are likely to be more successful if they take a neutral or sympathetic position.

So far I have discussed some of the difficulties I encountered in the early part of the fieldwork when I was collecting data on a wide range of topics. During this first year, I was also collecting data on the political system. I attended Municipal and County Council meetings, interviewed politicians, followed through several case studies of controversial issues and town projects, and conducted a reputational survey of political power holders.

Two general methodological points, of which I was unaware, emerged from this work on politics. First, I found that it was impossible to remain passive and uncommitted in a controversial political issue. People were constantly asking my opinion: did I think, for example, that a TAB office should be allowed to open in Bradstow. In such situations, it is as bad to be passive as it is to be provocative. I found that if I argued carefully people would listen and either agree or proceed to argue against my points. Further, in such discussions, other useful data that were previously ignored, and would not have been explored with even the best prepared questionnaire schedule, were often introduced.

Second, I found that I had to be constantly aware of what I was saying even in the most casual conversations. An anthropologist obtains some data from general gossip. Different groups have different norms or rules about gossip and these have to be learned and followed. This was fortunately brought home to me early in the fieldwork period. Three weeks after arriving, my wife was having a casual conversation with a patient in the hospital. Referring to an item in the paper, the patient said, 'The Council are still on about garbage collection. God they are a hopeless lot.' My wife replied, 'Yes, I agree with you. I've been to two of their meetings and they never get anything done. I think a benevolent dictator would go well in this town.' It was an incidental conversation that was soon forgotten, at least for the moment. Two days later, the President of Marston Shire Council, which adjoins the Bradstow Municipality, said to me, 'I believe your wife has been making acid comments about our civic fathers'. I asked him to explain and he recounted the story, informing me that the patient was his daughter-in-law. I replied that my wife had been to a Council meeting and was entitled to her own opinion. I could not have said much else, as it was obvious from his attitude that he thought my wife's comments originated from me. In this case the matter was soon forgotten and I had several discussions with him on later occasions, but it indicates why investigators must try to be aware of the possible consequences of all their actions as well as those of their spouses.

During the second year of fieldwork, I directed my attention to more specific areas on which I required more data. I selected a number of clubs and societies from different status levels, became a member, played an active part on their committees, analysed their membership and organisational structure, and the part they played within the stratification system. I collected comparative data on local politics from a nearby town and continued taking notes from general participant-observation.

By this time, I knew many people in Bradstow and I had a lot of qualitative data as well as some quantitative data from the census and from the reputational, issue and positional analyses of the political power system. I required, however, more quantitative material on such basic facts as amounts and sources of income, level and type of education, family backgrounds, and so forth. I also wanted further data on people's attitudes to class, politics and religion. I planned and carried out a random sample of 20% of the households which consisted of 326 interviews. I used a formal questionnaire and each interview lasted between one and three hours depending on the interest of the respondent. A response of over 94% shows that I was certainly accepted by the people at this time and the other 6% included those who were sick and whose houses were empty as well as the few who refused to be interviewed.[12] Surveys such as this, carried out on the basis of a thorough knowledge of the historical and sociocultural context of the area, can provide valuable, if somewhat limited data. Mass surveys carried out without any knowledge of, or reference to the socio-cultural context often provide misleading and meaningless statistics within a social vacuum, especially when they are concerned with such qualitative phenomena as class, status and political power. The survey was the last part of my fieldwork and I then started to collate the data and present it within an historical, social and cultural context.

It took me ten months, working almost every day, to collate, analyse, introduce comparative data, and finally write my Ph.D. thesis. The speed and ease with which this can be done depends largely on how the data were filed in the field. I, like most other participant observers, started by writing a diary. Comments from my notebook and other impressions were entered in my diary each evening. I continued this procedure for just over two months. At this stage I had enough knowledge to start filing on significant topics, such as council politics, controversial issues, voluntary associations, status divisions, and so forth. Data were entered on separate pieces of paper and put into the relevant file with a cross-indexing reference on the information that was relevant to more than one topic. I put the material from the sample survey onto manual punch-cards and produced a series of tables by cross-tabulation.

The historical dimension of community studies has often been neglected, yet such sociological analyses are never complete until the contemporary data have been placed within an historical context. Many social patterns that can be established from historical sources can be seen operating in the present, and without the historical context such patterns cannot be fully understood. Local traditions, ideologies and forms of action, although undergoing transformations in the present, are, nevertheless, rooted in the past. In my study I used five major sources. First, before I went to Bradstow I read as much local history as I could find. Most of these sources were general descriptive accounts, but they gave me a picture of what the town was like in previous years. Second, I used records kept by the Municipal and County Councils. These did not yield a great deal, but they were useful for such things as examining the development of local government and patterns of residential settlement. Third, through a local historian I gained access to every local paper printed since the first edition of 1883. Newspapers form, perhaps, the most important sources of historical detail for this type of work. I read every one over a period of four months and obtained a great amount of data from them. Fourth, I sought out people who had kept scrapbooks and diaries. I found one old lady who had kept a scrapbook on a gentry family in which she had hundreds of newspaper cuttings of their births, weddings, deaths and general social events, yet she had never met the family. Finally, some old people have valuable historical knowledge if you are prepared to spend many hours reminiscing with them. From one old man I obtained personal histories of five businessman, all of whom were mayors in the early part of this century.

I wrote three drafts for my thesis before the final copy was typed. After it had been submitted and examined in August 1970, I started work on converting it to a manuscript for publication. This process took three more drafts as I removed the comparative data, left out many of the tables, and edited it generally for expression and repetition. There are, however, more than mechanical difficulties in preparing an anthropological or sociological study for publication.

After fieldwork, most anthropologists find themselves with data that may harm people if it is published: the harm may be real, as for example, in counter-insurgency anthropology,[13] or it may be in the people's minds. Both are significant. In the writing of Bradstow I considered what might rather pretentiously be referred to as two broad ethical tenets in order to help me determine what I could publish and in what form. First, I was concerned with scientific enquiry; that is, the pursuit of knowledge, of free enquiry and free publication. Second, I took into account my own responsibility to the people and the confidences they shared. If this responsibility is not taken, personal confidences will be divulged, privacy will be infringed and reputations may be damaged.

Open enquiry and publication and responsibility may,

however, conflict — especially in an anthropological study which traditionally refers to individuals, families and case studies. Howard Becker[14] has pointed out that any good community study deals in some way with the differences between reality and the ideal: the veil of public relations is removed, and resentment is necessarily caused. According to Vidich and Bensman 'Any organization tends to represent a balance of divergent interests held in some equilibrium by the power status of the parties involved. A simple description of these factors, no matter how stated will offend some of the groups in question.'[15] In other words, most community studies create a hostile reaction through the very nature of their research material. How then can anthropologists deal with such a situation of conflict where, in terms of scientific enquiry, they should demand complete freedom but where, in terms of their responsibility to the people studied, they must take care not to reveal confidences? There is no absolute answer. Each case must be determined separately by the individual's conscience. In my view, anthropologists should attempt to strive for the freest possible conditions of reporting within the strictures of what they consider their responsibility to the people. This does not mean that one need have no conscience at all, but rather that each case is a matter for individual judgement.

Such considerations have to be carefully examined when the author is writing for publication. It is not easy to decide what to put in and what to leave out. Generally, the writer should not publish items that are not necessary to the argument or that would cause harm out of proportion to the intellectual benefit. This, of course, is open to wide interpretation but any stricter approach would unduly shackle the principal scientific enterprise of free enquiry and publication.

In Bradstow I left out several social drama situations because they could have been a source of severe embarrassment to some people. One of them, for example, later involved legal proceedings. I changed all local place names and all personal names in an attempt to retain the privacy of as many people as possible and to avoid any undue publicity on publication. I did not suppress details such as occupations, club memberships, case study material or similar data, for to have done so would have been to distort the social context.[16] Some people in Bradstow will, of course, recognise those who are described in the book. This is unavoidable in a study of this nature. Most of these people, however, are in public office or concerned with public affairs and should be accountable for their actions.

A further issue relating to this discussion concerns the restrictive laws of libel found particularly in New South Wales, and in Australia generally. Under these laws it is impossible, for example, to publish such examples of political corruption as Vidich and Bensman used so well in *Small Town in Mass Society*. I had to spend several sessions with the publisher's lawyers rewriting sections, omitting one case study, and pruning some quotations. I fought successfully against some alterations and agreed with others to enable most of the data to appear.

One effect of this has been to weaken one of my arguments and, therefore, partly affect the quality of scholarship. Another effect was the delay of publication. The manuscript was completed in 1971. It took several months for Sydney University Press to reject it 'because of the legal problems which relate to possible defamation'. Several more months passed before Cheshire Publishing decided to reject it because 'our sales research indicates that we could not sell any more than a few hundred copies'. It took further time for Melbourne University Press and McGraw Hill to reach the same conclusion. When Angus and Robertson finally accepted it, the legal difficulties caused some delay, the reorganisation of the publisher's educational section created a further deferment, and finally the first print run disappeared under the Brisbane flood. The book, *Bradstow*, eventually appeared in July 1974.

Reactions
The saga of community studies rarely ends with publication:

this is the time for the media and the people who were studied to have their say. The publication of Vidich and Bensman's book, for example, created a furore on publication, with newspapers providing the medium for a dispute between Cornell University, the townspeople and the authors.[17] Some of this heat was translated into action when the political leaders rode down the main street for the Fourth of July celebrations wearing hoods with their fictitious names on the back followed by an effigy of 'The Author' bending over a manure-spreader full of rich barnyard fertiliser. The story of Bradstow did not proceed this far, but some sensationalist-type publicity preceded publication.

A feature writer for the *Daily Telegraph* obtained a copy of the page proofs from the publisher (without my knowledge), who asked him not to mention the real name of the town. The journalist rang me to ask for an interview and to find out the real name. I refused both. Some time later I was awakened at 6.30 a.m. on a Saturday morning by a telephone call from a friend in Bradstow. He said 'Have you seen this morning's *Telegraph*?', I replied 'no'. He continued 'Then you had better get a copy because they have blown the lot on your book and it's all round town'. Feeling shaken I dashed to the newsagent's and bought a copy to find a double-page spread headed 'We are a nation of snobs: shock survey shatters the Aussie myth'. Below this was a map with an arrow pointing to the town and the comment 'Wild's Bradstow'. As I read on I became more and more furious. 'Cringe! Crawl! Tug your forelock in shame. The bronzed Anzac, the bar-bellying I'm as-good-as-you Jack Australian is a grotesque fraud. In reality he is a class concious, self-seeking, ladder-climbing — oh it hurts to go on — besotted snob who kicks those beneath him and slavishly apes his betters.' I felt worried, furious and frustrated. I was worried because of its possible effects in Bradstow. I was furious about the atrocious standard of journalism and the complete misinterpretation of the book. I felt frustrated because there was nothing I could do.

I thought about it after I had calmed down and I rang

the publisher, who was sympathetic. I then wrote a letter to the *Bradstow Press* which in part read,

> I should like to make it clear to all my friends in Bradstow that I was in no way responsible for the embarrassing publicity given the town in a recent article in the Daily Telegraph. The journalist in question did not interview me, neither was he authorised to use a photograph which he obtained from other sources. This incident has embarrassed me both personally and ethically...

The *Daily Telegraph* article, shortly followed by the publication of *Bradstow*, led to other sensationalist stories in both city and country newspapers. The *Sunday Mirror* referred to it as 'The Book That Set A Town Afire' and the *Brewarrina News* under the heading 'General Sporting Review' wrote 'Englishman writes Controversial Book on Australia'. In an attempt to create interest, the popular newspapers stressed almost exclusively the chapter on status and translated the results from one small town onto the nation. These journalists made it clear that the people who read their papers are very much concerned with patterns of status and prestige and want to read about it.

The more serious journalists' reactions to *Bradstow* were interesting in that they split into two camps. The reviews in *The Australian* and *The Age* saw the book as having something to say about Australia generally. According to Ian Moffitt 'it is a first-rate source book for the nation'.[18] But others saw Bradstow as unique. The *Bulletin*'s reviewer wrote 'Fortunately Australia as a whole is not so stuffy and rigidly compartmentalised as Bradstow'.[19] This was echoed by John Edwards in *The Financial Review* who commented '... one may wonder what relevance *Bradstow* has for the rest of Australian society, particularly the cities where most people live. It can't be like that everywhere, can it?'[20] The journalists' ideological slips were beginning to show. For some, it provided evidence of a class-structured society; for others it was an aberration that affronted their egalitarian beliefs. Clearly, the results from Bradstow cannot be generalised to Australia[21] and perhaps community studies are better at showing the heterogeneity of modern societies rather than their homogeneity.[22] Nevertheless, Bradstow is typical of a type of town that developed historically on the outskirts of many major cities, and the structural and institutional constraints are similar to those operating in other towns. Consequently, much of what goes on in Bradstow can be seen operating in a similar way in other places.

There was one newspaper review that was quite different from the rest. It was written by Maslyn Williams[23] who first went to live in Bradstow in 1931 and has maintained a continuous association with the district. He now lives in a neighbouring town and has many of the qualities of a professional Grange-ite. This review, which does not mention any of the data from the book, suggests I should not have published it because 'a lot of anthropologists have become pretty cagey about what they publish' and because 'it is of limited public interest'. He makes the elementary error of quoting the dustjacket as the author's prose and outlines one criticism that 'he does not mention the quite impressively deep-seated pride in the uniqueness of the district ...' Williams could not have read page 32 where I wrote '... exclusiveness, and the desire to keep the place a prominent country town are characteristics of the upper status groups, but such values have partly pervaded the middle, and in some cases, the lower rungs'. And later on the same page, 'the people are proud of the scenic beauty of the countryside'. The reviewer gives his own position as a Grange-ite away when he writes of Bradstow 'I consider it my home village' and 'It has always been a nostalgia town, a wish fulfilment village created by people whose spiritual and cultural affinities existed — and to some extent still exist — in the idealised rural scene ...'. He would get short shrift from the no hopers and some of the workers for these views. Finally, Williams does not mention that after I had completed fieldwork and was visiting the district, we had dinner at a mutual friend's house and the evening ended with a most acrimonious discussion of anthropology and academics. This review is interesting because it reflects the views of several Grange-ites I have spoken to and to which I shall return shortly.

The third category of reviews are the academic ones.[24] Most have raised useful sociological questions, but this is not the place to pursue them. I shall now turn to the reactions of the people living in Bradstow.

Shortly after the book was published, I received a telephone call from an interviewer on the Australian Broadcasting Commission's documentary programme 'Four Corners'. He explained that they wanted to go to Bradstow and interview people about their reactions to the study. I was reluctant to take part but when I found out that they intended to go ahead with the project regardless, I decided to present my point of view in an interview. The filming and the film developed a renewed interest in the book. As the interviewer commented 'Last week's best sellers at the town's two newsagents were *The Exorcist* and David Niven's biography. This week *Bradstow* is outselling all the rest'. The film also portrayed some interesting reactions. The following is an extract from an interview with one of the workers, an unskilled labourer with six children.

Interviewer:
Do you think there are social divisions in Bradstow?
Worker:
I think myself that it is divided into two different sections. There's the working-class people and then there's the Pitt Street farmers, let's put it that way, you know. They are made up of Sydney businessmen who have bought land and property here and...
Interviewer:
What are they like as a group?
Worker:
A percentage of them are pretty good and then there's another percentage of them that are a little bit classy, you know.
Interviewer:

In what way?

Worker:

Well, you go there (to do a job) and you look at them and they look at you and they think he's not up to scratch, he's not the sort of fellow I want to associate with, you know.

Interviewer:

Do you think the ordinary man gets much say in the way the town is run?

Worker:

Well, I've lived here for 31 years and I have never ever had any say in the way the town is run. But then again you wouldn't expect me to have much say. I am just an ordinary old labourer.

Interviewer:

Still, in a democracy one would expect that you would have some sort of say.

Worker:

Well, you're never given the opportunity are you. You are never asked your opinion. You're never invited along to any meetings or anything like that to be able to voice your opinion. You've just got to get onto the member of the Council who you think could put your case forward and hope that he does the job for you.

Interviewer:

Do you think it's right and proper that there should be these divisions between social groups? Is that just nature?

Worker:

Well, it appears that way. I've met quite a few people from Grange right down from the would-be's to the millionaires. You go and work for them, carry it out satisfactorily, and then run into them in the street and they just don't recognise you. They don't know you.

Interviewer:

Are they tough employers? Do they want their pound of flesh?

Worker:

(Pause) They want two pound. They want two pound of flesh.

Along with almost half of the other workers,²⁵ this man saw the stratification system as a dichotomy. He displays some antagonism to the Grange-ites yet he is deferential to those running the town, as is clear in his statement that 'You are never *invited* along to any meetings . . .' This is a typical reaction of one section of the workers.²⁶

The film team did not interview any tradesmen, but from two informants I have been able to gauge a reaction. In the Bowling club, the tradesmen's centre, the dominant reaction was 'Well, we all knew about it, anyway. Why bother writing a book about it'. A tradesman was heard to utter in a pub 'It shouldn't have took that long to find that some have money, some would like it and some don't have it, and that money talks to money while others drink in pubs'. This is typical of the tradesmen's tendency to concentrate on one or two status variables and is remarkably similar to one tradesman's views I quoted.²⁷

The film team interviewed several of the bosses. I shall reproduce extracts from the interviews and then discuss their implications.

Interview With the Elliott Brothers

Interviewer:
  It has been suggested that as a family you are influential in town affairs.

Tom Elliott:
  I don't think we have any influence at all. I think it's quite the opposite. If perhaps we are influential, as the book sometimes suggests, in community affairs where it has a wide range of consequences over the community as a whole, I think the fact that the four brothers who serve in such a wide sphere of activities in charitable affairs – then perhaps we do have some influence at these meetings, and in that case perhaps we could be classed as influentials. I wouldn't know. That's what others call us, not what we call ourselves.

Interviewer:
  Do you see big divisions in society here?

James Elliott:
I don't think there's any divisions at all. We might get one or two people sticking out or making statements and you feel that they might be a class above you or a class below you but I don't think there has been any divisions here at all.

Interviewer:
Yet it has been written up that the people in Grange wouldn't have people in trade in their golf club. Have you ever been made to feel that class distinction?

James Elliott:
Well, it's been said that often and it has been practised on one or two occasions here. I know of people in trade that have been refused admission to the golf club. I was offered honorary membership while I was mayor but that didn't suit ... I never wanted to join Bradstow Golf Club just for the class distinction.

Interview With Alderman D. Wilson
(Mayor at the time of filming)

Interviewer:
Do you see a conflict of interest between a man who has strong business interests in the town taking an active part in local government?

D. Wilson:
No I don't. It just so happens that when the time this book was written what was good for the Elliotts was good for Bradstow. The people who have the most say in the town, the most to gain, or the most to do with the actions of the town, should be represented on the Council.

Interviewer:
Surely from time to time it would lead to a conflict of interest. Such as a town planning matter where a businessman as a businessman has certain interests but as an alderman he has different interests.

D. Wilson:
Yes, that's quite true. But you must remember he's not the only one on Council. There are nine on Council and the other eight aren't just sitting there for the sake of it. They've got

to express their opinion. No one man can dominate the Council.

Interview With Alderman J. White
(Alderman White was the only Labor Party supporter on the Council)

Interviewer:
How powerful are the businessmen in running the town?
J. White:
They're a very powerful mob. A powerful mob. That's all I can say.
Interviewer:
Has everyone got free access to Council or is it one particular group that has always tended to dominate the Council?
J. White:
When I first entered Council nine years ago, the service clubs seemed to dominate it. But then when we talk about service clubs we better remember that the members of the service clubs are also the local businessmen in the town.
Interviewer:
It's all a bit incestuous isn't it. Everyone seems to be doubling up in roles. Is that a bad thing do you think?
J. White:
I think so, yes, for the running of the town. I do, yes.

Interview With Two Members of the Rotary Club
Rotary member 1:
The Rotary Club is a complete cross-section of the whole community. In no way do we meet to make basic business deals, or suchlike, through the town itself.
Rotary member 2:
It's purely a fellowship and a service club and there is no sense that they are trying to gain power or influence other people to become involved in some activity that they are interested in.

In the first interview, Tom Elliott starts by saying that the family are not influential and finishes by stating that they are. Similarly, his brother comments that there are no status divisions and then adds that people in trade have been rejected for membership of the golf club and that he felt slighted when offered honorary membership for the period of his mayoral office. When I interviewed James Elliott in 1967, he said in answer to the following questions:

Question:
  Do you feel that there are class differences in Bradstow?
Answer:
  There used to be three separate classes in Bradstow: the higher class, the businessmen and the working class. There is no real upper one now. Bradstow used to rely on country homes but this is not as true now. [He then listed seven Grange-ite and Gentry families.]
Question:
  In your opinion how do these differences show themselves?
Answer:
  It's mainly in the golf clubs. The Bradstow Golf Club won't allow businessmen in and they have a lot of Sydney members. The Country Club is where everyone is average.
Question:
  Do you feel that you belong to a definite class?
Answer:
  No.
Question:
  Why?
Answer:
  Well, I suppose I belong to the business class.
Question:
  Can you recall any recent occurrence in Bradstow that has brought the matter of class vividly to your notice?
Answer:
  Yes. The golf club offered me membership on an honorary basis while I was mayor. Well, I wouldn't accept that, I ask you.

Further, in his nominations of town influentials, James

Elliott nominated himself as most influential and his brother Tom as fifth from a total of thirteen.

The second and third interviews with Aldermen Wilson and White concern the Municipal Council. Alderman Wilson maintains an ideal democratic model of the operation of the council, whereas Alderman White is aware that the councillors primarily represent one group and are extremely influential in running the town. The latter's views are in direct accord with his more detailed comments made to me in several interviews in 1967 and 1968. The former alderman, however, rejects the evidence in favour of an official ideology of how the council is supposed to work.

The final interview with the two members of the Rotary Club indicates how some people pay no attention to factual data and cling to their cherished beliefs. The Rotary Club is not 'a complete cross-section of the community'. In fact, Rotary is one of the most elitist and narrowly represented voluntary associations in Bradstow.[28]

One of the bosses' typical reactions has been to deny the evidence of influence, authority, power and substitute ideological facades. For Tom and James Elliott, an egalitarian facade was used to reject notions of influence and prestige; for Alderman Wilson, it was a democratic front concerning the proper functioning of councils; and for the Rotary members, it was a belief about the representativeness and moral quality of their club. It is partly the job of community studies, and of sociology generally, to penetrate such ideological facades in order to expose the actual structure of social relationships. It is to be expected that when this has been done, attempts will be made to cover or mystify them by appealing to commonly accepted ideologies.

The film crew interviewed two prominent Grange-ites on the golf course. The conversation went as follows:

1st Grange-ite:
    I think this is a club we can be very very proud of. It's 75 years old in June and people have worked very hard for the club over the years, and they have been generous to the club.

You see it's good exercise and it's the company, you see, and as Freddie says, if you have people of comparable outlook and that, well you can play with any of them, enjoy your game, you sit down afterwards and have a natter away and tear everything to bits, you see. But as I say we've just got comparable interests whereas a lot of the younger fellows couldn't possibly have the same interests as we older, retired people.

2nd Grange-ite:
It's not that we don't enjoy talking to the young people.

1st Grange-ite:
Look, a lot of them come here when we have open days, and what's more, they enjoy it. But quite frankly, we pay double the subs they pay at the Country Club and the young fellows can't afford it. It's an economic business. All clubs are getting too expensive and there's nothing worse than a rich man's club.

Interviewer:
Is this a rich man's club?

1st Grange-ite:
No, but I say there is nothing worse than a rich man's club.

Interviewer:
Why is that?

1st Grange-ite:
Well, the fact of having money is not sufficient.

Interviewer:
What more is needed, do you think?

1st Grange-ite:
Oh, manners, a bit of personality, and comparable interests with other people, and that sort of thing.

Interviewer:
Would you be concerned about local political developments in Bradstow? The question say of whether a building should be built out here or whether a quarry should go in somewhere. Would that concern you?

1st and 2nd Grange-ites in unison:
My word, oh yes, my very word.

2nd Grange-ite:
> My very word. That's why I made the protest about the blasting of the quarry. I am most concerned about local development. I think they have made some grave mistakes, particularly in the building of a couple of motels which do not fit in with the landscape at all.

Interviewer:
> Is this something you think as Grange-ites you would have more say over?

1st Grange-ite:
> No. Grange-ites have less say because as a matter of principle anything we say is trodden on.

Interviewer:
> You don't think your position in society gives you a stronger sway over what the council does.

1st Grange-ite:
> It gives you less, gives you less.

In a similar manner to the bosses, the Grange-ites reject the evidence of their influence and fall back on stereotyped ideologies but in the course of conversation they give themselves away, emphasising those very status characteristics that make them Grange-ites. The fact that the Grange-ites' reaction to Bradstow was the most virulent of all is partly explained by the gap between their behaviour and their beliefs when asked to state them in a public arena. They are the status seekers par excellence, but they do not like to be seen in this light. Some Grange-ites invited a Sydney friend on a ski-ing holiday. When the book appeared one evening in the ski lodge, the Grange-ites' comments were 'What are you reading that radical rubbish for?' and 'Don't show that book around here'. They want to forget the evidence of Grange-ite prestige and power and all its implications for their rationalised beliefs and return to their exclusive world of the golf club, old-boy networks, dinners and cocktail parties.

The gentry, as far as I know, have maintained their traditions and offered no comment.

Reactions such as those outlined are not surprising in a study of this nature and they parallel the effects noticed in similar studies overseas. Nor is it surprising that the status groups react in different ways, for they perceive the study from varying perspectives. Each group, especially the tradesmen, bosses and Grange-ites, has attempted to defeat the book and its results in their own way so enabling them to return to everyday life as though nothing had happened.

There were some tangible effects. Some of the bosses established a property development company called Bradstow Industries Proprietary Limited. Social planners, development consultants, politicians' research assistants and people concerned with the care of the aged have all used some of the data for their own purposes. However, the effect on the behaviour of the townspeople has been minimal. There was almost certainly a greater impact on lay people from other towns and cities who read the book. Personally removed from the data, they were more easily able to see the implications of such a sociological analysis. Judging from the letters and comments I have received, many were able to transpose the Bradstow data onto their own social situations. Through this process such studies help, to borrow a phrase from John Rex, to demystify the modern world for the educated layman.[29]

As Richard Simpson commented,

> Studies of communities in depth are not only the raw material for cross-community comparisons; they are valuable in themselves. Even if we take the construction of abstract theories as the major goal of sociology, an additional goal is to shed light on how people live, here and now, in a way that cannot be done without the insights of sociology. It is significant that a goodly number of community case studies have made their way into commercial paperback editions; this seems to indicate that the educated reading public outside the field accepts community studies as a contribution to social understanding in which sociologists excel in a distinctive way.[30]

NOTES AND REFERENCES

1. Glass, R. 'Conflict in Cities in de Reuck', in A. & J. Knight (eds), *Conflict in Society*, Churchill, 1966, p.143. For further discussion on this type of criticism, see Bell, C. & Newby, H. *Community Studies*, Allen & Unwin, 1971, Chapter I.
2. Vidich, A. J., Bensman, J. & Stein, M. R. *Reflections on Community Studies*, Wiley, 1964, p. ix.
3. Vidich *et al.*
4. Dahrendorf, R. *Essays in the Theory of Society*, Stanford University Press, 1968, pp.151-78.
5. These involved the problem of travel and a low budget. My scholarship was worth A$3250 per year and I had no other source of research expenses.
6. There are, of course, status divisions within the Grange-ites. See pp.42-48. of R. A. Wild, *Bradstow: A Study of Class Status and Power in A Small Australian Town*, Angus and Robertson, 1974; reprinted 1976. One solicitor's wife, for example, referred to the Real Estate Agents' wives as 'the blue rinse brigade'. Nevertheless, they mix together at the Golf Club and refuse membership to those who are in trade in the town.
7. For further details see Wild, pp.47-48.
8. See Wild, pp. 41-42.
9. See Wild, pp.93-95.
10. See Wild, p.84 and pp.93-95, respectively.
11. Gans, H. J. *The Levittowners*, Allen Lane, 1967, p.440.
12. For further details, see Wild, Appendix A.
13. See, for example, *Newsletter of the American Anthropological Association* 12, 3 (1971), concerning ethics and fieldwork.
14. Becker, H. S. 'Problems in the Publication of Field Studies', in Vidich *et al.*, p.275.
15. Vidich, A. J. & Bensman, J. 'Comment on Freedom and Responsibility in Research', *Human Organisation* 17 (1958), p.5.
16. In one or two cases I did change the occupation in the text to avoid embarrassment. None of the occupations were changed in the survey data.
17. See Vidich, A. J. & Bensman, J. 'The Springdale Case', in Vidich *et al.*, *Reflections*, pp.313-349.

18. Moffitt, I. 'Review of *Bradstow*', *The Australian*, 10 August 1974.
19. Plowman, P. T. 'Review of *Bradstow*', *The Bulletin*, 27 July 1974.
20. Edwards, J. 'Review of *Bradstow*', *The Financial Review*, 9 August 1974.
21. For a discussion concerning W. Lloyd Warner's generalisations from his community studies, see Kornhauser, R. R. 'The Warner Approach to Social Stratification', in R. Bendix & S. M. Lipset, *Class, Status and Power*, Free Press, 1953, 1st edn, pp.224–255; and Bell, C. & Newby, H. *Community Studies*, pp.189–199.
22. On the comparability of Australian community studies, see Wild, R. A. 'Localities, Social Relationships and the Rural-Urban Continuum', *Australian and New Zealand Journal of Sociology* 10, 3 (1974), pp.170–176.
23. Williams, M. 'Review of *Bradstow*', *The Sydney Morning Herald*, 28 September 1974.
24. See, for example, *New Society*, 31 October 1974, p.30; *Australian and New Zealand Journal of Sociology* 11, 1 (1975), p.69; *Sociology* 9, 2 (1975), p.377; *Sociological Bulletin* 23, 2 (1974), pp.257–259.
25. See Wild, *Bradstow*, p.126.
26. This approach is described in Wild, *Bradstow*, p.123; pp.127–28.
27. Wild, *Bradstow*, p.122; p.128.
28. Wild, *Bradstow*, p.77 and pp.86–89.
29. Rex, J. *Sociology, the Demystification of the Modern World*, Routledge & Kegan Paul, 1975.
30. Simpson, R. L. 'Sociology of the Community: Current Status and Prospects', *Rural Sociology* 30, 2 (1965), p.149.

WORDS, DEEDS AND POST-GRADUATE RESEARCH

Bill Bottomley

A senior colleague remarked recently about students with a 'radical' orientation to social science: 'They can be as anti-positivist as they like in the classroom, but when they come to actually do some field research they'll all end up being empiricists, like just about everybody else.' I had to agree with him, though reluctantly. The conventional wisdom of social science — its world-taken-for-granted — is still at bottom positivist/empiricist, despite the clearly heterodox condition of social science theory at the moment. To borrow an image from Koestler, the unexamined assumptions of positivist/empiricist orthodoxy 'are diffused through all the strata of the social sciences like the invisible bubbles of air are diffused in the waters of a lake, and we are the fish who breathe them in all the time through the gills of intuition'.[1]

This chapter is about doing research, specifically postgraduate research, in such an atmosphere of orthodoxy. I have written elsewhere about this at a more formal and abstract level:[2] this chapter focuses more on the personal, experiential dimension. In particular, it is my contention that a sort of intellectual Gresham's Law operates, in which the higher ideals of scholarships and scientific advance are driven out, mediated or otherwise made subservient to the more practical demands of the research experience; the chief demand being the necessity not to violate too much the world-taken-for-granted of orthodox social science.

Six years ago, in 1971, I enrolled to do a postgraduate research degree; in 1975 I abandoned the project unfinished. The experience of those intervening four years moulded most of the ideas in this chapter. The substantive content of the research I was doing is not central to the matters I am discussing here, though I will refer to aspects of it where the context warrants. But mainly I am concerned here to try to document the way my research experience shaped and moulded some of the ideas I have come to hold about the enterprise of social science.

I enrolled for the higher degree in 1969, but it was not until late in 1970 that I finally settled on a topic. Even then it was after many false starts — two of them quite time-consuming and fairly well advanced — before I discovered that for various reasons I would have to jettison them. One of these interests — an investigation of the effects of technological innovation in industry on the family life of workers — had led me to spend some time among coal miners on the New South Wales south coast. At the time, in best Lazarsfeldian tradition, I thought of this work as the 'exploratory participant-observation' phase of my research. So much of what I set about doing as a keen and diligent researcher seems almost astonishingly naive to me when I look back on it now. I really believed then that the only rigorous way to go about things was to eventually get to a stage where I could operationalise my hunches and submit them to the test of empirical observation. Yet the more I worked towards such methodological goals, the more trivialised everything I was doing became. And the longer I spent in the field, the more I kept coming across potentially more interesting questions to look at — questions that I was forced to ignore in order to get on with the business of being scientific and rigorous. In the end, one of these other interesting questions continued to thrust itself onto my attention until eventually it became The Topic of the thesis. I was then spending a good deal of my time in the field 'participant-observing' with a small group of coal miners who also happened to be Communist Party members. I was repeatedly struck by the conventional conformist/consumer cast to much of their lives, despite sincere socio-political convictions on their part to the contrary. Further, they were apparently oblivious to the discrepancies which seemed obvious to me as an outsider. So I resolved to make this question the focus of my research, using the miners as an outcropping of what is a more generalised phenomenon. I tentatively titled the project: 'An Investigation of the Discrepancy between Belief and Behaviour'.

While I was going through these preliminary stages of sorting out a viable topic I felt inadequate, a bit flighty and scatterbrained even, because I kept changing topics. Even though I was aware that many other students doing higher degrees had been through the same hoops, the sheer weight and subtle pervasiveness of mainstream orthodoxy was such that I didn't seriously entertain the possibility that this indecisiveness on my part might stem from structural faults in the system I was working within. After all, the process had been developed by generations of scholars much abler than I was, and I would have felt arrogant to question it too trenchantly. I hadn't realised how back-to-front this part of the postgraduate research experience really is, how out of kilter it is with the way historians and philosophers of science have shown us so much scientific advance comes about. I began to realise just how much doing research as a postgraduate student in the social sciences is a highly artificial business (unless you are very lucky). Not only is it common for students to enrol for the degree without having a question in which they are genuinely interested, but finding a suitable (and tractable) topic is made even more difficult by the minimal resources available to most postgraduate students. Aside from the limitations imposed by the convention that such research will nearly always be done solo,[3] there are stringent constraints stemming from lack of money and lack of time. Although most tertiary institutions have a certain degree of flexibility in the time they allow for completion of a postgraduate thesis, there is nonetheless a sense of urgency about the whole business. Anyone who has had a topic turn into a blind alley after a couple of years' work will know what I mean — especially if they are reliant upon some form of subsidy or scholarship for their livelihood during the period of the research. My own feeling of urgency was also reinforced by the solicitous queries from friends and colleagues: 'How's the thesis coming along?', 'When do you think you'll be finished?' and so on. The questions were genuine enough, but they heightened my awareness that I was involved in completing a *package* and that I had only a finite time in which to do it, especially since eighteen months had passed already and I had just changed my topic for the third time. In other words, I realised that whether or not you get off to a good start depends a lot on luck.

What strikes me as interesting, in retrospect, is the way people viewed my tardy topic change as a problem, as though I were opting to handicap myself, in effect. It seemed as though there was more concern for the smooth passage of my *degree* than there was for the progress of any *ideas* in the research itself. I would have found it encouraging if more people had supported my decision to research a question that I had become genuinely intrigued by, rather than getting that uncomfortable look in their eye and cautioning me to be practical. 'Don't be misled by that "significant and original contribution to knowledge" business', said the old hands, 'What a Ph.D. really does is demonstrate that you have satisfactorily completed your apprenticeship and are eligible to join the club'. 'Don't try to buck it. Get the ticket their way first and then be critical.' It is this pragmatic aspect of postgraduate research — the fact that ultimately it is a process that has more to do with accreditation than with knowledge — that makes it much safer to stick to conventional and orthodox research techniques and noncontroversial topics and theoretical positions. Besides, the stakes for a student are pretty high, and to take risks with four or five of the most vital years of one's life takes a brave student indeed (or one who cares little for the ticket at the end). Everyone, including Ph.D. examiners, operates more comfortably in a world they can take for granted, and theses which do not upset the disciplinary world-taken-for-granted can look forward to a smoother passage than more innovative, creative or speculatively questing attempts. Gradually I was beginning to learn the informal rules for survival: don't take the ideals too seriously, and above all be 'practical'. As I experienced each of the major phases in the research process, the same message was reinforced; and I began to realise that the disparity between belief and behaviour, or ideals and action, or words and deeds, is just as evident among social researchers as it is among coal miners.

After I had been working on the belief/behaviour topic for about eighteen months, I was asked by my supervisor for a progress report. In this report, I spent some time explaining the various methodological considerations that had led me to work with south-coast miners. Previously, having decided to concentrate my interest on all of those miners who were communist (because they had an identifiable set of beliefs about society which they formally subscribed to), I had been considerably taken aback to find that there were only twenty in the area. One of these was a hospitalised pensioner on his last legs and another was over seventy and could no longer speak coherently. But I came up with an explanation for why I should stick with the other eighteen — couching it in terms of the entire universe being accessible, and the need to minimise the intrusion of confounding variables. Not that I did this with any conscious cynical intent — it was simply one of those explanations which were needed to make the research methodologically acceptable. But nowadays I would say that I used those men as my sample because it was with them that the question originated. I was among them because my previous topic had taken me there, and the way their behaviour contradicted their espoused beliefs kept intruding itself as a question. Why go somewhere else when I knew these men well already, and had established a useful rapport with them? It was as good a place as any to look closer at the matter. But if I felt such things at the time, I certainly didn't consider talking about my sample choice in those terms. I still think that to do so would have been foolhardy in practical terms, because honest reporting is not always acceptable science. Throughout my field experiences, I was constantly struck by the fact that social existence is disordered, ambiguous and humanly messy (and this applies to the researchers as well as to the researched); yet we try to make sense of the social world with methods that are conspicuously unable to take account of this messiness, and which appear stainless, sanitised and hopelessly inappropriate in comparison to the subject matter.

It is in the realm of data-gathering techniques that the discrepancy between the ideal and the real — what the textbooks say, compared to what really happens — is most apparent. Somehow it doesn't seem to matter how much you read about research methods and their problems, once you experience the research process at first hand in the field, when you are genuinely *involved* with a research question of your very own, the understanding you previously had seems to take on a new dimension. In my own case, this deepening of understanding most often took the form of a heightened awareness of the amount of almost unconscious self-deception that is necessary if one's work is to have a patina of 'scientific' respectability — of how much gets swept under the rug in order to mould real life experience into a shape that will fit the categories of a positivist/empiricist social science. This happened to me in a number of ways, and I'll recount some of those instances which are conspicuous in my memory.

One day I was talking with a group of communist miners over a beer or several,[4] and the conversation had drifted around to the necessity for a revolutionary solution to society's problems. 'But if you're prepared to blow up the pit when the crunch comes', I said to one, 'would you still do this if you knew it was going to kill a whole bunch of your non-communist workmates?'. His response was a little hesitant, but in the end he said he would be prepared to do this. My own *feeling* at the time was that in other circumstances his answer might well have been negative. I suspected that his reply had something to do with some of the other people present in the group, but there was no way I could check on this. The man I was talking to was a rank-and-file Party member, but also present were two Party functionaries, and my suspicion was that I got the answer I did because he wanted to be seen to be tough-minded and committed. But if my suspicions were well-founded, there was no way that I could see to check it out, because of the socially sensitive nature of the matter. No matter how I might have chosen to push the question further, either there or alone with him later, I realised that the delicacy of the topic, and its implications for his identity and 'presentation of self' meant that any answers he might give would be at best highly suspect. So, because it would have been socially awkward for me to pursue the matter further, I let it drop. (Methodology books tend to underestimate the amount of compromise in research techniques that arise from social constraints in the actual research context itself.) Subsequently, in a different context (this time in the respondent's own home, where I had eaten with them and would stay the night), I taped him answering 'No' to the question mentioned above (though it should be admitted that the question was approached differently this time). But the partial corroboration of my earlier suspicion set off a train of questions, many of which I still cannot answer. What was I to call his first response? According to many texts I should record a 'Yes' because that was, after all, the verbal utterance (observed behavioural outcome?). On the other hand, I could hardly call it a 'No' just because I had a strong feeling in my water about it. And 'Don't know' would have been an unsatisfactory category. Maybe the most honest and truly scientific thing to do would be to record it as closely as possible in all its ambiguity? But what implications does that have for the later processes of classification and analysis? (Some of these thoughts were to make me initially very receptive to the ideas of the ethnomethodologists when I came across them some time later.) But which of his responses, the positive or the negative, was *really* his answer? Was there necessarily only *one* correct answer for him? It would seem that the context was an important mediating factor. Maybe context was crucial and should always be specified? (Which, in turn, attracted me to some of the ideas of the symbolic interactionists.) But what if he didn't have any personally felt belief on the matter at all? What if he had never seriously thought about it before? How could I know if his response was merely an action called for by the social dynamics of the occasion on which the question was asked, and he was just being seen to be saying *something* — as expected? Or could he perhaps have genuinely felt both the positive and the negative responses on each different occasion? Maybe we assume too much consistency in people?

The ideas of Berger and Luckmann about the social construction of reality were the next to take their toll. If *all* human perceptions (including those of social researchers) are mediated by the perceiver's own subjective interpretations, then what are the consequences of this insight for us when we observe and record an event? Just what *is* an 'event', then? Even more contentious, what is the *meaning* of a given event? Take the following instance: I was told by one miner that militancy in the pits was on the decline. He nostalgically related stories of men underground who would throw handfuls of bolts into the gearbox of a continuous mining machine in order to disrupt production. To him, this was a display of healthy anti-boss sentiment, and an example of militancy. But I referred to this practice in conversation later with another miner (also a communist) and, although he recognised the phenomenon, he said it didn't happen all that often, and was only irresponsible larrikinism anyway. Which was it? Can we know for sure? How useful is such information to shed light on industrial militancy? Of course, disagreement between respondents is common enough in any form of social enquiry, but what if a respondent says that something happened and you, the researcher, think it didn't? Who is right? How can you assign any primacy to either view? So what do you do? Ask everyone else present (assuming you're lucky enough that there are more than two of you in the episode?) And then presumably you end up with the 'event' being that which most agree on. Which is only another way of saying that the notion of 'objectivity', so dearly cherished by so many, is just another word for 'majority opinion'. (Mannheim's distinction between relativism and relationalism proved to be some help in untangling some of the strands in that particular knot, and the recognition of this essentially *social* aspect of objectivity prepared the ground for later realisations about the social nature of scientific endeavour as a whole.)

I am sure that anyone with field experience will recognise what I am talking about. Only the most heavily blinkered have not had to confront squarely the profound ambiguity and often sheer unintelligibility of so many social situations from which we draw our data — no matter how we may choose to 'draw' them. As Pirsig says: 'We take a handful of sand from the endless landscape of awareness and call that handful of sand the world'.[5] And so do the people we are researching. But what I find intriguing is the way the very real problems of knowledge which these thoughts raise are so resolutely ignored. Ignored not only by those who see traditional scientific method as adequate to explain the social world, but also by that subtle, orthodox atmosphere I mentioned at the beginning that covertly implies that the social world is tractable and quantifiable.

I suspect that much of the disaffection with academic social science evidenced by more percipient students stems from their awareness of these problems and the fact that so many professional social scientists seem content to pretend that the problems don't exist. They can see that social scientists are not practising an important part of what they preach. In the university department that employs me for instance, where it *is* acknowledged that there are legitimate methodological considerations that are not quantitative, quantitative techniques nonetheless dominate the courses on research methods — and I suspect that it is much the same in most other Australian universities. At other times, our research methods courses have been labelled 'Measurement', with all of the linear and concrete overtones that word conveys. Not only is the bias predominantly quantitative, but a student majoring in sociology would be unlikely to come into contact with notions like 'studying up' that Colin Bell refers to in his chapter in this book. There is nothing about researching those in positions of power and privilege who are reluctant to divulge information, let alone any systematic and rigorous course on 'muckraking' research or advice on how to find your way through the back-corridors of power and the informal networks therein. (These thoughts helped me realise whose side orthodox social science is on — and the realisation had a stronger impact than when I had earlier read Howard Becker's well-known article on the subject. The fundamentally political nature of social science became heavily underscored as I realised the multitude of ways that the under-privileged and exploited, who are the subject of so much concerned attention from social scientists, always miss out in the end.) I know we all know about this double standard — the ostrich approach to these important epistemological problems — but I kept wondering why, if we all know about it, do we continue to do so little seriously to encourage attacks on the problem? Why is *counting things* still the oxygen in the atmosphere of orthodoxy? Why do we still covertly encourage students, in the name of numeracy, to apply mathematically sophisticated tests to raw data when this can only be done by ignoring the extremely arbitrary and precarious nature of those data?

There is another consideration, which overlaps with the qualitative problems just mentioned. I find it difficult to express, though I have alluded to it earlier, and it has to do with the depth of understanding involved. I don't want to suggest that my undergraduate studies had left me entirely unequipped to do social research. I knew that social data were rarely as straightforward as those of the physical sciences; I knew that you could never be sure when a respondent might be lying; I knew that the respondent may distort his or her response unwittingly, for deep-rooted psychological reasons, and all that. But somehow, merely to 'know' these things is not enough. Bishop Berkeley used the device of subscripts to make a similar sort of distinction to the one I am trying to make here. To borrow from Berkeley, then, perhaps I am trying to capture the difference between the understanding$_1$ something and understanding$_2$ that same something. 'Understanding$_1$' is the rational, cognitive, rather superficial comprehension, whereas 'understanding$_2$' is the full experiential realisation — a qualitatively different kind of awareness. But the snag is that it is not until you reach the level of understanding$_2$ that you realise you were only at the stage of understanding$_1$ previously. This is a most unsatisfactory way to try to articulate what I mean here, but I have wrestled with it for some time and it is the best I can do. Like the taste of passionfruit, it is something that has to be experienced; and if you have experienced what I am talking about, you will know$_2$ what I am trying to describe.

Here is an example of what I am trying to articulate, again from my experiences among coal miners. One of the phrases that became familiar to me was 'there's no such thing as unskilled labour'. I agreed with this, I suppose, though I felt that there was an element of self-justification in it as it was usually said by shiftmen, who were unskilled labourers in the eyes of mine management. About the time I first heard this saying, I made the following field notes from a conversation I had had with a retired miner: 'There is a sort of unconscious physical exhilaration in the work. You can't go underground and shovel for a long time and not get blisters. The experienced man can. There is a knack in knowing how many wedges are needed to fill a space. When a shiftman has put a timber up good and solid you can see 'em walking back with their chest stuck out.' I considered that worth noting after the discussion, but it was, in retrospect, only a superficial appreciation of the meaning of the words — a sort of pale shadow of their full meaning. It wasn't until I had been down several pits and had a go at shovelling grunched coal into skips whose sides were above shoulder height that I *really* knew what he was getting at. After that, when rereading my field notes, I put two fat pentel lines alongside the passage in my notes. I understood$_2$ what was being said in a way that I hadn't before. (Mind you, it had little to do with my thesis, but . . .)

Again, there is nothing new in what I am saying. For instance, Weber's notion of *verstehen* (as I interpret him) is close to the sort of understanding$_2$ that I mean; less scholastically acceptable, we have Robert Heinlein's neologism *to grok* standing for much the same thing.[6] But given that the idea has been around for so long, both inside social science and out, it only makes it all the more fascinating that orthodox social science should so steadfastly ignore its significance, and the important problems of analysis that it brings with it. (Consequently, it was with some enthusiasm that I read Murray Levine's paper on what he calls the 'adversary method'[7], which is grounded in the conviction that human judgements come from *weighing* evidence, not from just counting responses which have been stuffed into (usually only approximate) categories; and it recognises that the *subjectivity* of the researcher mediates that weighing all the time. Such a method challenges the orthodox injunctions that objectivity must be preserved at all costs, yet faces up to the curbs placed on the operation of the questing human intellect by the ideology of traditional scientific method.)

Things had begun to get very spongy indeed. The more I thought about qualitatively different ways of knowing, the more precarious and confusing everything seemed. What is it to *know* something, and how can we be sure about it? Introspecting, I began to see the inconsistent nature of many of my own beliefs, the way the expression of them altered according to context. Which is the one I *really* believe? I saw that in many instances I couldn't answer many of my interview questions even when applied to myself, and I was in much closer touch with my own situation than I possibly could be with that of others. Yet even when I examined them carefully, I was frequently quite unsure of my own motivations for many everyday actions. It seemed unlikely that I could ever manage to investigate the gap between belief and behaviour in others if I had no understanding of it in myself. It seemed to me (and still does) that little can be done on this sector of the epistemological frontier until we understand more about the nature of consciousness — and this will require diverting energy and resources away from current safe research pursuits towards work which has to be done 'out on the edge'. But such work does not enjoy the legitimacy of more orthodox topics, so the chances of anything substantial happening in this regard are slim.

My reading took me from Barzun and Bronowski to Suzanne Langer; from Koestler's stuff on paranormal psychology to the recent material on explorations 'beyond the mechanical mind'. Conventional methods of measuring attitudes via highly sophisticated scaling techniques that I had been taught began to look even more misguided than I had considered them to be in the past. It was like assuming that a cloud is made of concrete and that you can say something useful about it by trying to measure it with a ruler.

Again I felt the atmospheric pressures of the orthodoxy. Up until then I had tended to dismiss, along with most of my colleagues, the recent rekindling of interest in the occult sciences. (I still don't know what to make of most of it.) But writers in this area claimed to be delving into the *hidden,* and that seemed to me to be a pretty good place to start looking for some of the answers to the questions I had. But while I was reading about it (in the best open-minded scientific fashion) I knew I felt strange about it. There was a furtive feeling about it all, and I felt myself wanting somewhat apologetically to justify having books by people like Gurdjieff or Ouspensky on my desk. It was as though it was an admission of intellectual adolescence to be reading such ideas. It is an oddly effective form of scholastic censorship, and I suspect it goes deeper than most academics would care to admit. (Even writers as established as Maslow and Rogers are almost apologetic that some of their ideas and methods are not 'scientific' in the traditional sense — no matter how valid they may be in terms of broader scientific precepts.)

The inadequacy of traditional scientific method alone to cope with the social world was further underlined for me when one of the members of the small group with whom I was most friendly let his Communist Party membership lapse. Over the three years I knew him, his views had changed perceptibly. But because of my friendliness with him, he had been one of the first people I interviewed. From the opinions he was expressing towards the end of my fieldwork (fieldwork: four years of disparate experiences, all of which we are enjoined to assume are commensurable), I felt that a similar interview with him then would paint a different picture of his beliefs than the initial one did. Which one would I say was 'him'? Are we correct in unconsciously assuming so often that a person at Time A is the same person at a later Time B? Time is a crucial variable, and one that it is impossible to hold constant — which violates one of the most basic precepts underlying the hypothetico/deductive method. (I was later to read with vehement agreement Derek Phillips' effective demonstration[8] that the nature of social science subject matter makes it impossible to meet many of the assumptions required by traditional scientific method, and that this has always been so. It also helped me to view the phenomenological notion of 'multiple realities' in a renewed favourable light.) Similarly, not only did the respondents change over time, but so did I as well. My interviewing technique had changed with practice (hopefully, for the better); but so had my perceptions of the problems I was working on. The very problem itself was in a constant state of flux and redefinition as my ideas about things were moved about and reshaped to accommodate significant events and other data inputs as they built up. (Glaser and Strauss' *Discovery of Grounded Theory* is a helpful attempt to capitalise on this and turn it to methodological advantage,[9] but I hadn't read the book then, and was instead overwhelmed by how arbitrary, in the final analysis, are what we decide to call 'data'.) The research experience was for me a cumulative educative process. But this means that each new level of understanding or awareness that I felt I had reached invalidated or made inappropriate much of the previous data that I had gathered, because they were quite often gathered on different assumptions — ones that I had subsequently come to reject. This brought with it serious practical problems, since I was going to have to call a halt and write it all up eventually.

As well as the field thoughts noted above, and a myriad others of a similar kind, the process of classifying and analysing the data collected hammered home the same sort of message. The progressive loss, the increased distortion in the name of generalisation, of the uniqueness of each response and event, became almost painfully evident when it was being experienced directly, compared to being read about. The maxim that abstraction is a defence against complexity took on new force. Not only had the reduction to Gutenbergian 'data' lost everything but the grossest aural aspect of any occasion, but *that* emaciated representation was then *further* distorted to fit the closest homogeneous category that I happened to have created under the blind assumption that an analytic approach was the only thing called for. To think of performing complex mathematical operations on data of that order appeared almost laughable, as one would need faith indeed to expect the resulting numbers to reflect much of truly human relevance to any particular aspect of the social world under study.

Before I decided not to finish the doctorate, I had completed the fieldwork and written about half of the first draft of the thesis. It was during the writing that I felt most acutely the limitations on language that are demanded by scientific respectability and conventions of expression. Again, the result was to leach even more from the human richness of the social world. Assumptions of linearity meant that the dissertative mode conveyed a spurious coherence, a more orderly progression (both actual and theoretical) than is really the case. There was a very bad fit between the means I had to convince an interested reader of my point of view and my own personal experiences in the field. The subjective dimension had been almost completely excised, yet it was often crucial to a full understanding of why I had come to the conclusions I had. (Maybe Nisbet is right, and sociology is more an art than a science.) The sterile mode of serious scientific discourse is quite unsuited to capture the experiential richness of social life, yet to deviate from the convention in this regard makes it that much harder to be taken seriously. Gifted playwrights, poets and novelists seem to come close to communicating human complexity and ambiguity, and looser forms of the novel since the advent of stream-of-consciousness techniques may well prove to be a useful methodological tool in this regard. This perhaps helps explain why so much good sociology is being written these days by non card-carrying sociologists — like Patrick White, Doris Lessing, Tom Wolfe and some sociologically sensitive television scriptwriters (to name a mixed few).

Aside from its bloodlessness, the scientific literary style also has a decidedly mandarin character about it. Because it is really a dialect of the educationally privileged, much of its meaning would be obscure to a reader unpractised in the manipulation of abstract concepts, or with a limited vocabulary. Which means that my knowledge gained about, say, underprivileged groups is largely inaccessible to the underprivileged, and tends to be used against them by the privileged, rather than providing a resource that they (the underprivileged) might use to their own advantage. (It wasn't until a colleague remarked on it after reading the first draft of this chapter that I realised that my whole research operation was an exercise in 'studying down'. No matter how sympathetic I may have been to my 'subjects', I was still engaged in the study and dissection of working-class lives, and investigating the beliefs of the powerless in society.[10] In the final analysis, I was in it for my *own* sake, and for *my* interest, not theirs.) In much the same way, there is a ludicrously large gulf between a real, live, alienated coal miner and the theoretical jargon that describes him as a person 'who is making totalities when he should be making totalisations, springing from his propensity for reification when he need not go past objectivation and objectification.' We may as well be speaking in tongues as far as the coal miner is concerned. This is the Brahmin face of science, and it belies any naive notions about free-floating ideas.

By this time, I had begun to give some consideration to the end portion of the postgraduate process — submission of the thesis, its format, how it is examined and how long that takes. I had already been told that the system could not accommodate a thesis that was not in written form, and that any attempts to utilise other media of expression could not be stored by the library along with all the other 'proper' theses. My arguments that there should be no technological holds barred in most effectively communicating one's ideas fell on deaf ears.

Once again, I *thought* I knew what happened after theses were submitted, but it wasn't until it was *my* thesis that was about to go through the hoops that the inadequacies in the procedure hit me with any real impact. Suddenly it was much more disturbing that it could be rejected because an examiner might turn out to be on the opposite side of the epistemology debate to me. It seemed particularly unsatisfactory that candidates rarely have a right of reply to examiners' criticisms. It seemed almost mediaeval that the student has no formal right to even see the examiners' reports, or to have a say in who the examiners are to be (at my alma mater, anyway). It was this firsthand contact with the bureaucratic dimension of the postgraduate degree process that brought me up against yet another discrepancy between belief and behaviour. More correctly, it is a clash between the ideology of scholarship and the functional needs of the institutions wherein scholarship is carried on (and I say 'carried on' with some deliberation). Just as within scholarship itself scientific ideals become subordinated to everyday practical and social demands, so too are the ideals of scholarship subordinate to university administrative requirements. Ideas 'floated freely' among a 'community of scholars' have a turbulent passage in an atmosphere charged with career interests, departmental jealousies, personal rivalries, status aspirations and disciplinary parochialness other sociological matters, the realities of power can never be left out of account, and consequently considerations of administrative expediency usually prevail. The high ideal of learning being a personal growth experience of crucial importance to each individual becomes translated into lectures, practicals, examinations, and all the other techniques of what passes for education these days. Quantitative competitive assessment procedures cling on tenaciously as the major dynamo behind modern institutionalised education practice, in the face of overwhelming evidence of their inappropriateness and inadequacy.

My conception of social science was now considerably different to the ideas I'd had when I began my research. I came back to Kuhn and Feyerabend and read them again with different eyes. As Gouldner would say, their ideas resonated harmoniously with my changed domain assumptions. It was with that deeper understanding$_2$ again that I realised the implications of the fundamentally *social* nature of *all* scientific enterprise. Science is just as subject to fads, fashions and foibles as any other social activity (though it insists that it isn't), and the sanctified aura we bestow upon it is hugely misplaced. It is this social dimension that explains the shortfall of practice from the higher ideals at all the levels I encountered it, and it made particularly good sense when applied to disputes at the level of abstract theory and to the problems of organising scholarship institutionally. But the ramifications of the intrusion of organisational demands, their situational inflexibility, and their primacy over the more lofty principles traditionally associated with universities go much further than I realised at first. The operational arrangements that prevail in universities are the product of ruling bureaucratic oligarchies who make the rules and who are not elected. Not only are they not elected, but they are also not representative of the various interests within the university (women, for instance) or even accountable for their actions in any wide social sense. Consequently, any activity not within the rules (written or unwritten) is seen as a nuisance, dysfunctional, 'stirring', or even disruptive and worse. The durable links between the university and the *status quo* outside it are most visible at this level of analysis. Mills' 'interlocking directorates' can well be applied to the nexus between the representatives of the institutions of growth-oriented industrialism and university councils. As Anthony Arblaster says: 'That the normal functioning of the institution is itself a political issue, and that the institution may, in its normal activities, serve certain political ends, are suggestions which the oligarchs can afford to ignore. For they can be confident that the politicians, the bulk of the press and the bulk of their own staff will share their apparently neutral preoccupation with order and constitutionality.'[11] Such institutional inertia, bound tightly into its current form by a complex web of sociological factors, makes the acceptance of even small innovations difficult and slow. Small wonder that challenges to sacred scientific assumptions get such short shrift.

I want to stress again that I had become acquainted with most of the ideas I've discussed here during the course of my honours undergraduate degree (though I would still argue that it is too easy to emerge with an honours degree and remain largely sociologically insensitive). I knew a lot of the iceberg was not visible, but it took the research experience to teach me just how extensive is the submarine portion, to use another marine metaphor! Religious terminology always seems apt when talking about science, and in many ways the process for me was rather like giving up religion. For a long time, I lived with the growing realisation of the shortcomings of the prevailing orthodoxy, but not until the crucial link was made between the intellectual realisation and my own *life* could I dare to take the leap of non-faith and say I was now an atheist.

Most colleagues with whom I discuss these matters agree that there is a serious rupture between the way we say things are and the way things actually are. The growing number of books (such as this one) devoted to exposing the vulnerable underbelly of everyday social science attests to the fact that, even if you still think the emperor is wearing *some* clothes, at least his underwear is undeniably grubby. And growing numbers of social scientists are beginning at last to take account of the facts of power and politics which lie behind the fact that he is an emperor. But most people (and social scientists are people) have an uncanny ability to insulate themselves from the implications of their theoretical insights for their own actions. Despite the accelerating demystification of social science, many social scientists still seem to lack a consequential dimension to their 'professional' beliefs. As I mentioned earlier, one result of this is that the menu offered to undergraduates by most Australian social science departments that I know of is still heavily flavoured with positivist assumptions. It is still almost axiomatic that students should confront Chi-Squares before Cicourel.

Not until the majority of social scientists withdraw their tacit assent to the adequacy of traditional scientific assumptions will the hegemony of 'hard' science cease to be legitimated. This would require that social scientists bring their actions into closer line with their ideas. Then perhaps we might be able to get on with the job of asking some bold new questions, interesting and humanly important questions, without being encumbered by the conceptual baggage of an inadequate epistemological philosophy.

For myself, I came to the conclusion that the rite of passage called Ph.D. research demanded a higher personal price than I was prepared to pay for admission to the club. Besides, doggedly sticking to the thesis was preventing me exploring other interesting ideas. It was like a gilt-edged sword of Damocles hanging over me all the time, and it was getting in the way of my education. Not that the experience was not educational; quite the contrary, but the lessons I learned made my continued progression through the expectations of postgraduate study no longer relevant for my own life.

It was rather ironic that soon after formally abandoning the doctorate, I should discover Robert Murphy posing what he sees as 'one of the thorniest questions in social science: What do people really do, and how does this correspond with what they think they are doing and what they think they should be doing?'[12] My research gave me a better understanding of just what is involved in asking that question, and convinced me that if we are ever truly to understand the phenomenon and others like it, we will have to go far beyond the methods and assumptions of the received orthodoxy. And stop kidding ourselves about what we are really doing.

NOTES AND REFERENCES

1. Koestler, A. *The Heel of Achilles*, Picador, 1974, p.29.
2. Bottomley, W. 'The Relationship of the Doctorial Dissertation to Scholarship', *Australian University* 11, 3 (1973).
3. Look at 'Reflections on *An Australian Newtown*' in this book; and see the hoops that Bryson & Thompson were put through when they tried to work for a thesis together.
4. This was an indispensable and unavoidable fieldwork pastime for my topic, and I feel sure most researchers would at some time or another have experienced the difficulties associated with fieldwork and alcohol. Significantly, the textbooks do not address themselves to the matter. It is as though they believe that the human researcher really is an objective observer who is never forced by social circumstances (?) to get drunk and who only goes to the toilet to make furtive and hurried research notes. If we are going to be truly rigorous, as we are so often urged, shouldn't we at least distinguish the sober observations from the drunken ones? But does this suggest we would also have to report on the manic moods of the researcher, as well as the depressive and just plain neutral?
5. Pirsig, R. *Zen and the Art of Motorcycle Maintenance*, Bodley Head, 1974, p.82.
6. See his (sexist) science-fiction novel *Stranger in a Strange Land*, New English Library, 1965.
7. Levine, M. 'Scientific Method and the Adversary Model', *American Psychologist*, September 1974, p.661.

8. Phillips, D. *Abandoning Method,* Jossey-Bass, 1973.
9. Glaser, B. & Strauss, A. *The Discovery of Grounded Theory,* Weidenfeld & Nicolson, 1968.
10. Witton, R. personal communication.
11. Arblaster, A., *Academic Freedom,* Penguin, 1974, p.124.
12. Murphy, R., *The Dialectics of Social Life,* George Allen & Unwin, 1972, p.49-50.

A MARXIST AT WATTIE CREEK

Fieldwork among Australian Aborigines

Hannah Middleton

It is a strange experience writing this. Probably the most exciting and the most frightening aspect of writing an anthropological thesis is fieldwork. Rereading my field journal brings back in sharp focus all the early uncertainties and worries, and the later grief at having to leave what had become a valued home. Not every anthropologist will be fortunate enough to move from shyness and strangeness to respect and love, but with genuine concern for the people among whom we work and a willingness to treat them as individuals and not as subjects this should be possible. And from such an approach the student gains far far more than just research data.

Robert Jay in *Reinventing Anthropology* wrote that:

> In future field work I shall place first a mutual responsibility to my whole self and to those I go to learn from, in agreement with my desire to relate to them as full equals, personal and intellectual. I shall try to use my relationships with them to find out what topics are relevant to each of us, to be investigated through what questions and what modes of questioning, and for what kinds of knowledge. I should wish to make the first report for them, in fact with them; indeed it may be that written reports would seem to us redundant.[1]

In April 1970 I arrived from the icy winds of a Berlin early spring in the humid heat of a dry season in Darwin on the Northern Territory coast. I had travelled widely in Europe and worked briefly in West Africa, but it was my first visit to Australia. I was amazed by the blood-red earth and almost as much by the beer bottles on it. A few weeks later I found my way 'down the track' (learning the new language was very important at that stage) about 580 kilometres south from Darwin to Wattie Creek where the Gurindji people had been squatting, demanding the return of their traditional land, since March 1967. I lived with the people until the end of October and then again from December until mid-January 1971.

Some of my experiences were clearly typical; I began with the usual 'honeymoon' stage when everything is new and exciting, and passed on then to 'culture shock', an awareness of what I missed from my own culture and how clumsy and ignorant I was in theirs. Finally I achieved an adjustment that expressed itself in a sense of belonging, in choices of individuals whose company was a stimulus, and pleasure in an acceptable and accepted work pattern and a position of involvement and partisanship in relation to the goals of the group.

Most of this was at an emotional, subjective level and the painful phase was mercifully brief, partly because of the courtesy and consideration of the Gurindji generally and partly because of my adoption by a particular family not only into their kinship system but also, with considerable patience in training me (and I *never* learnt how to select dead trees to chop down for firewood), into their daily lives. The process was also facilitated by an event that I had not planned: my mother in London wrote regularly to my Gurindji mother. I had to read and explain the letters to her and also write her replies. Those two women, talking through me about me — about me being a good girl, about their other children, about their lives — made a bridge between the two cultures on which I perched, forced to analyse and come to terms with the differences while feeling secure in the love from both sides.

My research was much easier than my subjective life. All the work I could do for the Gurindji (reading and writing letters, discussing their plans and possibilities, speaking for them when instructed to do so, going on all kinds of errands and so on) was as much part of the information I required as was my participation in the events of daily life. My explanation that I wanted to learn about and then write about their strike, their ideas about the land, their relationship with white Australia and their plans for the future, was not only accepted but was approved of and I was actively encouraged, supported and assisted, especially by the senior men.

It is only fair to point out that this situation could hardly have been better for an anthropologist (and if you want to learn about the opposite pole – the hell it can sometimes be – read *The Mountain People* by Colin Turnbull[2]), but in fact it was better. Most of my information came from participating in Gurindji life, keeping my eyes and ears open and getting it down on paper or tape before I forgot anything, but when the role of participant and that of observer might have clashed the Gurindji solved the problem for me.

I had read all the accounts of fieldwork I could before I arrived in Australia and – very properly – I had ideas in my head about how I would deal with the problems that might arise. The one thing for which I had been totally unprepared was the perception, sophistication and authority with which the Gurindji elders themselves dealt with the contradictions that arose.

Early on I learnt which men were my brothers. Brother/sister avoidance is still practised: siblings may not speak or give anything directly to each other, may not use each other's names nor come into physical contact. Quite often, however, it became necessary for me to break these rules. In a personal situation I would be publicly shamed for forgetting that someone was my brother. When it was my turn to sell in the Wattie Creek store or if I was discussing relationships (when doing the periodic checks on who was in camp or working on genealogies) or when I had to travel in an overloaded vehicle on some job, it would be publicly pointed out, the discussion being initiated by an older man and then taken up by everyone else present, that the verbal or physical contact with or the actual naming of the brother was not really proper 'Gurindji way' but that since 'she is working for we, this time she can do it cuddia (white man's) way and no one can swear at her'.

The shuttling from white observer to Gurindji daughter could sometimes get a bit confusing (for me) but the concern to reassure me that I was behaving in an acceptable way was warming. And the situations were often enlivened by humour. My field journal for July 28, 1970, includes the following entry:

> Apparently I was included in the 'Register of Wards' until the Sister realised later ... She was helping the Welfare Officer do the census. M.R. with a straight face apparently included —
> European name: Hannah
> Tribal name: Lauwie
> Skin: nangari
> Tribe: Gurindji
>
> Lauwie is the name of what everyone knows is my favourite place — the beautiful, deep, dark-green, peaceful, permanent rock pool and spring about one mile down the river. From this time on I was always addressed as and referred to as Lauwie or nangari.

Choice

The initial basic problem facing any social anthropologist considering work in the field is 'why?' and 'where?'.

The particular world view — or, more precisely, political orientation — of the individual involved, together usually with unavoidable academic and financial and sometimes chance factors, will finally determine the theoretical and geographical area chosen and the purpose of the research.

In my case the world view is still best expressed in Marx's eleventh thesis on Feuerbach, that 'the philosophers have interpreted the world, in various ways; the point, however, is to *change* it'.

I was reared, academically speaking, in the British school of structural-functionalism with Radcliffe-Brown and

Malinowski as my adolescent culture heroes. Part of my move to Marxist anthropology was concerned with the trauma of finding that Father Christmas Radcliffe-Brown did not come down the chimney with the neat, fitting theoretical models. The theory I did find was only the first, although the crucial step towards understanding and changing the world. As Ho Chi Minh described Marxism, it is 'not a map but a compass'.

Functionalist social anthropology has provided very pretty models showing society as an elegant self-regulating system tending towards equilibrium and stability. This analysis, while often complex and sophisticated, has been so deliberately static that the possibility of an historical approach has been rejected. But the fact that societies do change, even if anthropologists frequently fight shy of studying them when they do so rapidly, shows that a static analysis must be based on a dynamic one.

Marxist historical and social theory has been specifically designed, as no other has, to analyse the simultaneous dialectical play of forces tending constantly to 'destabilise' a society (that is, to make it evolve) and those constantly tending to keep it, sociologically speaking, a going concern.

Marxism has also made an impact on social anthropology not only by the application of certain special ideas, but by the use of the dialectical method. This has chiefly meant an insistence on the historical character of all phenomena and on the fact that historical change proceeds in certain complex but defined ways such as the quantity/quality interrelation, the importance of internal contradictions, and so on.

The dialectical and historical approach is particularly important today in practice as well as in theory, for the chief problem facing social anthropologists now is not the stable and fairly insulated 'primitive society' but 'detribalisation', a term whose very negativeness underlines the limits of a synchronic or static analysis.

There are two significant quotations from Engels that elaborate on and illustrate the materialist conception of the history of human society — the theoretical approach I used as my compass. In his 1883 speech at the graveside of Karl Marx, Engels said:

> Just as Darwin discovered the law of development of organic nature, so Marx discovered the law of development of human history: the simple fact, hitherto concealed by an overgrowth of ideology, that mankind must first of all eat, drink, have shelter and clothing, before it can pursue politics, science, art, religion, etc.; that therefore the production of the immediate means of subsistence and consequently the degree of economic development attained by a given people or during a given epoch form the foundation upon which the state institutions, the legal conceptions, art and even the ideas on religion of the people concerned have been evolved, and in the light of which they must therefore be explained, instead of vice versa, as had hitherto been the case.[3]

And in *The Peasant War in Germany* Engels explains in more concrete terms the way in which he himself had used this approach in his analysis:

> My presentation ... attempted to explain the origin of the Peasant War, the position of the various parties that played a part in it, the political and religious theories by which those parties sought to clarify their position in their own minds, and finally the result of the struggle itself as necessarily following from the historically established conditions of the social life of these classes; that is to say, to demonstrate the political constitution of the Germany of that time, the revolts against it and the contemporary political and religious theories not as causes but as results of the stage of development of agriculture, industry, land and waterways, commodity and money trade, then obtaining in Germany.[4]

When I returned from the field — as so often happens — I considerably altered the original drafts of my thesis. In the new introduction I wrote:

The marxist view of ethnography is that it is an historical science and that the societies studied are at any given time both the result of and undergoing historical processes. Societies are never static; both before and since colonisation of the Australian continent by white men, Aboriginal society has been undergoing changes determined by objective material factors. It is an examination of this process of change and development in the material basis of the society and its reflection in the ideological superstructure — through the specific example of the Wattie Creek Gurindji — that forms the basis of this research.

The developing struggle of the Australian Aborigines against economic exploitation and discrimination, against racial discrimination and for the right to determine their way of life and culture themselves cannot be limited to an analysis covering only a few months. Nor is it sufficient just to fit the contemporary movement into the general constellation of political forces existing in Australia today so as to assess the Aborigines' tactical allies and alignments. A scientific understanding of the developments in Australia can only be obtained by the use of an historical materialist approach: historical in that a political situation at a particular period must be regarded objectively as in dialectical movement; materialist in the sense that these political movements are not the causes but the results of material factors which themselves are subject to dialectical historical change.

I have quoted at some length from my own work partly because it is vital to realise that one of the most important aspects of fieldwork is the writing-up process,[5] whereby the data from months or years in the field are pulled together into a respectable and digestible form. I have and will quote from other authors partly to try to show how essential it is to draw on the experiences and ideas of as many people as possible. Briefly, fieldwork is always complicated and often traumatic, so get as much help as you can.

In terms of my orientation, another point must be considered and that is the question of the relationship between objectivity and partisanship. The most succinct analysis of this that I know was made by the Englist Marxist Maurice Cornforth[6] and so again I will quote at some length from what he said:

> There is no such thing as 'a theory' in the abstract. Theory is made by people, used by people and kept going by people. Without people active in a society there is no theory. So the actual circumstances and interests of people and in particular of people socially related in classes determine how theories are worked out, what questions they deal with and what they say ...
>
> It is an objective fact that *all* social theories are partisan. *Our* partisanship consists in recognising this objective fact. *Their* partisanship consists in denying it and trying to cover it up.
>
> From the very nature of their class position, exploiting classes always have, in theory, to try to cover up the fact of exploitation and class struggle. They cannot recognise the fact of their own way of life, which consists in exploiting and oppressing others. They have to conceal this fact from the exploited ... Thus they are partisan in theory in ways that depart from objectivity. But they practise this partisanship by trying to make out that they espouse objectivity and not partisanship in theory...
>
> We are in no way interested in covering up, distorting and falsifying social reality. On the contrary, we are interested in understanding it as it is, in order to be able to change it. Evading the recognition of fact, distorting it, does not help the working-class struggle at all. On the contrary, the *interest* is as *scientifically* as possible to recognise the facts and understand them.
>
> So working-class partisanship demands objectivity. And *socialism* becomes a *science* — to grasp and understand the objective conditions, the possibilities and necessities contained in them, and to work out, on that basis of scientific understanding of objective fact, what is to be done.

Cornforth also pointed out that value judgements are in fact made in the social sciences (in contrast to the natural sciences) in terms of evaluating what has been and is being done, social aims and methods of achieving them, and so on. He stated that:

> ... for Marxism, the scientific understanding of social reality is the basis for value judgements, and is incomplete without them ... This can be seen clearly, for example, in *Capital.* Marx did not only deliver an *objective analysis* of capitalist society but a *condemnation* of it, based on that very objective analysis. And he did not only make a scientifically-based *prediction* about socialism but a *call* to fight for it with a *practical policy* for doing so.

Given these models for my theory and method, plus the accident of a professor who directed my attention from West Africa to Australia (not without 'withdrawal symptoms' until they were cured by reading Donald Stuart's *Yandy* – an example of what I meant earlier by chance factors), it was logical that I should choose what might be called a politically sensitive area or group to apply to for my fieldwork.

It would probably be useful here to go into some detail about the professor whom I just mentioned, since this will give some additional information about the circumstances and influences that were as much part of the baggage I brought to Australia as the notebooks, camera, taping equipment and so on.

I had graduated in African Studies from the School of Oriental and African Studies (London University) and was working with Professor Frederick Rose at Humboldt University in Berlin, German Democratic Republic. Born in London in 1915, Fred was educated at Cambridge University, England, then came to Australia in 1937 and, funds being scarce, got a job in the north as a meteorologist so he could study the Aborigines. He was first at Groote Eylandt (a small island in the Gulf of Carpentaria off the north coast of Australia) in 1938–39 where he set up a weather station and spent much time living with and investigating the Aboriginal people. He spent five years in north Australia, and for a time after the war worked with the office of Post-War Reconstruction dealing with Aborigines and Industries in the north.

For some years he was persecuted by the Commonwealth Security Police: he was followed, his phone was tapped and mail was opened. This culminated in the 1954 Petrov Commission when he was called as a witness. It is worth pointing out that with not one witness, communist (he had been a member of the Communist Party since 1942) or otherwise, was there sufficient evidence for charges to be laid. It was after this that he was offered the Chair in Social Anthropology at Humboldt University and chose to move to the academic freedom and economic stability of the German Democratic Republic.

In an interview with the Australian newspaper *Newcastle Morning Herald* (28 June 1968) he commented 'there was plenty of smearing, though, and a lot of it stuck. Not that it worries me that much: I'm used to it by now, but it's a pity I can't get to Groote Eylandt'. Here he was referring to the Government's refusal to give him a permit to go to Groote Eylandt in 1968 for research partly funded by the Australian Institute of Aboriginal Studies. The same thing had happened in late 1962 when he was not permitted to enter reserves and settlements in central Australia.

Rose is not alone in suffering from this political discrimination. Several other top-ranking researchers sponsored by academic institutions have been refused permission in the past to enter Aboriginal reserves (and parts of Papua-New Guinea) on the basis of Australian Security Intelligence Organisation reports.

The issues of academic and political freedom involved in such decisions and the permit system generally were well expressed in a letter that Dr Les Hiatt of Sydney University's Anthropology Department wrote to *The Australian* on 7 June 1968:

'The Government's decision to prevent Professor Rose from carrying out anthropological research on Groote Eylandt exemplifies the kind of State tyranny from which such decisions are allegedly preserving us. Under the permit system, authorities in many parts of Australia have the right to decide who may enter an Aboriginal reserve. This is a continuation of the old policy of protection, which assumes that the Aboriginals need to be protected both from themselves and from unscrupulous white adventurers. Naturally, there is no provision for the possibility that Aboriginals might need to be protected from the authorities.

Nor is there ever any official admission that the system helps to protect the administration itself from adverse criticism.

This is by no means the first occasion on which the authorities have shown a willingness to obstruct the work of social scientists sponsored by reputable academic institutions.

In no case has the Government, in preventing or hindering them from proceeding with their scientific work, indicated what it is afraid of. Mr. Wentworth [then Minister of Aboriginal Affairs] has said that Professor Rose has 'a particularly bad record of treachery and of prostituting his position as an anthropologist to further the aims of communists'.

The minister may or may not be able to substantiate these allegations made under parliamentary privilege; but in either case it would be interesting to know what harm he thinks Professor Rose could do. Although the latter has spent lengthy periods on Groote Eylandt since 1938, he seems to have failed completely to convert the people to Marxism.

If he really wished to stir up trouble among the natives, he could spend his time in Australia much more effectively around cattle centres in the north, or even among Aboriginals now living in working-class suburbs of our major cities. Mr. Wentworth has brought a new style to Aboriginal affairs and deserves the full support of all who wish to see the cause of Aboriginals advanced. Already he is in danger of being called a 'red' by sectional interests who want him to give up his attempts to obtain land for the Gurindji. I have no wish to embarrass him over the Rose case, but the incident raises a wider issue with which Mr. Wentworth must come to terms.

To revert to my earlier point about the choice of where to work, it was clear that my acknowledged wish for integration of theory and practice, a unity of academic and political work, just underlined the nature and direction of this choice. The following historical outline is intended to indicate why it was equally logical that ultimately I contacted the Gurindji people in the Northern Territory for permission to live and work with them.

Aboriginal history in Australia is about 40 000 years old, a time in which a complex stable society was evolved which was a highly sophisticated adaptation to the environment and was based on an incredibly detailed and intimate knowledge of that natural environment, on communal ownership of the basic means of production — the land — and on reciprocity between groups and individuals.

In only half of one per cent (less than 200 years) of that time, white colonisation and settlement have destroyed the traditional economy and the social and spiritual life of nearly all the people, as well as causing the physical death of hundreds of thousands of them. For those who did survive the white intrusion, the changes were appalling: seminomadic hunters and gatherers became sedentary unskilled cheap labourers and free self-determining people became degraded dependents.

The mission and government settlements established when the Aborigines were expected to die out became pools of controlled cheap labour, while official policy and legislation were designed to control Aboriginal movement and labour power as the people were slowly moved into the labour force. The gradual but accelerating process of ethnic[7] consolidation (whereby the old, narrow tribal affiliations broke down and were replaced by new, wider bonds) that was inevitable among the Aborigines under the impact of white colonisation tended more and more to take the form of proletarianisation (involvement in the money-commodity economy as members of the working class) as white society began to realise and exploit their labour potential in particular fields but especially in the pastoral (beef cattle) industry in the north.

Political consciousness and protest action in a modern form began to develop among the Aborigines during and after the Second World War. The political and social struggle that has grown among black Australians since the war is an integral part of the world-wide national liberation movements. What has and is occurring in their fight against the form of colonialism existing in the Australian continent is an example of the extraordinarily rapid growth of liberation consciousness and organisation among a numerically small people. Scarcely twenty years before the Gurindji first took action, the majority of the Aborigines in the north were still living in a hunting and collecting society or had just emerged from it and were held in subjection by monopoly capitalism under conditions that were more like slavery than wage labour. The development of their struggle nor emancipation and self-determination has gone hand in hand with the extremely rapid growth of their consciousness and political organisation. Before the war the Aborigines' horizon was bounded by the tribe or local group; today their movement is Australia-wide and they have developed from an amalgam of separate units into a national minority.

In 1942 an industrial award was established which covered white workers in the pastoral industry in the Northern Territory. In 1948 the North Australian Workers Union applied for a review of the award seeking that Aboriginal pastoral workers should be included within its provisions. The application was rejected.

Under the influence of international and internal pressures and also the fear of the threat posed by a cheap Aboriginal labour force, in 1965 the North Australian Workers Union again applied — in what became a test case on equal wages for Aborigines — to the Commonwealth Conciliation and Arbitration Commission, asking that the clauses in the Cattle Station Industry (Northern Territory) Award discriminating against Aboriginal workers should be deleted.

In March 1966 the decision of the Commissioners was handed down. It agreed to the removal of the discriminatory clauses but a 'slow worker' clause was added whereby the pastoral employers were free to designate any of their Aboriginal employees as slow workers and to pay them less than the award rate. In addition, the Commissioners accepted the argument that full award wages should be introduced gradually and set 1 December 1968 — almost three years later — as the deadline for their full implementation.

The reaction to the decision was swift and for many startling. On May 1st Aboriginal pastoral workers from Newcastle Waters station went on strike and most of them left the station with their families. They were followed shortly afterwards by employees from the British monopoly Vesteys station at Wave Hill and a number of its out-stations together with workers from some of the out-stations of the Victoria River Downs holding (owned by the Hooker corporation). The majority of these strikers were Gurindji although there were members of other local groups among them, predominantly from the Bilinara and Mudbara people, and the stations they had worked on were all in the west of the Northern Territory and within 240 kilometres of Wattie Creek. By the end of the month most of the strikers and their families had moved to a temporary camp on the banks of the Victoria River near the Wave Hill Welfare Settlement.

In 1970 the story of the walk-off was a favourite, an epic told to visitors and at meetings as well as informally with individuals adding their personal anecdotes to the mainstream of the story. I remember particularly Lily Punai, a woman of about 50. She was doing the ironing at Wave Hill homestead where she was employed as a domestic. A white stockman came in and told her that everyone had gone and asked if she would stay. She said she would go. She put the iron away, rolled her swag, and set out alone to walk about 24 km through the bush to join her people.

In its early stages the Gurindji action could be and was

easily categorised as an industrial dispute and the influence of unionists both before and during the strike is recognised. But in March 1967 the people took a further step which, from personal accounts and written sources, seems to have been exclusively their own decision and to have taken most of their supporters by surprise. They moved their entire camp to Wattie Creek and a month later, at their request, were helped to send a petition to the Governor-General asking for the return of 1300 square kilometres (500 square miles) of their traditional land.

It was this group, the Gurindji at Wattie Creek, that I wrote to from Berlin and later contacted in Darwin, asking for permission to live and work with them for a year.

Arrival
My field journal for Thursday, 21 May 1970, reads:

> Blood-red earth interspersed with grey stretches and dry creek beds. New road being graded with plenty of detours. Dust and strong winds — you go grey and eat and breathe it all the time. I am anxious for the camera.
> Wattie Creek at last ... The wind is hellish ...
> Flies!!
> Rigged up tent as a windbreak — Unpacked and sorted out food and dishes. Made lunch of tinned meat and potatoes. Wood and water brought up for us already and a small fireplace of bricks built ready for us. Cooking in the open in this wind is almost impossible ... Later sat around with some of the old men and a billy of tea, yarning in the dark. Clouds like lace before the moon. Night never really dark but like an English late twilight with a million stars I cannot recognise. And the wind goes down in the evening.

The initial impressions were entirely of powerful natural beauty, considerable physical discomfort and great confusion. People moved often between camps that appeared to be randomly scattered, they did not always seem to end up the day in the same camp and the flies and the dogs attacked me with dedicated persistence while the rounded, weathered hills grew purple in the evenings, the earth was a colour I had never imagined before and the gums were as white and gaunt as I had expected. Human and natural phenomena combined to overwhelm me.

I had been taught that there was only one rule for good fieldwork — be patient and flexible. And looking back it seems to me that this is the best lesson I was taught, for I just relaxed and decided not to do any work for at least two weeks. And in those two weeks I not only began to enjoy life but I slipped relatively painlessly into the resocialisation phase.

23 May 1970:
>   Made my first damper which came out pretty well and was praised by P. and M.
>   While sitting in the sun and wind I showed around photos of my family to several women who showed great interest. The men all crowded round too. Wrote the names in the sand. Washed clothes. S. and M. deputed to help me... then we had tea together and gossiped.

Adjustment
As I described earlier, my role was quickly and explicitly established for me by the Gurindji themselves and my training as a daughter was conscious even when the expectations were waived. My period of resocialisation was therefore relatively easy and brief (although in the first month or so, when I felt the need to refer back to my own culture, I learnt parts of Jane Austin's *Pride and Prejudice* almost by heart) but it is only fair to point out that this is not always the case.

Rosalie Wax writes:

>   During this first stage of fieldwork, the fieldworker lives in a kind of social limbo, trying to behave as if he 'belonged' and as if he knew what he was doing...
>   Indeed, it is no accident that the few professionals who tell

us anything about their first-stage, pre-involvement experiences, almost always adopt a comic or whimsical style. Painful and humiliating experiences are easier to talk about 'if one does not take them too seriously, and it is less distressing to picture oneself as a clown or a figure of fun than as a dolt or a neurotic'.

Once this stage has been passed, the fieldworker reaches one of three conclusions — that with an increasing sense of relaxation and competence he or she can begin useful work, or that it is just not possible to do the research projected, and/or that fascinating new areas of research have appeared.

If this seems too brief an examination of the most crucial and trying phase of fieldwork, I can only point out that my experience of it was remarkably agreeable and problem-free. The best weapons with which to meet it are, as I pointed out, patience and flexibility. In addition, it is a specific concrete problem that varies in time and place so that general advice must be of limited use.

The student who expects to be told precisely how to construct this kind of field relationship would do well to read a number of the available descriptions carefully. If he has the wit to be a good fieldworker, he will perceive how different were each of these situations and he may also understand why honest and experienced fieldworkers frequently tell beginners that there is not much they can tell them, because each situation differs from every other.[8]

The role or roles that fieldworkers find may be waiting for them or may be created by their hosts alone or with the fieldworker. One thing roles can never be is simply adopted or assumed by fieldworkers. The choice, both morally and pragmatically, must lie with the members of the receiving society. And the roles are best played or assumed by fieldworkers who are conscious of their place in their own culture but able to learn to be conscious of and to respect what their hosts are and what they want the fieldworker to be.

Again there is no precise instruction or advice which can be given to facilitate this, just as my initial reading and training were a poor preparation for many of the personal (usually with white Australians) and practical hazards I found I had to face.

Hazards
It occurs to me, looking back now, how much I enjoyed experiences that were mildly hazardous or unpleasant while contacts that were decidedly difficult still leave bitter memories. Perhaps it would be best just to quote here some entries from my field journal and hope that you reach the same conclusion that I have — that a fieldworker must have a sense of humour, a strong constitution and unlimited curiosity.

24 June 1970:
> A gasket has gone on the Toyota so I ended up cutting a new one from a piece of leather (so that is what a gasket is) and climbing over the truck with a spanner putting it back with B. who fortunately seems to know about engines.

2 August 1970:
> Several more people are sick ... I went round with the thermometer, finding several between 39 and 40, so I handed out fever-reducing pills and prayed the flu epidemic does not hit too hard. J. has a bad cold too and A. is boiling up eucalyptus leaves for him to drink in between feeding me tinned cake for lunch.

13 August 1970:
> An old door and old nails and bits of wood were taken from K.'s camp and brought up to mine — 4 nails held the door to 4 legs and I had a shaky table. ... I cleaned out all the boxes and loaded the table up — very proud — and in classic style it collapsed slowly sideways scattering my lunchtime cup of tea all over letters, notes, etc. Rescuers rushed up and

we hammered lots more nails in ... and it felt more secure so I put everything on it again and this time it stood!

15 August 1970:
Got up feeling ill — temperature, shaky and chest pains (bronchitis?). A. put me in a bed in the shade and W. put her hand on my chest and sat with me for hours. M. wailed. G. was worried and said he could not eat while I was sick and then he found and cooked beef and onions for me 'to eat properly' at lunchtime. Finally I staggered upright to stop W. going on foot to the Settlement to get the Sister ...
In the evening ... J. made a fire for me by the tent to keep warm by. G. said, 'Look at me, my daughter. You look beautiful. Before you were crook, but now your face has really changed.' J. said that they had to look after me and had been afraid that I — a white person — would die at Wattie Creek.

6 September 1970:
Threatening rain — a lot of cloud and *very* hot and somewhat humid. And willy-willys of frightening force rushing through the camp. The dogs go insane and it takes ages to find anything afterwards and to clean up the swags and rebuild. The first couple terrified me but I am getting used to them now.

7 September 1970:
Went shopping to the Welfare Settlement. The car steering broke en route and we ended up in a konkerberry bush — *very* spiky. Mended it with wire and continued. Who needs *Notes and Queries*?[9] — I should have a motor mechanic's handbook and a nursing qualification.

10 September 1970:
One of the puppies rescued from the policeman's gun has bitten my leg and it has gone septic.

20 September 1970:

About midnight sterilised a **needle in the camp fire** and with Savlon, and lanced my leg — **quite disgusting** but at least the pain is reduced so I can **walk** ... went back to bed only to be woken to move the **books and the child** J. into the tent because of rain. Storm **and high winds so no sleep.**

24 September 1970:
Despite the rain, water for **drinking and washing all** comes now from soaks in the river **bed** ... **The water is poor and** the work of ladling it out and **into drums and then** carrying it with a yoke up the cliff side **is backbreaking.** How the hell do I keep my leg clean **with only 2 bandages** left and lousy water — I boil them in **salt water** and put them on immediately but am not sure **if this will work** — and dust and flies don't help.

27 September 1970:
In the late afternoon B., stripped **to the waist, began** running up and down and swearing. **He threw a couple of** spears and clashed boomerangs ... **His wife** ... **wanted to come** up to me for protection ... **on the grounds that she is my** sister but on the assumption **that this would work** because B. would keep away because **I am white.** L. interfered on the grounds that despite her **claim on me as a sister** which was justified, as a white I **could not be involved** in the row because B. was so furious that **he could not be trusted** to keep away and it was not right **that spears should start** flying around her (L.'s) sister and it **was unthinkable** that a white person should be injured in **that way** at Wattie Creek.

27 December 1970:
[The policeman, who had already **questioned** me two times was reported as commenting that] **because I wore no** powder on my face or perfume and **because of the way I** dress and am living, I have lowered my **status as a white** woman among the Gurindji.

7 January 1971:
   I was thwarted (in a questionnaire) because the truck came to take the children to be weighed and a lot of adults went for the trip: Then F. arrived and took a load for an overnight fishing trip and finally my biro ran out ... I have sent for more but it is a bloody inefficient scientist who loses her bag of biros and pencils somewhere and arrives back in the field with just one!

14 January 1971:
   Drove on to A. Station ... The manager was very unfriendly but faced with two women and me introducing myself and being polite ... he finally gave in and said we 'were most welcome'. He was decidedly racist — when in reply to his question about my work I said it was on the attitudes of Aboriginal women, he commented that he 'didn't think gins could think' and when I managed to reply that every human being did, he said 'yes, like a horse or cow thinks about the next meal'. (That was the price paid to meet the people working at this station.)

16 January 1971:
   Set out early to drive home, taking the bitumen ... Crossed two small springs then came to a really big one running. N. and I waded in waist-deep and barefoot to find the stony ground and then stood to mark the road while J. drove the Toyota through with the others holding up the rifles and swags as the water came up above the floor. Then we came to the Victoria River which has a concrete causeway and was only knee-deep but running strongly. After prolonged paddling and discussion we risked it and got across with no trouble.
   There was a tremendous storm in the night and the bough shelter collapsed on to the tent and the rain came in, so my books went under a tarpaulin and remained dry and I curled round on the bed and remained wet and cold all night.

Analysis
Before I left for Australia my professor told me to write down *everything*. At the time I thought this a trivial remark, but I learnt its value while in the field. It is not just a question of memory becoming a very inadequate tool under the staggering impact of so very much that is new and strange. A more important factor is that distance can turn events or information into something far more interesting or significant than they appeared to be at the time. In the field it is often difficult to see the wood for the trees.

As an example, on 7 July 1970 I recorded in my field journal a story that at the time I thought was just an interesting version of a typical creation myth.

> First there was water here and then it went back so that there was the Northern Territory. Then a thousand million Aborigines were here and lived on the land for a long time. The first cuddia who came was Ned Kelly and he brought with him the first horses, a stallion and a mare, and the first bullock, a very hairy one whose picture you can see on some rocks in Victoria River Downs country. Ned Kelly was a friend of and helped the Aborigines. The second cuddia who came was Captain Cook. He looked at the land and saw that it was very good and wanted it for himself. He decided to clear the Aborigines off the land. So he shot many of them and he shot Ned Kelly too and he stole the land. But now we want the land back.

Months later, back in Berlin, I had time to think about this story and the analysis I finally reached went through two stages: the first in which I put the story into the context of the time and circumstances in which it had been told; and the second in which I began to draw some theoretical conclusions.

The first stage began by pointing out that since the beginning of their strike in 1966, the Gurindji received material support from various sections of the white population but particularly from unions and it was initially channelled through the unions in Darwin. The contacts that the people had with the unionists (and other visitors) obviously had an influence on their consciousness generally and on their attitudes to white people.

Most of the unionists, students and others who visited Wattie Creek shared in varying degrees views about the history and structure of Australian society which to some extent have been communicated to and internalised by the Gurindji people.

The story may not fit historical facts but it makes sense. 1970 was the bicentenary of Captain Cook's landing and was a day of mourning for Aborigines — for the account of his discoveries contributed to the British decision to found a convict colony in 1788.

Ned Kelly, in contrast, is a folk hero and has passed into popular legend as the man who stole from the rich to give to the poor and who fought against established authority.

The Aborigines have taken over and adapted to their own use these white symbols: Cook as negative who stole the land and murdered the people, and Kelly as positive and friendly to the oppressed Aboriginal people. And the interaction of these two symbols prepares the stage for the Gurindji's own campaign — 'but now we want the land back'.

The second stage of analysis moved on from these statements to the generalisation that the Gurindji land rights campaign appears to have the characteristics of a modern political struggle by a national minority against imperialism in their own country, but in fact this is an oversimplification. The development of black consciousness and organisation in the remoter areas of the north is by no means an even and steady process and while certain actions do take place in a modern context, others make use of traditional ideology and concepts. The resistance of the Aboriginal people has often been expressed in mystical or religious form.

This conclusion was reinforced by another story I was told in which the *form*, the traditional beliefs about the powers of shamans, was widened to express a new *content*, the antagonism of the Gurindji towards white pastoralists.

It was also clear that the process of development of Aboriginal consciousness and the clarification of their position in their own minds still retains much of their traditional ideological superstructure. There is a dichotomy at Wattie Creek whereby resistance to exploitation is still being expressed in beliefs and concepts whose forms are derived from the ancient society and which are comprehensible for all the members of the community, while at the same time the leaders — the senior Gurindji men — appreciate the need for and use of modern forms of political organisation which are not yet generally understood.

My attention was drawn to this aspect of the processes of change at Wattie Creek when I left the field and was able to read again, specifically the following:

> ... the dual effect of Munzer's activities appears particularly pronounced — on the one hand, on the people, whom he addressed in the only language they could then comprehend, that of religious prophecy; and, on the other hand, on the initiated, to whom he could disclose his ultimate aims.[10]

The story was about Yauwalyeru, a 'clever man'.

> One day a mob of mumbit [Aborigines] were in the middle of an open plain. They had just killed a cleanskin [unbranded bullock] when they saw three cuddia riding up. They were frightened so they all ran away except for Yauwalyeru. The cuddia rode up to where he was standing right by the dead bullock. They asked him if he had killed it and he said he had. They said that blackfellers were not allowed to knock off cattle, but he replied that he was a stockman and that whenever he wanted to eat beef he would. One of the cuddia drew his gun and shot the old man for this answer. Then they made a big fire to burn his body and when that was done they rode away. Later on as they were riding along they met an old blackfeller. 'Hey, don't you know me?' he called out. They looked at him and saw it was the man they had shot and burnt but they couldn't believe it. But he told

them that he was Yauwalyeru, the man they had shot and burnt. And he asked them if they could do that. They were very surprised and agreed that they couldn't. And then he said that he was going to kill them. Then Yauwalyeru took a very long chain with a big lock and key on it out from his guts and with it he hung the three cuddia in a tree. And they died.

Conclusions
There are a number of conclusions to fieldwork. An obvious one is the affectionate memories and gratitude that you carry away with you, less concrete but as tangible as all the notebooks and tapes and photographs. The last days are a trial — all the questions and ideas that at the time seemed less significant suddenly rush to the surface and demand answers for which there is no time left. But more poignant for me are the last two entries in my journal:

18 January 1971:
M.R. made a speech saying I was the first to come from a foreign country and I had been here a long time. They were sad I was going and hoped I would come back ... My father left early to work and camp again at Wave Hill Welfare Settlement — and told me to send word to his cuddia relations to write to him and to send me back to Wattie Creek again soon. He also said he gave me permission, it was alright, he allowed me to go away to see my cuddia mother and father.

19 January 1971:
I said rather determinedly casual goodbyes to various people and then K. came up and held my hand and kept on saying 'don't forget' and his wife came up and held the other hand. Then A. came and wept and I was quite finished. K. left and all we women sat together and just cried while A. and P. wailed aloud.

The crucial conclusion, however, is the use to which all

the material gathered in the field is put. This is the area where the anthropologist is concerned with choices he or she can make about what to write and where to publish (if at all), about applied anthropology, involvement in planning and other agencies, about political activity and so on. This really is a response to what Berreman has called 'the searching questions of the peoples of the third world and others: namely, "What has been the effect of your work among us? Have you contributed to the solution of the problems you have witnessed? Have you even mentioned those problems? If not, then you are part of those problems and hence must be changed, excluded, or eradicated along with their other manifestations. If you are not part of the solution, you are part of the problem".'

My response to this 'searching question' has been to try to follow the model of *Capital* described on page 9: objective analysis, condemnation, prediction and practical policy. There is not room for all these aspects here, but what follows is intended to indicate some of the major aspects of analysis and policy making.

To a degree, content influences form and so there is a corresponding change in style and language. This does not in any sense mean that there is any loss in my sense of commitment at many levels to the Gurindji people. On the contrary, this section in part reflects what I learnt at Wattie Creek (as well as later work in other parts of Australia). It is partially a way of repaying my debt to my hosts; it is also for me the most significant and the most deeply felt part of this account of fieldwork with a group of Australian Aboriginal people.

The Aboriginal National Minority
There are two dialectically linked aspects of the situation of the Aboriginal people which must be considered if we are to make a correct analysis in order to change this situation. These are the class and the national aspects; in other words, their position as workers and as black workers.

Classes are primarily and predominantly determined by

the relationship of their members to the means of production and the place they occupy in the social system of production. In capitalism the direct producers, the workers, are alienated from the means of production and are economically dependent upon the capitalist system.

Ideology is a secondary, although important factor. Class consciousness is clearly not developed among the Aborigines (and many white workers), but this does not alter the objective process of class formation.

A worker does not cease to be a member of the proletariat because the capitalist system forces him or her into unemployment. Thus the very high level of unemployment among the Aborigines does not alter their position as members of the Australian working class.

Two forms of proletarianisation, both so far at a low level, have been and are taking place: pastoral and other workers mainly in the north tend to be in a transitional stage (living in traditionally orientated groups) or are rural workers. In the south they tend to be wage workers but are isolated, unorganised and atomised.

Thus we have an Aboriginal working class at a number of stages of development towards fully fledged industrial wage labourers: from groups with much of their social organisation and ideology still traditionally orientated through rural workers to urban workers and some members of the industrial working class.

The Aborigines continue to suffer racial discrimination and oppression, segregation and isolation, and represent the lowest stratum of Australian capitalist society under conditions of deprivation, extreme poverty and backwardness.

As a result of this position, the process of spontaneous assimilation to the (white) Australian nation (a process inevitably produced by the economic integration of the Aborigines into the capitalist system) has been held back. The Aborigines have retained in varying degrees many traits of their traditional way of life and thought (culture, speech, customs, institutions), often with new meanings and functions, and have adapted elements of the Australian capitalist nation to their particular needs and imposed low levels in distinctive forms of their own (e.g. Australian pidgin English).

Moreover, in their resistance and struggle against racial discrimination and deprivation they have begun to organise themselves on the level of the whole of Australia and have begun to develop an Australia-wide common consciousness of themselves as a people of their own and distinguished from the (white) Australian nation.

It is essential to move from such an analysis on to the question of what can be done to right some of these wrongs, to build a new situation with and for the Aborigines in which they have economic and social equality and dignity.

From the proletarian class point of view the land question has been central. This key issue has two stages: rural and mining.

Land rights do not mean leasehold (as have been given to the Gurindji) or a form of freehold — as recommended by the second (1974) report of the Woodward Commission of Enquiry into Aboriginal land rights in the Northern Territory set up by the Labor Government in February 1973 — they mean communal and inalienable and ownership.

Communal rights in land approximate most closely to the Aborigines' own demands and to their traditional form of land ownership. They also carry a degree of protection from future land alienation, for collective ownership makes it far less likely that individuals can be persuaded or forced to sell the land.

The demand for inalienable land rights also involves protection from the danger of having the land stolen again, this time by subtle, legal means or from imposed economic necessity. The demand also implies a recognition of the unbroken rights of Aborigines to their land from a past of at least 40 000 years into the future.

This picture, however, is unbalanced if we do not also consider the revolutionary aspects of the land rights demand — the demand for the return of part of the basic means of production.

Land occupation is an illegal activity. By their example of combining legal methods (petitions, demonstrations, etc.) with illegal action against the discriminatory class laws of Australia, Aboriginal groups have not only exercised a profound influence on the struggle of Aborigines throughout the continent, raising it to a qualitatively higher level, but have also contributed to strengthening the revolutionary tendency in the consciousness of the white working class.

Aboriginal groups are also resisting the exploitation of tribal lands by mining companies and directly play a part in the fight against multinationals and imperialism. Others are confronting representatives of overseas monopoly leaseholders of pastoral land.

In the fight against monopoly landed property, the demand for Aboriginal communal inalienable landed property has an antimonopoly, revolutionary character. This is because it sets an example of the expropriation of private property generally and because it creates a counter-position to State monopoly or private landed property.

Up to the 1970s, the key issue was landed property for the Aborigines and the struggle that waged around this question related to all Aborigines and played a major role in the development of their organisation and the growth of their Australia-wide consciousness.

More recently, however, the question of mineral rights has moved to the forefront of the struggle. There is a contradiction between north and south with this aspect of the Aboriginal struggle now being centred in areas such as Arnhem Land (in the far north of the Northern Territory) where there are significant natural resources.

If the demand for communal inalienable land rights is to be realistic, then the people must be able to control the exploitation — in whatever form, if any — of those lands and also be able to develop economically viable communities. Both these aspects demand Aboriginal rights to natural resources.

However, communal rights hold back the development of natural resources since they transcend the abilities of the individual groups to exploit such resources.

Recognising growing Aboriginal unity and the specific problems of mineral exploitation, it is necessary now both to maintain and protect local group rights and also to acknowledge that land and mineral resources belong to *all* Aborigines — that they are Aboriginal national property.

Concretely, this would mean that groups such as the Gurindji (there are no significant mineral deposits in the Wattie Creek area) should retain whatever profit they make from projects based on communal landed property. Where there are natural resources, 50% (as a tentative figure) of the profits should be used to finance general projects for all Aborigines (under the planning and control of an independent national Aboriginal organisation) and also to provide particular support and developmental assistance for communities on whose land the mining is actually taking place.

Where the exploitation of the resources in the communal lands transcends the capacity of the local group (in mining, extraction and processing, oil exploitation and drilling, use of forest resources and so on), the Australian Government should be charged with establishing the wishes of the group, reaching voluntary agreements on leasing with the community and, if the lease is granted, taking over the activities. This would involve a significant reversal of the present situation in which leases for such enterprises would be available only on a voluntary basis and only to the Government, not to private firms or monopolies whether Australian or foreign.

There is a great deal more than could be written here, for I have not included issues such as housing, health, education, employment and culture, but I have tried to show the basic features of the analysis and the crucial aspects of the political demands that came from my fieldwork at Wattie Creek in 1970–71.

When the Gurindji men and women tried to explain their approach to members of the group and to visitors they judged to be sympathetic, they used to say: 'No matter who you are, we are here to look after each other'. And when the women described the things they wanted to improve life at Wattie Creek, they included items such as double beds, mirrors, tables and chairs, childrens shoes and 'flowers to make Dagu Ragu pretty'.

This has been, of course, the account of only one person's fieldwork and the conclusions built on it. Faced with such generosity and such need, only deep involvement and commitment could be possible. I hope that other social anthropologists who go into the field also bring back lasting emotions of love and commitment.

NOTES AND REFERENCES

1. Jay, R. in D. Hymes (ed.), *Reinventing Anthropology*, Vintage Books, 1974, p.379.
2. Turnbull, C. *The Mountain People*, Jonathan Cape, 1973.
3. *Selected Works of Marx and Engels*, Progress Publishers, 1968.
4. Engels, F. *The Peasant War in Germany*, Progress Publishers, 1956.
5. Wax, R., *Doing Fieldwork*, University of Chicago Press, 1971. On page 45, she writes: 'It is a horrid but inescapable fact that it usually takes *more* time to organise, write, and present material well than it takes to gather it. The notion that one can work in the field for a year and then write a good report while one is carrying on a full- or part-time teaching lead is idiotic. (People do write in this fashion, but this is one reason why so many monographs are uninspired.) The sensible researcher will allow as much free time to write his report as he spent in the field. If he is really astute and can get away with it, he will allow himself more.'
This is an exceptionally useful book for fieldwork and anyone contemplating such activity *must* read at least the first 55 pages.
6. Lecture delivered to the Philosophy Section of the Communist University of London, 29 July 1973. Reprinted in *Marxism Today*, January 1974, London.

7. 'An ethnic community is a social organism consolidated on a definite territory from groups of people under the conditions — (already present, or achieved by them in the course of the development of economic and socio-cultural connections) — of a common language, common features of culture and way of life, a number of common social values and traditions, and a considerable intermingling of racial components sharply differentiated in the past. The basic characteristics of an ethnic community are ethnic self-consciousness and a common name for themselves (self-naming), a common language, territory, peculiarities of psychological traits, culture, way of life, and a definite form of social and territorial organisation (or an aspiration to create such an organisation).' Kozlov, V., 'On the Concept of Ethnic Community', in Yu. Bromley (ed.), *Soviet Ethnology and Anthropology Today,* Mouton, 1974, p.86.
8. Wax, p.20.
9. *Notes and Queries on Anthropology,* 6th edn, revised and rewritten by a committee of the Royal Anthropological Institute of Great Britain and Ireland, Routledge & Kegan Paul, 1951. This is a book that was recommended to me by lecturers at London University; I would not pass on that recommendation to you as I object to some of the values implicit in it. One quotation from page 32 will illustrate what I mean: 'It is important that not even the slightest expression of amusement or disapproval should ever be displayed at the description of ridiculous, impossible or disgusting features in custom, cult or legend.'
10. Engels, p.77.

NOTES ON CONTRIBUTORS

COLIN BELL is a graduate of the Universities of Keele and Wales. He has been Professor of Sociology in the University of New South Wales since 1975. Previously he was Reader in Sociology at the University of Essex. His other publications include *Middle Class Families* (1968); with Howard Newby *Community Studies* (1972), *The Sociology of Community* (1974), *Doing Sociological Research* (1977) and *Property, Paternalism and Power* (1978); with Margaret Stacey *Power, Persistence and Change* (1975). He is currently working on books on the nature of sociology and aspects of the political economy of property.

SOL ENCEL is a graduate of the University of Melbourne. His academic career was interrupted by the 1939–45 war, by marriage, and by employment in the Australian Public Service. He was Tutor and Lecturer in Political Science at Melbourne 1952–55, Senior Lecturer and Reader in Political Science at the Australian National University 1956–66, Rockefeller Travelling Fellow in 1960, and Visiting Fellow at the University of Sussex in 1968–69 and again in 1973. Since 1966, he has been Professor of Sociology at the University of New South Wales. His other publications include *Cabinet Government in Australia* (1962 and 1974), *Equality and Authority* (1970), *Women and Society* (co-author), *Australian Society* (co-editor, 1965, 1970, 1977), and *The Art of Anticipation* (co-author, 1975).

HUGH STRETTON was educated at the Universities of Melbourne and Princeton and graduated from the University of Oxford. He has been a Fellow of Balliol College, Oxford, then Professor of History at the University of Adelaide, where he is now a Reader. He was a member of the Australian Housing Corporation and the Cities Commission while they existed, and has been a member of the South Australian Housing Trust since 1971. His other publications include *The Political Sciences* (1969), *Ideas for Australian Cities* (1970), *Housing and Government, the 1974 Boyer Lectures,* and *Capitalism, Socialism and the Environment* (1976).

LOIS BRYSON is a graduate of Melbourne and Monash Universities and is currently a Senior Lecturer in the Department of Anthropology and Sociology at Monash University. Also a trained social worker and secondary teacher, she worked in these fields before joining the Monash staff as a Tutor in 1965. From 1972-75 she was editor of the Australian and New Zealand Journal of Sociology. Her current fields of interest are the sociology of the family and of welfare.

FAITH THOMPSON has found that living is interrupted by a career and so now works only part-time. She is a graduate of the University of Western Australia and Monash and is a qualified social worker with ten years' practice and research experience, mainly with the Walter and Eliza Hall Institute of Medical Research and the University Department of Medicine of Western Australia. She has taught courses in Anthropology and Sociology at Monash (1964-65, 1972) and Melbourne University (1974-75). During 1972-74 she worked as a sociologist with a consultancy practice of engineers and town planners, and contributed to a variety of planning reports. She is currently a Research Fellow in the Department of Social WORK AT La Trobe University, where she is running seminars on urban development and planning.

EVA COX, after a career in commercial research, belatedly graduated in Sociology from the University of New South Wales, where she subsequently taught for two years. She is currently the Director of the New South Wales Council of Social Services and undertaking a Ph.D. on the human consequences of social research.

FRAN HAUSFELD is a graduate in Philosophy and Government from the University of Sydney where she is currently a Tutor in the Department of Government. She has submitted a Ph.D.

thesis on 'Popular and Professional Conceptions of Democratic Politicians and Politics' and is awaiting her fate.

SUE WILLS has degrees in Arts and Economics from the University of Sydney. She is now a Tutor in the Department of Government of that University and is completing a Ph.D. thesis on 'The Politics of Sexual Liberation'.

BETTINA CASS is a Lecturer in Sociology at the University of New South Wales.

MADGE DAWSON retired in 1976 from the position of Senior Lecturer in the Department of Adult Education at the University of Sydney.

HEATHER RADI is Senior Lecturer in History in the Department of History, University of Sydney.

DIANA TEMPLE is Associate Professor of Pharmacology, University of Sydney.

SUE WILLS is a Tutor in the Department of Government, University of Sydney.

ANNE WINKLER is a Lecturer in the School of Health Sciences at the Western Australian Institute of Technology.

Individually, they have published in the fields of women in the family, the workforce, and education; the psychology of sex roles; the feminist movement; Australian history, and pharmacology. Their co-authored book on women in universities will be published by Australia International Press in 1978.

ALEXANDER MAMAK studied Anthropology and Sociology at the Universities of California (Berkeley) and Hawaii, and is currently a Lecturer in Sociology at the University of New South Wales. He was Research Anthropologist for the University of Hawaii's Research Corporation in 1974-75, undertaking a study of urban change associated with copper mining in south-east Bougainville. He returned to Bougainville in 1976 to study the first Provincial Government elections. His first fieldwork experience was in Fiji in 1970-72, concerning pluralism and social change. Since then he has returned several times to Fiji to undertake studies of development at the local level. His recent publications have included *Bougainvillean Nationalism: Aspects of Unity and Discord* (1974) and *Compensating for Development: the Bougainville case* (1977) with Richard Bedford. Recently, his main interest has been focussed on action research and research for development.

RONALD WILD is a graduate of the University of Sydney where he was the Drapers' Company Commonwealth Scholar. He completed his Ph.D. at the same University in 1970. From 1970–74 he was a Lecturer in Anthropology at the University of Sydney and is presently a Senior Lecturer. His other publications include *Bradstow* (1974), and papers on social stratification, community studies and ageing. He is currently working on books on social stratification in Australia, and English and American comparisons with Bradstow.

BILL BOTTOMLEY is a graduate of the University of Sydney and of the University of New South Wales where he is a Lecturer in Sociology. He is currently working on a book on ecologically sensitive alternatives in domestic housing.

HANNAH MIDDLETON is a graduate of the School of Oriental and African Studies, University of London and of Humboldt University in Berlin (German Democratic Republic). She has been a Lecturer in the School of Sociology, University of New South Wales since 1974. She has worked for the African Service of the British Broadcasting Corporation and as a Lecturer in English Language and Institutions, an employment officer, travel clerk, shop assistant and barmaid. In 1960–61 she was Mayoress of the London Borough of Greenwich. She became a member of the Communist Party of Great Britain in 1962 and in 1974 joined the Socialist Party of Australia. The majority of her publications are in political and trade union journals, but include *But Now We Want the Land Back* (1977).